MW00480025

ACKNOWLEDGEMENTS

About this book, Jim said, shortly before he died, "it's all there." It was all there, but the book could not have been completed and published as it is without the efforts of Clayton Beltran, a cousin, Larry Townsend, Jim's friend, Steve Giovannoni, his brother, and above all Betsy Giovannoni, his wife.

DEDICATION

Dedicated to Jim's daughter Jessica.

"It doesn't matter to me whether I sell any books.
I'm writing this book for Jessica. I want her
to understand what it was like."

dangerous laughs

Occupational Hazards of a
Life in Standup Comedy

BY JIM GIOVANNI

Jim Giovanni

PROLOGUE

I love black and white movies. Most of my favorite movies are old black and white movies. I think one of the reasons I love them so much is the fact that my earliest childhood memories are of a world right out of an old black and white movie. If you think about it, black and white movies aren't really black and white at all. Images in them consist mostly of shades of grey. It is shadow and light and dark and bright like the world of Sam Spade in *The Maltese Falcon*.

I enter the world in San Francisco in 1949. Hey what do you know? I'm a San Francisco 49er. My parents live in the Sunset District less than a mile from the ocean. Fog City. Like an old movie everything is grey, the sidewalks and the buildings and the sky. Men look like Bogie, dressed in dark suits and grey fedoras with brims pulled down. Women look like Mary Astor with fancy feathered hats and gloves and stoles wrapped around their shoulders, the heads of minks still on them with their beady little eyes staring at you, daring, "Go ahead kid. Give her a kiss. What do you got to lose? What's the matter? You afraid I'll bite?"

Grey people riding around in grey cars down grey streets. Foghorns and screeching seagulls, even the sounds are grey. Alcatraz, the Bay Bridge, the Ferry Building, all grey like I'm living in a film-noir movie. The thing with film-noir movies is, bad stuff happens in them. At age two, I drive a car into the garage wall, paint our black dog white and put my baby brother in a drawer of the television stand, which falls over and Steve narrowly escapes injury. Two, and I already have a rap sheet.

Jim Giovanni

Jim at two

THE BIRTH OF A COMEDIAN

Jackie Mason and me, we have a lot in common. His parents wanted him to be a rabbi, mine wanted me to be a priest. We both became comedians. I don't know about Jackie, but in the fourth grade I knew I had the calling. God spoke to me. He said, "From now on, you are a designated funny person. Now go into the world funny person and make people laugh." It happened in fourth grade Religion. How appropriate. God works in mysterious ways. It wouldn't have happened if it wasn't for the nun.

Getting up in front of a crowd is not my idea. It's the nun's idea. This is a pre-Vatican II nun. These nuns are not like the nuns like you see nowadays. These nuns mean business. Still, I don't think kids like me are covered in the nun's manual. I'm an ADD kid before they know what ADD is. No matter what the subject is, my mind isn't on it. So here's the scene. It's 1959. My body is in a fourth grade classroom in San Anselmo but my mind is in Kezar Stadium in San Francisco. It's a big game between the San Francisco 49ers and the Baltimore Colts. Y.A. Tittle and Johnny Unitas are the quarterbacks. I'm a wide receiver for the 49ers. I go out for a pass and I get open and Y.A. throws an "Alley Oop" pass and I catch it and I am running for the game-winning touchdown...

"Mr. Giovannoni!"

I'm jarred back to reality: "Uh, yes, Sister..."

"Stand up."

I stand up.

"Mr. Giovannoni, go to the front of the classroom!"

I go to the front of the classroom and stand facing the blackboard with my back to the class. I already hear the laughs.

The nun shushes the class and says, "Turn around and face the class!"

I turn around. At this point she still thinks public humiliation will work.

"Mr. Giovannoni, what subject are we discussing?"

"Uh, Religion, Sister."

"And what in Religion are we discussing?"

I look around. Everyone has a Baltimore Catechism on his or her desk, the Baltimore Catechism being the basic training manual for Catholic school children, so I kind of have a hunch that's what we are talking about. I say, "Uh, The Baltimore Catechism, Sister?"

"And what are we discussing in the Baltimore Catechism?"

I'm stumped.

"Mr. Giovannoni. What are we discussing in the Baltimore Catechism?"

I desperately fish for an answer. My eyes are rolling around in my head and my tongue is getting a pretty good workout too. I'm doing Tommy Smothers before I ever heard of Tommy Smothers. And like Tommy I'm getting laughs doing it. The nun is getting really irate. She sternly shushes the class, then turns to me and says. "Mr. Giovannoni, This is your last chance. I'm going to ask you one more time. What specifically are we discussing in the Baltimore Catechism?"

The tittering is getting louder. My tongue looks like a snake that's trying to escape.

"Mr. Giovannoni! We're waiting for an answer!"

I blurt out: "Johnny Unitas and the Baltimore Catechism?"

Boom! The class explodes in laughter! It's my birthday and Christmas and the Fourth of July all rolled into one. The nun stands there red-faced. She tries to shame me further but it's no use. Nothing works. No matter what she says, my response gets laughs. I'm not even trying to be funny. It just comes out that way. Finally, she tells me to sit down.

I say, "But I'm...!"

"Sit down!"

"I'm...!"

"SIT DOWN! NOW!"

Never again does the nun give me the stage. From then on she does everything she can to keep me off the stage. Nothing works. If I sit up front, I get laughs. If she makes me sit in the back, I get laughs. Even when I'm not trying to get laughs, I get laughs, although, I admit when I'm in the back I am actually trying to get laughs. I'm doing Crazy Guggenheim impersonations: "Hi ya, Joe! Hi ya Mr. Dunahee! Who-a ha hee hee hee...!"

Crazy Guggenheim is sure fire. The nun isn't exactly sure what is going on but she can see and hear the reaction it's getting. One kid, every time I do it it's like he has comedy Tourette's. He thrashes around in his seat laughing uncontrollably making pig-like snorting sounds. He does it every time. You know I'm going to push his buttons. So now the nun knows seating me in back isn't a good idea, so she seats me up front where she can keep an eye on me. The problem is now everybody can keep their eyes on me, and that's what they all are doing in anticipation of me doing something funny. I get laughs even when I'm trying not to, especially when I'm trying not to. Every time the nun asks a question or says anything to me, I'm like Tommy Smothers, and it gets laughs.

The nuns are flummoxed. It's not I'm a bad kid. It's I'm a goofy kid. It's catch-22 for them. They don't know what to do. My parents don't know what to do. I get F's in deportment and report cards with comments: "Disrupts the class" and "Disrespects Authority." Everybody tells me acting like an idiot is never going to get me anywhere, and they are absolutely right. The validity of their assertion is not in question. The question is: Who says it's an act?

The good news: I expand upon my talent for mimicry, which is great for laughs. After Crazy Guggenheim, I learn to do: Klem Kaddiddlelhopper, Ralph Kramden and Ed Norton in The Honeymooners, Sgt. Bilko, Rupert Ritzik and Doberman, Jack Benny and Rochester, Groucho, Bugs Bunny, Elmer Fudd, Yosemite Sam, Daffy Duck and Porky Pig! By fifth grade I have an act!

Moral: Beware the Law of Unintended Comedians.

Jim in high school

CLASS CLOWN

High school is the first time I have male teachers. I quickly learn how to imitate them, doing impersonations of them in the hall between classes, during recess, at lunchtime in the cafeteria, after school in the locker room, whenever and wherever I can gather a crowd. I improvise routines casting the teachers in various offbeat scenarios, such as Westerns and Horror films. My talent at vocal mimicry is so accurate that I actually call my parents on the phone and impersonate our History teacher who is also one of our football coaches, telling them all the bad stuff I've been doing. It's quite a tale, total B.S. of course, but my parents believe it and really think I am the coach, who they know personally because we all go to the same church. They're going: "Oh boy! Wait 'til he gets home! He's in big trouble now! He's really going to get it this time...!"

It's everything I can do to keep a straight face and not laugh out loud. I get home and my dad says, "We got a call from Mr. McCann today."

I say, "Oh, yeah?"

He says, "Yeah!" and proceeds to run off a litany of all the bad stuff I've been doing.

Now I'm doing McCann's voice, " Oh yeah? What else did he tell you?"

Dad realizes he's been had, and now he's doing Paul Ford the Colonel on *The Phil Silvers Show*: "Well, you did it again, Bilko!"

JONATHAN WINTERS

By 1965 my classmates are calling me Jonathan Winters II. I have all of Jonathan's records and know all of his routines by heart. I come up with an original idea for a parody of the TV series "Branded" in which Jonathan Winters portrays the title character. I act it out for my classmates. They think it's funny and encourage me to write it up and send it to Jonathan Winters. I do and much to my surprise, my hero writes back. I still have the letter framed on my wall. It reads:

"Jonathan Winters

May 1, 1965

Dear James:

Many thanks for your very nice letter and your suggestion.

I just want you to know that your interest and encouragement are really appreciated!

All the best to you.

Warmest regards,

Jonathan Winters"

It's signed by Jonathan Winters himself and, I must say, as much as Jonathan has a reputation for being a wild man, he has very good penmanship, much better I expect than most of his psychiatrists. I show the letter to my dad. My dad says, "Great. A lot of good it's going to do not to encourage him when he's got Jonathan Winters encouraging him."

In June 1967, The Summer of Love, I graduate.

JONATHAN WINTERS

May 1, 1965

Mr. James Giovannoni
265 Tulane Drive
Larkspur, California

Dear James:

Many thanks for your very nice letter and
your suggestion.

I just want you to know that your interest
and encouragement are really appreciated!

All the best to you.

Warmest regards,

Jonathan Winters

JW/lm

Letter from Jonathan Winters

FUNNY MAN
ON CAMPUS

In the fall, my childhood daydreams turn out to be oddly prophetic. I play football for real in Kezar Stadium. Our college team plays on Saturdays. The 49ers play on Sundays on the same field. Unlike in my daydreams, in real life I'm a defensive player. I don't start, but when I get in, I get tackles. I also get lots of laughs impersonating the coaches. My teammates think I'm a riot. Without telling me they sign me up for the freshman talent show. I don't want to do it, but they literally drag me over to where the show is being held. My act goes over big that night. All of a sudden I'm "funny man" on campus.

ALL-AMERICAN SCHIZOID HOUR

Junior year I quit football, become a longhaired hippie and team up with a comedy partner. We're "The All-American Schizoid Hour" and are an instant hit in student reviews and coffee houses both on and off campus. Unfortunately, our partnership is doomed from the start. He is politically correct before politically correct exists. We constantly argue over material. We are the Cheech and Chong version of The Sunshine Boys. "'Grass' is funny. 'Acid' is not funny."

We are the Orange Sunshine Boys.

SOLO ACT

In 1969 my comedy partner turns on, tunes in, and drops out. He joins a commune and moves to Tennessee. I'm back to being a solo act with no one to answer to but the audience. Now all I need is the audience. Somehow I find one at an outdoor peace rally/concert in Berkeley with Country Joe and the Fish among others. I get up and do my impersonation of Richard Nixon, sitting on the shitter in a public restroom, reading graffiti off the walls, complete with Nixon facial expressions and gestures: "'Fighting for peace is like balling for virginity.' Who wrote that on this wall? 'Dick Nixon before he dicks you.' I want the name of the person who wrote that on this wall...'There once was a fellow named Dick who could pile it high and thick. Some thought him a sickie, others quite tricky and an insufferable prick.' Bring me the testicles of the person who wrote that on this wall!"

The crowd eats it up.

Then Country Joe comes out. "Give me an 'F'..."

Little do I know Nixon is actually keeping an enemies list.

"I'm ready for my close-up, Mr. Hoover!"

THE DRINKING GOURD

In 1970, there are only folk clubs or large venues like Fillmore Auditorium and The Avalon Ball Room. The larger venues feature headline acts like Janis Joplin or Jimi Hendrix or Howlin' Wolf and no comedians. The coffee houses and smaller rooms feature mainly folk acts. This is the pre-comedy club era. "The Hungry I" and "Purple Onion" are no longer happening, so there is a gap between the Jonathan Winters Bob Newhart Smothers Brothers generation and the wave to come. There really are no venues for guys like me. The only places I know of that have open mikes are the Lion's Share and the No Name Bar, both in Sausalito, and The Drinking Gourd on Union Street in San Francisco.

One night I decide to go over to the Drinking Gourd and do the open mike. I'm the only performer in there without a guitar. They give me ten minutes to get up and do a comedy set, and I don't know why, but my first time performing solo in a club, I suffer true stage fright. It's one of the few times in my career it happens like that, I don't know why. Well, maybe I do know why or at least part of the reason why. Both on stage and in the audience that night are several name folk acts, so there is actual pressure to be good. It is odd though, isn't it?

I get up in front of thousands at a peace rally/Country Joe concert, and I'm unfazed. I go on in a small venue like the Drinking Gourd, and I'm utterly terrified. The MC introduces me, I get up and I am afraid to look at the audience.

I know they know I am scared witless up there. My entire set I focus on a spot on the back wall and deliver my routine to the spot on the wall, getting a few laughs and mild applause at the end.

I walk off feeling like I bombed, but a famous folksinger who is so famous I can't remember his name comes up afterwards and says, "You're good, kid. Keep it up. Don't quit."

BACKSTORY TIME

The Holy City Zoo is the first time I actually get paid to make people laugh, but, before I go any further, allow me to share a little backstory. Holy City is a small town in California located on Highway 17 in the mountains between San Jose and Santa Cruz. Holy City once had a zoo, a children's petting zoo cleverly named the Holy City Zoo. At some point in the late sixties, the Holy City Zoo goes defunct and decides to sell off all its assets, which consist mainly of old barn wood and a faded tin sign with "Holy City Zoo" hand painted on it. I have no idea where the animals end up, but my guess is it's on some commune or another, since those mountains are loaded with hippies. In fact, I suspect offspring of both hippies and animals alike are, at this very moment, loaded in the Mountains of Santa Cruz.

"What do we do with the shake?"

"Feed it to the goats, dude."

Before it becomes The Holy City Zoo, 408 Clement Street is a bar ironically named: The Library. The Library's main customers are college students, who come to drink beer and shoot pool and escape the drudgeries of the real library. But in 1970 the times are indeed a-changing and the owners of The Library decide to sell the business and move on. Bob Steger, a folk singer and former co-owner of The Drinking Gourd, takes over the lease. About the time the Holy City Zoo in Holy City is going under, the partnership between Bob and his partner in the Drinking Gourd is going under. So Bob decides to sell his half of the Drinking Gourd and use the proceeds to open his own club out on Clement Street. Bob, a true Renaissance man, is not only a musician, but also a carpenter and very creative and skilled with his hands. So Bob ventures forth into the hinterlands in search of old barn wood with which to create the interior of his new folk club. He finds it in Holy City. Since the hand painted sign comes along as part of the deal, Bob mounts it on the front of the building at 408 Clement St. and names his new club the Holy City Zoo.

MEANWHILE

I can only go so long, like maybe ten minutes, without hearing laughs before I feel an overwhelming urge to perform for someone, anyone who will listen, friends, total strangers the guy who spritzes the vegetables in the supermarket. One day I'm out jogging in Golden Gate Park and before I know it I'm doing a comedy act for what starts out as three winos sitting at a picnic table and ends up a crowd. Not just winos, there are tourists, hippies, people I recognize from school. There's one of my professors.

Before I know it, we're taking up half of a small meadow. It's a concert I smell weed people are drinking wine. I do about a half hour of spontaneous hilarity, have no idea what I'm doing, but I'm inspired and the crowd is rolling with it. Even the cop on the horse is laughing. His presence inspires me to do an impression of John Wayne reciting a litany of every Indian tribe he ever got in an altercation with: "I fought the Shawnee, the Pawnee, the Piute, the Kiowa, the Iroquois and the Sioux, the Navajo, the Apache and the Cheyenne. I fought every tribe but the Puqaui (pronounced puck-ow-ee!) Like Christopher Columbus said when he got to America: 'Where're the Puquai?'"

Now even the cop's horse is laughing. Someone says, "You're funny. You ought to go over to the Holy City Zoo. They have an open mike over there on Thursdays. You should go sign up."

"The Holy...what?"

"The Holy City Zoo."

"Holy City Zoo? What's that?"

"It's a new club over on Clement."

"What kind of club?"

"A folk club."

"Do they allow comedians?"

"I don't know. Why don't you go ask them?"

"Where is it?"

"Where The Library used to be."

"Don't tell me they moved the library. I have finals next week."

"Not that library, numb nuts, the bar 'The Library'."

"'The Library' is not there anymore?"

"That's what I'm trying to tell you. It's a folk club now."

"What did you say the name was?"

THE HOLY CITY ZOO

The first time I enter The Holy City Zoo it's like entering a whole new world. The interior of The Zoo has a warm feel to it that's impossible to describe. Old barn wood, some of it with animal hair still embedded in it, cut into intricate patterns and carefully inlaid by a skilled craftsman, whoever put the place together is an artist. It's impossible to describe, but the vibe is unmistakable. Right away I know this place happening. Like walking into a hippie wonderland, it's like I found a home. Of course, after a few years go by and all the old barn wood gets a chance to absorb all the old spilled beer and wine it can absorb, the place ends up smelling like a barf factory. The new owners rip out all the old barn wood and paint the interior black. The Zoo loses her charm along with the barf smell. Admittedly there's a trade-off there. But I am getting ahead of my story. In the beginning The Zoo is a strange and wonderful place, a magical world where hippies and hobbits and other mystical creatures of alternate universes co-exist in peace and harmony. Can you dig it? So, I walk into The Zoo for the first time, cozy up to the bar. I'm looking around taking it all in.

The bartender says, "Can I get you something?"

They have Guinness Stout on tap, a good omen. I say, "Guinness, please. By the way, whom do I talk to, to sign up for the open mike?"

The bartender says, "Talk to Bob."

"Which one's Bob?"

"The guy with the beard."

It's 1970. Everybody has a beard. I say, "Which guy with the beard?"

The bartender says, "The short guy with the beard who's losing his hair."

I walk over to where the short guy with the beard who is losing his hair is standing.

"Are you Bob?"

"Yeah, I'm Bob. What's your name?"

"Jim. I'm here for the open mike. Are you the guy I talk to about signing up?"

"Yeah, I'm the guy. You want to sign up?"

"Yeah."

"Where's your guitar?"

"I don't have a guitar."

"Do you have somebody with you?"

"No. Just me."

"What do you do? Sing a cappella?"

"I don't sing."

"You don't sing? What do you do? Are you a poet?"

"No, I'm a comedian."

"A comedian? That's a first. Okay, we could use a few laughs around here. I'll give you ten minutes. I'll put you on early, so don't go anywhere."

There is a fairly good crowd in there that night. I do my impersonations and it gets a good response. I go back the following week and Bob gives me a better time slot. I come back three weeks in a row. Each week, he gives me a better slot and each week the crowd gets bigger and the response gets better. After the third week, Bob says, "You're funny. The crowd loves you. If I give you your own night, would you be interested?"

Without hesitation, not thinking where the hell am I going to come up with all the material, I say, "Sure."

Bob says, "Here's the deal. Fridays have been weak. I don't know why. It's one of my worst nights. It shouldn't be. It's Friday, it should be my best night! I'm thinking maybe your stuff will work. I'll put you on with this chick singer I've got booked. You and her do three sets each and alternate sets. Start at eight thirty, and try to keep it going 'till at least one or so. I'll pay you twelve-fifty a night and your bar, whatever you want to drink, your Guinness or whatever, is free. Sound good to you?"

"Sounds great!"

"Can you start tomorrow night?"

"Yes!"

Now I'm in a panic. I've got less than twenty-four hours to get three sets together. I have one. Where am I going to come up with two more? I spend all the next day frantically searching the mental rolodex, making up lists of every character I've ever done: Famous people impersonations, cartoon characters, high school teachers, long haul truckers I worked with, characters I met the summer I worked as a Gandy dancer on the railroad, any funny true story I can think of, funny songs, anything and everything I can do to consume time on stage and entertain a crowd. I come up with three sets, two of which I have no idea if they are going to work or not.

That night I get to the Zoo, and my name is on a handpainted sign in the little window in front of the building along with the name of the other performer, a depressed woman folk singer, whose entire act is singing depressed woman folk songs. I mean there's not an upbeat song in the repertoire. I've heard more toe tappers at a wake, which is apropos because it might as well be a wake – ours! It's no laughing matter, and that's the problem.

Our debut turns out to be a disaster. I do my best, but every time I go on stage it's like trying to pull an elephant out of quicksand by the tail. Just when I think I got the elephant halfway out of the hole, she digs a deeper hole. The crowd is sparse to begin with and gets sparser. By the end of the night only two people are left in the place, seven if you count the folk singer and me and Bob and the bartender and the waitress. Now I understand why Fridays are a bust. By the end of the night I'm doing my William Bendix "Life of Riley" impersonation: "What a revoltin' development this is!"

I am thoroughly convinced it's over the first night. Bob comes up afterwards and says: "This isn't working."

I'm thinking: "Brilliant deduction, Watson!"

Bob says, "You and her aren't a good fit. I'd like to try it again only this time I'll book you with an act that's more compatible with what you do. Do you want to give it another shot next Friday?"

"Does Nixon shit in the White House?"

I have a week to get it together for Friday and I make the most of it. I come up with so much new material I can't wait for Friday. I come back for the Thursday night open mike just to see if the material works. The crowd is hot. The material kills. I close with an impersonation of Ed Sullivan doing a tease for Friday Night: "Be sure to come back tomorrow night for our really big shoe. The little Italian mouse, Topo Gigo will be here, Senior Wences, and our special guests, The Beatles!"

Friday rolls around and The Zoo is packed. The Beatles are

a no show, but there is a new sign in the window, "Jim Giovannoni & The Strand Brothers."

THE STRAND BROTHERS

Here's the story on the Strands. The Strand Brothers is the name of a band but they are more than that. The Strands are guitar players and singers who are actual brothers. Rick is older in his thirties. An ad man by day, Rick's claim to fame is that he's the guy who came up with the Qantas commercial with the Koala bear in it. He also plays a real sweet guitar. Rick has a twinkle in his eye and wears a fedora and has longish brown hair and mustache with muttonchops. Jim is the younger of the two and is not as meticulous with his grooming as his older brother. Brother Jim has obviously not visited a barber or picked up a razor blade in years. He has long brown hair and beard and looks like an everyday hippie as opposed to an upscale hippie like his brother. The Strands have perpetual shit-eating grins on their faces, as if they are enjoying some private inside joke. Of course, with the amount of weed that is being consumed, pretty much everyone has a shit-eating grin on his or her face. Our first night is a smash. In fact as I recall, by the end of the night pretty much everyone is smashed.

THE GLORY DAYS

The Strands and me are Sympatico from the get-go. From day one, Friday nights are packed. Every Friday night there's always an overflow crowd outside waiting for someone to leave so that they can get in. The problem is, no one leaves. The bar routinely sets records for sales of beer and wine that I'm sure to this day remain unsurpassed. I love working with the Strands. I love what they do. I also love making musicians laugh and The Strand Brothers are great laughers. They think my stuff is hilarious. The Strands are absolutely the perfect guys to team me up with. It's a match made in hippie heaven. Before long, the whole thing turns into a major cluster pluck. The band grows from two to as many as ten pickers at a time, all playing acoustic instruments. One of the regulars is an upright bass player from Hawaii named John Yu. The place is tiny, but somehow John always manages to fit his bass in there, which is cool because John is a great upright bass player. The Strands keep the crowd thoroughly engaged and singing along all night long.

I alternate sets with the band and climax my third set by pouring a bottle of Guinness Stout over my head climbing into the balcony and jumping from the balcony back onto the stage. I don't know about risking life, but I definitely risk limb. It is The Zoo and I'm the biggest animal in it. I get laughs, lots of laughs. Outrageous laughs. Dangerous laughs. I know people come every week to see the wreck, but the wreck never happens. The bit gets wild applause every time I do it, which is every Friday night. For the grand finale, I get up with the band and sing "Okie From Muscogee" for all of the long hair San Francisco hippies. Fridays become such a hit that when The Zoo shuts down at 2 AM, the whole crowd piles out of there and heads off to someone or other's place in the vicinity to continue the party. The music and laughs go on until dawn. Afterglows usually last until about 6:00 AM. and end with hippies crashed wall to wall on the floor of whoever's pad it is. It is indeed a magical time.

TRUE BLUE FAN

One night a bunch of us are standing in front of the Zoo at a little after two in the morning. Bob locks up the place and leaves, so we're hanging out talking and someone pulls out a torpedo and fires up. A pungent aroma wafts through the immediate vicinity for about a city block in each direction. About this time, I realize I have to pee so I hop in a large empty dumpster which is conveniently parked in front of The Zoo. I'm in the dumpster and a spotlight hits me. At first I don't know what it is, but my buddies do. They immediately evaporate into the night. The only thing that doesn't evaporate is the smell of whatever is being smoked. So my buddies disappear and I'm left standing there alone in the dumpster with pot smell everywhere and my dick in my hand and a spotlight shined on my head and it dawns on me. "It's the bloody coppers!"

Sure enough, I look down and a San Francisco police cruiser is pulled up alongside the dumpster and that is indeed a spotlight aimed at my head, an indication I am undoubtedly a person of great interest to these cops. Just about the time I'm thinking: "This time I am definitely going to jail..."

The cop says, "What are you doing in the garbage bin, Jim, looking for some new material for your act?"

Now I'm doing my act from inside a dumpster with the lighting guys San Francisco cops. What a trip.

THE OLDEST GAG
IN THE WORLD

Around 1972, I get my longest duration laugh of all time ever. I am two years into my run at The Zoo and it's hard for any comedian to play the same club week after week for that long and not go stale. At some point, you run out of material. No matter how hot you are your jokes start to fall flat. Even the balcony-jump bit is by now wearing thin. "We keep waiting for him to crash and burn, but he never does."

At least if I did, it would be different. I feel an urgent need to come up with something new, something off the wall, something totally original. But I'll settle for one out of three. See, I figure the oldest gag in the world can be the most effective if no one sees it coming. Enter my bother. My brother Steve and I have a sibling rivalry that dates back to the early '50's. We're the Graziano-Zale of the toddler set. We fight so much our parents send us to different schools. Every summer they farm one or the other of us out to an actual farm in the San Joaquin Valley to keep us from killing each other. My favorite Mother's Day card has a picture of two babies in diapers with boxing gloves on. One is on his butt on the floor bawling and the other is standing over him with a beaming smile, holding his gloved hands up in victory. The caption reads, "Thanks, mom, for being such a great referee."

Mom reads the card and says, "Thanks for keeping it real."

But my brother and I are grown-ups now.

Right.

One day I get a call from my brother informing me that he is home from college and is coming to see my act. The same act that I always close by singing, "Okie from Muskogee." The same act that the same audience is used to seeing me do the same way every week. Hmmm. That's when I get the bright idea to pull the oldest gag in the world, but one I've never done on stage before. The audience has been lulled into a false sense of "this guy does the same act every week." No one will see it coming. Right before the show I go to a first class bakery and buy a large banana cream pie. A real one, baked in a real bakery, not some cheap mass-produced supermarket job. The only thing supermarket is the large brown paper bag I conceal the pie in. I ask my brother to meet me before the show. I tell him I need his help. He agrees and shows up early. I clue him in on my plan. "See this?" I show my brother the bag.

"Yeah."

"I got a banana cream pie in here, a real one!" I show him the pie.

"Looks good."

"It is good. The best. Here's the deal. I'm going to do three sets. After the third set, I'm going to get up with the band and sing, 'Okie From Muskogee.'"

"Okay."

"I want you to sit right up front. I'm saving a seat for you. Put the pie under the table. Don't let anyone see you have it. Wait until the end when I get up with the band. I'm going to sing three songs. The last song is 'Okie From Mus,ogee'. The last line of 'Okie From Muskogee' is, 'From Muskogee, Oklahoma, USA.' When I sing the last line, I'm going to stick my face out. Wait 'til the 'USA' part. I'm going to drag that out. When I do, I want you to hit me in the face with the pie. Don't throw it. Slap it in there good. Don't miss. And remember, wait 'til the end. Whatever you do, hold your fire until then. Got it?"

"No problem." My brother grins. He has a look in his eye that makes me more than a little nervous. I've seen that look before.

That night I get up and do my act the way I always do with as little variation as possible. I don't want anyone to suspect what is coming. I have a hard time containing my enthusiasm, which is contagious. The energy builds all night. Even though the crowd has heard it all before, my material goes over big. The fact of knowing what I am about to pull off gives me an edge that hasn't been there in recent weeks. The place is packed. It's a massive cluster pluck. At least 10 or so musicians are on or around the stage. The big moment arrives. I get up with the band. The Strand Brothers are sitting directly behind me. John Yu is behind me stage left with his upright bass. The instruments are acoustic but the energy level in the room is electric. I sing "Okie From Muskogee." When I get to the last line of the song, "From Muskogee, Oklahoma, USA!" I close my eyes, stick out my face, and really stretch out the last "A."

POW! My brother slams the pie into my face with such force that it doesn't just nail me. It nails everyone behind me and in the immediate vicinity on both sides. It's like someone fired a pie out of a blunderbuss, like if I were up there alone there would be a silhouette of me outlined in pie on the curtain behind me. The thing is I'm not up there alone. There are a lot of people behind me and on both sides and everyone gets a taste. No one is exempt. The Strands get hit hard because they are directly behind me, but John Yu and his bass is the biggest target and they get it the worst. Looks like half the pie ends up on John's bass.

A laugh tsunami ensues. As soon as the laughs start to die

down, a glob of pie drops off Rick's fedora or John's bass and another huge wave of laughter is released. It goes on like twenty minutes or more, laughs rolling on wave after wave. The expressions on the faces of the musicians are ones of shock and disbelief. Some are laughing, but they are the "you asshole" kind of laughs. They sit frozen in place, afraid to move, as hunks of banana cream pie drop off them, their instruments, the curtain behind us. The crowd loves it. Timing is everything. Soupy Sales eat your heart out!

FAST FORWARD

Twenty years later the original Zoo crowd gets together for old time's sake. We pick up right where we left off. The night becomes a cluster pluck like the old days. At some point, I ask Rick if he remembers the pie incident. Rick holds up the same beautiful old Guild guitar and directs me to look inside the sound hole.

"See that?"

"What?"

"See it? Right there."

Stuck to a strut inside the body of the guitar I see a petrified piece of piecrust.

"That's the night my guitar got a little sweeter."

Glen the Cop who I first meet in the dumpster goes on to become a highly respected inspector in the San Francisco Police Department. Glen is at the party and he tells me, "You know, I learned a lot about police work watching you imitate Colombo. Play stupid, pretend you don't know anything, keep leaving and coming back, 'Oh yeah, I almost forgot, there was just one thing...' It really works! You catch crooks off guard. They feel sorry for you and tell you stuff they don't mean to. You don't know how much you helped me in my career as a detective."

No shit. There's one for the book.

THE GUINNESS STOUT INCIDENT

Fireworks are great while they last, but alas, fireworks inevitably burn out. With The Zoo and me, the burnout is mutual. By The Zoo, I mean the current Mrs. Steger. Her being the linen tablecloth and proper place setting type and myself being the chug beer out of the pitcher type, you see where this is headed. I'm already working at the Zoo when her and Bob tie the knot. No sooner is the knot tied the handwriting is on the wall. And as anyone familiar with The Zoo knows, when the handwriting's on the wall, you're in the toilet! It sounds like an old joke but it's true!

One night I go into The Zoo Men's Room between sets, read the wall, and come out with three new jokes and a phone number. And this is before The Zoo is a comedy club. The guys writing on the wall are all musicians! There's musical notation on there, philosophical musings, poetry of the doggerel variety: "Here I sit broken hearted..."

But I digress. Suffice it to say once Mrs. Steger shows up, everything for me goes down the crapper. The conflict to me is obvious. Mrs. Steger wants control, and my idea of control is not breaking my legs when I jump out of the balcony. If this were today, liability insurance issues alone would force management to put a stop to my shenanigans. In 1972, it's not an issue. Who cares if I choose to be the recipient of a Darwin Award, especially if it has entertainment value and sells beer?

Unfortunately, Mrs. Steger finds no entertainment value in watching me evolve backwards every Friday night, regardless of beer sales and, Darwin's Theory or no, she makes no secret of the fact she considers me too big of an animal, even for The Zoo.

As bad as things are, they are soon to get much worse, especially for Bob. Not long after they get hitched, Bob is diagnosed with a brain tumor. He loses the rest of his hair and most of his hearing and vision, but Bob won't quit. Even as things go from bad to worse, Bob troops on. He keeps working even though he can't see, and cuts off fingers with a skill saw. It is indeed a dark time. When it becomes too much for Bob to handle the affairs of the club, Bob's wife takes over full time. I know it is the kiss of death for me. The more she makes it known how little she approves of me, the more I make it known how little of a shit I give. I still draw a crowd and my contract, albeit verbal between me and Bob who can't see or hear anymore says all the Guinness Stout I can drink and I take full advantage of the privilege until the bitter end. My run at The Zoo ends ignominiously when I accidently leave the Guinness tap running, a fresh new keg to boot. By the time the error is discovered, the keg is pretty well drained. This is the perennial final straw as it were. Mrs. Steger's parting words to me are indelibly burned in my memory: "OUT!"

"Sorry about that…"

"OUT!"

"I didn't mean to…"

"OOOUUUT!!!"

It would be years before I would set foot in the Zoo again.

THE BOARDING HOUSE

In 1972, David Allen is the owner of the Boarding House and a big dog on the San Francisco entertainment scene. And when I say "big" I mean in every sense of the word. David is a striking presence. Think Sydney Greenstreet in a Greek Sailor's cap. Hip before hip is happening, David is Enrico Banducci's right hand man at the Hungry I during the glory days. He's also Deputy Dave, a local television celebrity and kiddie favorite. I grow up watching Deputy Dave. I remember the first time I see the cartoon Deputy Dog, I think, "Hmm, this looks suspiciously like Deputy Dave."

One day I get a call to meet David Allen in his office at 960 Bush Street. I walk in and David is sitting behind his desk. I do a double take and I say, "You're Deputy Dave!"

David leans back in his chair.

"And you are…?"

"Jim Giovannoni."

"Oh, hi. I'm glad you came in. I've been hearing good things about you. I heard you've been working out over at the Holy City Zoo, right?"

I say, "That's right."

"You're a stand up, right?"

I say, "That's right."

He says, "What kind of stuff do you do?"

"I do impersonations mainly."

"Oh yeah? Like who?

"The usual, John Wayne, Walter Brennan, Kirk Douglas... pretty much the same ones Frank Gorshin does, but my material's all original..."

"Good. It's better to do your own stuff. That's the only way you're ever going to make it."

"I also do Patton and The Godfather. I'm starting to get Colombo down pretty good too."

"You look like Falk. That's half the battle. That's what makes Gorshin so terrific. He looks like the people he does."

"Gorshin's my favorite. Next to Jonathan Winters of course."

"Winters...the best! A genius, but man, is he out there! I could tell you stories. When he was at the Hungry I...He climbed the mast of the Balclutha you know..."

"I remember. I had a paper route at the time. I used to deliver the News-Call. I read it in the paper. Jonathan Winters climbed the Balclutha around the same time Superman committed suicide. It said in the paper Superman shot himself. I remember thinking, "How did he do that? He must have used kryptonite bullets.""

Dave chuckles. "Good observation" he says. "Okay, so you do impersonations. That's good. Audiences love impersonations. You'll be perfect to open for Dan."

"Dan?"

"Dan Hicks and His Hot Licks.' They're headlining here next week and I'm looking for someone to do the opening spot. I'm looking for a comic. You'll be perfect. Are you up for it?"

"Yes!"

"I'll pay you 90 bucks for the week and half off your bar tab. And I'll give you a meal…"

"Sounds great!"

"Be here next Tuesday by seven. First show is at eight. Try to get here early, at least an hour before the show so you can eat. Please, do me a favor. Don't just show up right at show time. I don't need a heart attack. Okay?"

"Are you kidding? I'll be here two hours before the show."

"An hour's good. Just get here early enough so I can feed you. See you next week." Dave sticks out his hand. We shake.

"Thanks, David."

"Any questions?"

"No. I'll see you next Tuesday."

I start to walk out but hesitate, scrunch up my face and do the Peter Falk eye thing, turn around, and look at David. Now I'm talking like Columbo. "Gee, I almost forgot, there was just one thing…"

Dave says, "What?"

"Gee, since you're Deputy Dave and I work for you now, do I get to wear a badge?"

"Only if it's part of your schtick."

THE BIG TIME

Getting a gig at The Boarding House is a big deal. The Boarding House books George Carlin, who is going through a metamorphosis, transitioning from straight button-down standup to bellbottomed counterculture icon. During his runs there, Carlin sits at the bar, writing fervently. Then he gets up in his next set and tries out material he just wrote at the bar. Steve Martin records three albums at The Boarding House. The reviews he gets in San Francisco launch his rocket to stardom. One day David says to me, "Be sure to come see the comedian I'm bringing in next week. He's out of New York, a new young guy. He's brilliant."

I go back the next week. Dave's right. The comedian is Robert Klein.

MORE BACKSTORY

At first it doesn't dawn on me, but I've seen Dan Hicks before, a few years earlier in 1968 at an open mike in the Sausalito Lion's Share. I remember it like it's yesterday. Dan is on stage, barely upright on his barstool, drunk off his ass, strumming his guitar and singing, the lyrics classic Dan Hicks: "He don't care about the way he walks. He don't care about the way he talks. Is that traffic light green or red? Is he alive or is he dead? He's stoned. Dead stoned…"

One day I'm on the houseboat. It is bright and sunny at about two in the afternoon. I am varnishing the deck. Just about the time I'm starting to hallucinate off the fumes, a bunch of musicians pile out of the houseboat next door onto the boardwalk with acoustic instruments and begin jamming, guitar, fiddle, upright bass, a couple of chick singers. It's no hallucination. I don't know it at the time but the group is Dan Hicks and His Hot Licks. I don't recognize Dan. He's sober.

FAST FORWARD

Three years later, I'm opening for Dan and His Hot Licks. My first week at the Boarding House is pure magic, one of my best ever as a performer. The Boarding House is a jewel. The room sparkles. Everything sparkles. There is a sparkling fountain in the back. It is a supper club, dinner and a show, a class joint. Dave knows his way around a menu. One look at him and you know Dave knows food. Performers get a free meal, always a plus. We do two sets a night. The first is dinner and show, the second, just show, but with a different crowd, which means I can do the same set twice. Dave gives me twenty minutes, so I do my best twenty minutes of "A" material twice a night for six nights. I get my first review from San Francisco Chronicle entertainment critic, John L Wasserman and it's a good one. It is dated Friday, March 31, 1972.

ON THE TOWN
John L. Wasserman, SF Chronicle

THE BOARDING House, the 960 Bush club which failed as a Troubadour North in 1970 but has since succeeded mightily as the Boarding House, is celebrating its first anniversary this week with Dan Hicks and his Hot Licks and comedian impressionist Jim Giovannoni. On Tuesday, opening night, a bad night for audiences, without any record company promotional party, the first set was standing room only. This is a tribute to Hicks and Company, of course, but also to the club, which is operated by the imperturbable David Allen, serves decent food at decent prices, keeps the noise down to a reasonable level, charges modestly for admission and bev-

43

*erage and has rather quickly become one of the most import-
ant clubs on the West Coast.*

*Giovannoni is primarily on impressionist, and an un-
usually creative one. Frank Gorshin, for example, is far
better at pure imitations, in voice and in style, but his raw
material-and this is also true of David Fry-is basically con-
ventional.*

*Giovannoni did, among other things, a model airplane en-
gine being started, Dustin Hoffman's Ratso Rizzo from
Midnight Cowboy, Bugs Bunny and Porky Pig, a character
reading graffiti on bathroom walls in a new non-existent
movie by Candid Camera's Alan Funt entitled "Pay Toilet";
John Brody throwing an interception, Tommy Smothers, Bill
Cosby and Wolfman Jack.*

It's a great week, one of my best yet on the planet. Dan
Hicks is on fire. The Hot Licks are at their hottest. I hear
"How Can I Miss You If You Won't Go Away" twelve times
that week. I love Dan's stuff but I don't get the feeling
it's reciprocal. I don't know whether Dan just doesn't like
me or he doesn't like Tommy Smothers, but on more than
one occasion, Dan makes droll comments about Tommy
Smothers and/or my impression of him. Dan's comments
are not intended as gentle ribbing, either. Dan's disdain
or the disdain of Dan, whatever you want to call it, there
is nothing quite like it, you have to experience it to fully
appreciate it. It's practically impossible to get Dan to acknowledge you, much less like you, so in a sense it's quite
an accomplishment, a badge of honor as it were. At the
end of the week, David Allen calls me in his office to settle up. He is sitting behind his desk.

David says, "Have a seat."

On Dave's desk is an old fashioned adding machine with
hand crank and paper adding machine tape streaming
out of it. Dave holds my receipts from the bar in his hand.
"I'm deducting these from what I owe you." He says.

Dave starts cranking the machine, adding up the receipts. "Okay, I'm giving you eighty-four bucks. Your bar tab is $6.50, but you did a good job so we'll round it off, make it an even six. "Six from ninety is eighty-four so I'm giving you eighty four bucks."

"Thanks, Dave."

"You did a good job. Next time I'll give you a hundred."

"That's great! Gee, thanks, Dave!"

Wow! I already got a raise! Dave picks up two large brown paper shopping bags and puts them on his desk. They are both stuffed to the brim with receipts. "Can you believe this? I'm going to be here all night!"

I say, "What's that?"

He says, "Dan Hicks' bar tab. It looks like Dan's going to owe me money."

THE GREAT AMERICAN MUSIC HALL

The Great American Music Hall opens around the same time as the Boarding House in '72. The owners are Jeanie and her husband, both healthcare professionals, married with no children. Since Jeanie and her husband are a childless couple and their favorite thing is jazz, they figure why not use what disposable income they have by not having children, to open a jazz club? It makes sense. Jazz musicians are like children. In fact, next to comedians, jazz musicians are the biggest children around. The only difference between comedians and jazz musicians is jazz musicians are funnier. "How many jazz musicians does it take to change a light bulb?"

"Who's worried about changes, man?"

One night I'm in the Great American music Hall opening for Buddy Rich. The show is supposed to start at 8. I'm downstairs in the dressing room. About 7:45 the stage manager comes up to me and says, "How much time can you do?"

I say, "Jeanie told me do twenty minutes."

He says, "Never mind what Jeanie told you. Buddy Rich and the band aren't here. The place is packed. It's 'standing room only' up there. We start at 8 no matter what. I'll introduce you. If Buddy's not here, go out and start talking and keep talking until I give you the sign to get off. Keep going no matter what. Got it?"

"Got it."

I hope I got it, enough material that is. I'm praying Buddy and the band show up, but 8 o'clock rolls around, and still no sign of Buddy. I'm standing backstage and the stage manager comes up to me. He does not look happy. He says, "Buddy and the band aren't here. Remember just keep going until I give you the sign. You ready?"

"I'm as ready as I'll ever be."

I'm more than a little nervous. I don't know how long I'm going to have to be out there and if I am going to be able to cover it time-wise. I can hear the buzz, feel the energy in the room. Lights dim. A hush falls over the crowd. The stage manager's voice comes over the PA. He says, "Good evening. Welcome to the Great American Music Hall. Buddy Rich and his band aren't here, but here's a comedian anyway..."

The guy doesn't even say my name and thanks for telling them the band isn't here yet. Turns out it doesn't matter. My act kills. I'm going strong thirty plus minutes into it and the stage manager gives me the "wrap" sign, so I go to the two-minute drill. Now I'm doing the Ape Man, the Zarathustra music is playing, I pour the Guinness over my head and I can't jump off the balcony because I can't get to it and the one in the Music Hall is too high anyway, but the light guy is a genius with the lights and he's doing all kinds of far out wild crazy effects, making the sun come up while the ape holds up the bottle Guinness rolling off my head, foaming out of my mouth and the crowd is going crazy. The music climaxes, I jump off the stage into the cheering crowd and exit stage right triumphantly drenched in Guinness. I get downstairs and Buddy Rich is standing in the hallway in front of the dressing rooms with a big Bugs Bunny looking grin on his face. I say, "Your audience awaits you, Mr. Rich."

Buddy says, "Who the fuck are you?"

I say, "I'd tell you to ask the stage manager, but apparently he doesn't know either."

He says, "What the fuck...?"

"I'm Jim Giovannoni. I'm your opening act."

Buddy says, "Oh, yeah. How is it up there?"

"Great. It's sold out. Hot crowd. They're ready for you."

Buddy says to the guys in the dressing room: "Hey assholes. Knock off the bullshit. Time to get up there."

Welcome to the big time.

THE COMEDY STORE

I don't know it at the time, but just as the Comedy Renaissance is getting underway in San Francisco, it's happening in Los Angeles, New York, Chicago, all over the country. Around the time David Allen is opening the Boarding House in San Francisco, Sammy Shore is opening the Comedy Store in Hollywood. When I first hear about the Comedy Store, I decide that it's time for this duck to fly to a bigger pond. I take the meager stake I've raised and head to Los Angeles. I get there, check into a room in a cheap motel in North Hollywood. The place is a cesspool of pimps and hookers and God knows what, but a necessary evil I must endure if I'm going to make a run at it in this business. My first night at the Comedy Store the first guy I see is Al Franken, who became a US senator. You can't miss Al. He's there with his comedy partner, Tom Davis. What strikes me most about Al Franken is he's got the best Afro I've ever seen on a white guy. At the time I think Al could have beat out Angela Davis in a best Afro contest. I try to grow one myself during my hippie period, but mine always lay down on me. At my best I looked like Frank Zappa on a bad hair day. I can't tell you much about their act, but I do remember being jealous of Al's hair. Nowadays I see Al on TV and I'm still jealous of Al's hair. The other guy with outstanding hair I remember from those days is Gary Mule Deer. Gary's hair is still outstanding. So is his comedy routine. As of the writing of this, both Gary and his hair are still out standing up somewhere. My act kills in those early days at the Comedy Store. In a tuxedo with slicked back hair and a moustache

49

and bar napkins stuffed in my cheeks, I'm a dead ringer for Marlon Brando in The Godfather. Ditch the moustache, fluff the hair, put on a raincoat, I'm Columbo. Of course everything revolves around Nixon. Nixon and the Godfather, Nixon and Colombo, the Watergate hearings. I close with Redd Foxx live at the White House. I also perform at the Troubadour and the Ye Little Club in Beverly Hills, soon to be under new management and renamed the Joan Rivers Club. The act is a hit everywhere I go. My star is on the rise until August 9, 1974, the day Nixon resigns. I try to do my act that night and it's like talking to a room full of mannequins. I soon find out this is not just an aberration either, an off night as it were. It's just as bad the following night and the night after that. Now painfully aware of the perils of basing one's entire act on current events, I pack my bags and high tail it back to San Francisco. It's years before I do Nixon on stage again.

MEANWHILE BACK AT THE BOARDING HOUSE

David Allen is a great guy, but he's all business when he needs to. I don't know it at the time, but Dave originally comes from New Jersey to San Francisco to open up a shooting range. I remember hearing this and thinking I'm glad he likes me. I love working for Dave, who himself is skilled at improvisation. He knows his way around a stage, has a keen sense of what works and what doesn't, so I always run ideas past him before I try them out in front of a crowd. I remember one conversation in particular. Like most comics, I'm constantly in search of new material. As a kid I played trumpet, so I tell Dave my idea of putting the trumpet in my act, maybe doing a Louis Armstrong impersonation. Dave says, "I don't believe you should burlesque an instrument unless you can play the shit out of it."

I never take a trumpet on stage in the Boarding House.

THE PETE HARRISON SHOW

Moving furniture has always been the perfect side job for me. That way I'm not tied to any set schedule. I can work whenever I want and, if I get a show business gig, I'm free to take it. One day I'm working furniture with an old boy who says he is a country music fan. I do my Merle Haggard impersonation for him and he says, "You know, you want to go over there to the Pablo Club. My cousin Pete Harrison's got a radio show over there on Sundays and they got a talent contest and I think you'd be good to go over there and sign up for the talent contest."

I get to the Pablo Club and it is a pure-d, bone-e-fide honky-tonk, located right there smack dab in the middle of the City of San Pablo. The minute I walk through the door I know I'm in Redneck Central. Every Sunday afternoon at 3:00 P.M., KSAY, the local Country music station on AM radio, broadcasts a live Country music radio show from the Pablo Club in San Pablo featuring Pete Harrison and the Pete Harrison Band. It's called what else? The Pete Harrison Show. One of the great things about the Pete Harrison show is, every week after the show, there is a talent contest. The winner of the talent contest gets to sing the following week in a featured spot on the Pete Harrison Show live on the radio. Pete advertises the event each week on his show. "Y'all come down to the Pablo Club, you hear."

That Sunday I get over to the Pablo Club, the place is jumping. The bar is three deep and the dance floor is packed with folks out there a two-steppin'. On stage in the middle of a song, up there a-pickin' and a-grinnin' is Pete Harrison. Pete's a good ol' boy who looks like a country singer. Best part is, he plays the kind of country music I like: Heavy on the twang! After the show is over, it's time for the talent contest. I ask Pete about signing up. "What song do you want to do?" Pete says.

I say, 'Harold's Super Service'. It's a Merle Haggard song. Do you guys know that one?"

He says, "Someone in the band will know it."

The contest is pre-karaoke karaoke with live musicians. The competition is strong. Every now and then you get a dud, but most are good. Pete introduces the singers. One by one, each gets up and sings a classic country song, backed by Pete and the band. A couple gets up and does a George Jones and Tammy Wynette duet. They are good too. My turn comes. I get up and sing my song. I know my voice ain't the greatest but it's a funny song and I sell it and get a good response from the crowd. I finish second. I know I can win if I punch it up with some jokes, so I come back the next week and ask Pete if it's okay if I do a couple of impersonations before I sing my song. Pete says, "Okay, but don't do long, no more than a minute or so and then sing your song."

My turn comes. I figure with this crowd I can't go wrong with John Wayne and Walter Brennan. Aside from the fact I don't do Nixon in my act anymore, I wouldn't do it for this crowd anyway because these folks look like they probably voted for Nixon, and I don't want to be attending no necktie parties anytime soon, especially my own. So I play it safe and do John Wayne, Walter Brennan, a cow, and a coyote. Got to have the coyote, especially since I'm fixin' to sing. What the heck, Ernest Tubb is tuned a little off too, ain't he? Ha! So I do about a minute or so, sing my song and when time comes to pick a winner I get the biggest response. A week later, I'm back at the Pablo Club singing "Harold's Super Service" live on the Pete Harrison Show on the radio. After the show, Pete asks me if I'd like to do a paid gig opening for him at the Richmond Rod and Gun Club. I agree and Pete says, "Okay, meet us here next Saturday at four and we'll all ride over together."

The next Saturday, I get to the Pablo Club and Pete tells me to ride to the gig with the guitar player. Turns out, the guitar player is the guy who wrote the biggest hit Country single of all time at the time, "Release Me." So now I'm with the guy who wrote "Release Me," stuck at a railroad crossing in a big old Pontiac Bonneville, sitting there watching a freight train rumble by, and it is a long-ass freight train, so we're there for a while, and I ask the guy how he came up with the song, "Release Me."

He says, "Well, I'm driving along in Mississippi with my brother-in-law and I'm married to his sister at the time and I wanted to get out of it so I says to him, 'Man, I wish there was a way I could get a release from all this stuff with your sister, I'd sure like to get a release from it all' and he says, 'You know that sounds like it would make a pretty good song, you ought to write that one' and we didn't have no paper or nothin' to write with, but there was an old broke pencil in the back seat there on the floor and I had a knife on me so I got out my knife and I whittled on that ol' broke pencil and we got to the honky-tonk there and it was an old gravel parkin' lot there and we pulled in the parkin' lot and got out and took that ol' pencil and wrote 'Release Me' on the trunk of his car and the next thing I know it's a hit, and you know that dang thang has been translated into over seventy languages."

I say, "You must have made a ton of money."

He says, "My ex-wives is all doing real good."

ARTIE MITCHELL

Speaking of guitar players, around this time I meet Mike Bloomfield. Mike is a lead guitar player in The Paul Butterfield Blues Band. Mike sees my act and digs what I do and asks for my phone number, says he might have a gig for me. I give Mike my number and forget about it.

One day I get a call. "Is this Jim Giovannoni?"

"Yes. Who's this?"

"Artie Mitchell."

"Hi Artie Mitchell."

"I got your number from Mike Bloomfield. Mike says you're a funny guy."

"I'm pretty funny."

"You do impersonations?"

"Yes."

"You do John Wayne?"

"Yeah. Doesn't everybody?"

"Mike says you're good, so I'd like to hire you to for a movie I'm working on. It's a feature film. Are you interested?"

"Yes. Absolutely."

"Good. Come by my office and I'll tell you more about it?"

I'm thinking, "Wow! This could be it. This could be one of Coppola's guys!"

Artie gives me the address on O'Farrell Street. I am so busy daydreaming about what a big star I am about to become I have no clue when I walk in there where I am. It doesn't dawn on me until I'm in the lobby that Artie's address is The Mitchell Brothers Theater. The first clue is the sound of fervent love making coming from inside the main theater. That's where the Mitchell Brothers current hit *Behind the Green Door* is playing on the big screen. Someone directs me upstairs to Artie's office. I get up there and Artie is sitting at an editing machine looking at dailies.

I say, "Hi. I'm Jim Giovannoni."

Artie says, "Hi Jim. Artie Mitchell. Check it out. This is our new project. It's the film you'll be working on. It's called, "Sodom and Gomorrah".

It's easy to see how the film got the title. On the screen is a naked couple coupling naked in a tree, the guy behind the woman, banging away doggy style, the only dialogue the chick saying,

"More olive oil! More olive oil!"

Gives a whole new meaning to the expression, "making it on the big screen."

The movie also features a naked yogi hippie demonstrating various self-gratifying poses. It blows me away, pardon the pun. I'm thinking: "Is this even possible?" If I saw this nowadays I'd say, "Surely this is computer generated."

Seriously, it reminds me of the old joke. "Why do dogs lick their balls? Because they can."

The reel ends. Artie says, "What do you think?"

I say, "I think if I was that guy, I'd never leave the house..."

Artie laughs.

I say, "Makes me wish I stuck with the yoga classes."

"Mike's right. You are a funny guy…"

"Seriously, Artie. What do you need me for? I mean I'm talented, but I'm not that talented."

"I don't want you for on camera. I want you to do voice-over. You are going to be the Voice of God only God is John Wayne…"

BOOM! RED FLAG! Catholic school indoctrination kicks in BAM! I don't know if it's true what they say about what God does to blasphemers, but I ain't taking no chances. I say, "Sorry, Artie. I can't do it."

Artie says, "Why not?"

I say, "I'm afraid I'll turn into a pillar of salt."

Artie's pissed. That's the last time I ever see Artie Mitchell.

THE ARTIST MANAGER

One day I pick up the Chronicle, look in the want ad section under entertainment, and see an ad: "Professional Artist Management seeks talent." I call the number and arrange to meet with the Artist Manager at his office, which is on the fourth floor of an old Victorian on Gough Street. There is no elevator, so I climb four flights to get to the top floor. I enter the main office and the setup in there is sparse. There's just a desk and a secretary sitting behind the desk and a locked steel file cabinet. There isn't even a chair for me to sit on. This should be a clue like maybe these guys don't stay in one place too long, but instead of thinking like Columbo, I'm thinking like a furniture mover: "This would be an easy office move if it had an elevator and didn't have all these stairs." I tell the secretary I have an appointment to meet with the Artist Manager. She picks up a phone and announces my arrival and tells me to wait. So I'm standing there waiting, finally a door to a private office opens, a casually dressed older gentleman appears. He's wearing dress shirt, no tie, slacks, dress shoes.

Writers note: Details are important, especially if this ever goes to court.

So this guy, who I am soon to find out is the Artist Manager's father, comes out and escorts me into the office of the Artist Manager. I get in there and the Artist Manager is sitting behind a big desk. He is dressed in an expensive looking suit and silk tie like he's Frank Sinatra's manager or something. There is a second chair in front of his desk and he invites me to sit, I suppose looking back on it, to soften me up for the kill. He then asks to see my promotional materials. I happily oblige, showing him my professional publicity photos and my resumé and good reviews from the Chronicle.

The Artist Manager proceeds to tell me how everything looks good, but he still needs to see me perform. He says he is going to have me audition in front of a live audience at the Travis Air Force Base Officers Club on Saturday at 8 and 10 PM. I should have figured the minute he said it was two shows that it was a scam to get me to work free, but being a young, naïve, dumbass furniture mover/comedian, I go along with it and say yes.

He tells me to dress up, wear a tux and to get to Travis by seven, check in at the Main Gate and tell them my name and that I'm with the show at the Officer's Club. He says he'll see me on Saturday and not to let him down. I rent a tux and get there Saturday night and it's a big event indeed. All the men are in dress uniforms or tuxedos and all the women are wearing evening gowns. There are flower centerpieces on the tables, the works. There is a six-piece band and the band members are all wearing tuxedos. The Artist Manager and his father are there. The Artist Manager's father is wearing a tux, but The Artist Manager has on a fancy Italian suit with a silk tie. I mean this guy is playing the role of Artist Manager to the hilt. He tells me to go out at eight o'clock and do twenty minutes and then bring on his wife, a chanteuse blonde bombshell Anne Margaret type singer. She's the headliner, there's a break after her, and then at 10 PM straight up we do it all over again.

It's a production. Le Chanteuse is going to change her outfit for the second show and everything. At exactly 2000 Hours Air Force time, I go out and do my twenty minutes. My act goes over like usual. The Godfather and Columbo are both hits, and John Wayne is an out-of-the-park home run.

I introduce the bombshell, and she's up there and everything is going fine until, like happens with a lot of bomb-
shells, there's an explosion. She's singing jazz standards,
everybody is digging it until she leaves the stage and goes
in the audience and sits in some officer's lap and starts
singing "Nothing Like A Man" to the guy and all of a sudden, a woman, I'm assuming it's the guy's wife, flips out
and blip, she lays a gin and tonic right in the middle of
Le Chanteuse's evening gown. A shit storm ensues, and Le
Chanteuse goes into her wounded diva routine and says
she cannot continue. The second show is mercifully cancelled. I am somewhat relieved, since I burned all my "A"
material on the first set, and all I have left are fart jokes.

THE AFTERMATH

Monday morning The Artist Manager calls and says he wants to see me in his office. I go up there and of course the secretary makes me stand and wait, and finally they let me in. The Artist Manager is behind his desk, and his father is there hovering as usual and The Artist Manager lays a contract in front of me. I look at the thing and it's pages of legalese which basically says that this guy owns me for the rest of my life and everything I make he gets twenty-five percent and anything over $25,000 he gets thirty percent,, and he has seven year options into perpetuity to renew my contract, but I have no option at any time to quit. Oh, and he doesn't actually have to get me any work. All he has to do is "manage" and "advise" me in my career.

I have a bad feeling about this so I decide to get my own father in on the deal to find out what he thinks. We arrange another meeting with my dad there and my dad, being the sort who sees good in everybody no matter how big a scumbag they are, meets Artist Manager and Artist Manager Daddy and thinks that they are lovely people, and I should sign the contract. I do, at which point The Artist Manager informs me that all of my promotional materials are now his personal property including all of my pictures and resumés. He basically confiscates the stuff and says that from now on I am only to go through him for future business transactions and further assures me that I have a brilliant future ahead of me.

Oh, by the way, did I tell you I am married? As of the writing of this book, we are going on forty-four years and

I could tell you stories that would curl your hair, but that's a whole other book. For the purposes of this particular work, think of my wife as Mrs. Columbo. I will talk about her from time to time, but if left up to her, she'd rather be left out. You have to understand that she and I are opposites. She is an introvert. I'm an extrovert. She is germane to this particular story, however, so I have to talk about her. We are still newlyweds, married less than a year, when all this business with The Artist Manager is going down. I'm still working my day job moving furniture, patiently waiting for the phone call that is going to change our lives, and she is working as a registered nurse and are in the process of moving into a rental flat in the Richmond District in San Francisco, which I spend nights painting in preparation for our big move.

She makes new curtains, I move all our stuff, we are just getting settled in and the Artist Manager calls and says he just booked me for six months at a club in Anchorage, Alaska. My wife is not happy it's a strip joint but The Artist Manager says I need to do six months there so that I can build up my chops and after that he's going to put me on the road opening for big name acts like The Serendipity Singers and Bob Hope. Hey! I'm desperate to make it in show business. I'll do whatever it takes. Moving furniture is getting old by now, so I agree to do what The Artist Manager says. He tells me to be at the airport on such and such a date and my ticket will be at will call. I immediately call my boss and quit my day job.

My wife, figuring it's probably not such a great idea to let her husband go off to Alaska to work in a strip joint for six months without her being around, decides to go with me. She quits her day job and I quit mine and we go to the landlord, who we've just signed a one-year lease with, and explain the situation. He says he'll let us out of the lease providing we do all the legwork of taking out an ad in the paper and finding someone to take over the lease, with his approval of course. We do all this and I move all our stuff into storage.

We show up at the airport on the ordained day and lo and behold, we get to Will Call, and there are no tickets to Anchorage. They haven't even heard of me at Will Call. I call the Artist Manager from the airport to find out what the deal is and I get the answering machine and hear my own voice doing Redd Foxx. This goes on for two weeks with The Artist Manager avoiding me the whole time. In the meantime, my wife and I go through the humiliation of having to ask our bosses for our jobs back and then the major hassle of finding a new place and signing a new lease and painting and moving all over again. All the while, I keep calling the Artist Manager to no avail. Finally, I get through, and he nonchalantly tells me that the deal fell through. I tell him that I'm really upset about what has happened and he casually blows me off like it's no big deal. "No big deal? It's a big deal to me. I've had it with this shit. I want out of my contract."

The Artist Manager says he can't do that and hangs up on me. Now I'm really pissed. I call and call and call but he won't answer the phone. Now I'm afraid to take a job at the Boarding House or the Great American Music Hall because I know he's going to find out about it when he sees my name in the newspaper. I definitely don't want to have to pay this prick 25% of what I make for gigs I already got before I ever met him or his asshole father, so I decide to take matters into my own hands and to go up to his office and confront him directly.

CRIME TIME

I get there and the door is locked. I knock and knock until finally Daddy Artist Manager opens the door a crack to see who it is. It's enough of a crack to stick my foot in where he can't close the door. I say I want to talk to The Artist Manager and I'm not leaving until I do so. He insists that his son is not there and that I should leave, but instead of leaving I gently but firmly push the door open. He is powerless to stop me. I enter the office. By this time they no longer employ a secretary, so it is just the two of us standing in the waiting room area. I tell him I know he's lying and that the Artist Manager is locked in his office like a little scared rabbit, avoiding me. He keeps telling me that I have to leave, but I say I'm not leaving without my contract and all of my promotional materials. I know exactly where they are too, in the locked steel file cabinet, which is right there in front of me. He insists he is not authorized to do that and he doesn't have the key to open the file cabinet. I say, "There comes a time in every furniture mover's life when he has an overwhelming urge to throw a locked steel file cabinet down four flights of stairs, tearing up hallways and stairwells and every other fucking thing as she goes, and the time has come for me! Yee haw! Stand back! Time to start the rodeo!"

I grab the file cabinet and start walking it. He's panicking, hollering: "Stop! You can't do that!"

He makes a move like he's going to shut the door to prevent me from leaving with his file cabinet, but I'm on a roll now and I ain't stopping for nothing. "It makes no bit of difference to me if it goes through the door or the wall I guarantee this motherfucker will be open by the time it gets to the ground floor!"

"No! No! Don't! Stop! Please! Oh, my God!" The asshole knows it's no bluff. Boom! Out come the keys! "Okay, okay. Stop! Stop! Please stop!" His hands are shaking so bad he has a hard time opening the file cabinet. He finally does and the whole time he's scouring through the file cabinet, he's shaking all over the place. He finds my contract and promotional materials, double and triple checks to make sure he's got everything, piles it all into my arms and says he never wants to see me again. I assure him it will not be a problem. I leave happy albeit somewhat unsatisfied. By the time I worked myself up to it, it's a letdown to not actually throw a locked steel file cabinet down four flights of stairs, but at least I got what I came for, which is to be out from under contract from these pricks. It does make me feel slightly better having at least scared the shit out of them. For the next few days, I keep thinking I'm going to hear from the cops, but I never do. About five years later I pick up the Chronicle and find out why. This article appears Wednesday, June 28, 1978 in the San Francisco Chronicle:

THEATRICAL AGENTS INDICTED – FRAUD

A San Francisco-based theatrical agent and his son were indicted yesterday by a federal grand jury here for allegedly defrauding state fairs and entertainment centers across the country by promising appearances by such stars as Bob Hope the Smothers Brothers Roger Miller and John Davidson and then failing to deliver.

Warrants were issued for George Stanton, 58, and his son David, 29, of Los Angeles, both officers of the Theatrical Corp. of America after the grand jury indicted the two men on 18 counts of mail fraud involving $450,000 in losses.

The Stantons were also charged with submitting false insurance claims totaling more than $600,000.

State fairs in New York, Texas and Minnesota invested in television specials to be filmed on location according to the indictment although some of the shows had to be halted or shelved because the headline acts meanwhile had not agreed to have their performances distributed.

The indictment also charged that Hope and others were unaware contracts have been drawn up for their appearances, or that the agents were charging inflated fees.

In addition the government charged that the Stantons refused to reimburse money to investors for appearances by stars who never performed.

Postal inspector, Lawrence M. Russell, who headed the 17-month investigation, said many of the show business luminaries-among them Liza Minnelli, Helen Reddy, Jim Nabors, Roy Clark and the Fifth Dimension would testify at the trial.

Russell said several insurance companies were bilked by the Stantons, who insured the purported TV shows then reported the films had been stolen and collected on claims.

The Theatrical Corp. of America, located at 1369 Post St. and headed by David Stanton, owns the name Serendipity Singers and books performers under that name for personal appearances.

The Stantons produced a Bob Hope show in Concord in 1975 but investors said Hope did not collect his entire fee.

Russell also claimed the Stanton kept $20,000 of an insurance settlement for themselves when the Serendipity Singers collected benefits stemming from a 1975 auto accident in Dallas.

Resort areas suffered the most in the scheme, according to investigators, who said investors in Reno, Tahoe and Vail,

Colo., lost $188,000 between 1974 and 1977.

Russell added that the state fairs were bilked out of $30,000 during the same period. The Stantons, in the meantime, collected $91,000 in false insurance claims, the indictment said.

The California labor commission suspended the agencies license in 1971 for not dealing fairly with artists.

Which goes to show, once again it proves the old adage: If you're going to rob somebody, rob a crook. Crooks don't tell.

THE GAME

Around this time, my main way of staying sane is playing tackle football on weekends. There is a regular tackle game I play in from 1970 till about '75 at College of Marin Football Stadium in Marin County. It happens every Sunday of football season starting with the first pre-season NFL game and ending the day of the Pro Bowl, August through January every Sunday. The regulars for the most part are guys who never played in high school or college. Most of them are Juvenile Hall alumni. If the Honor farm had a team, these guys would be on it.

On any given Sunday one might ask, "Where's Ria?"

"Ria's in jail, man. Ria rolled his car."

The next week it would be "Where's Clark?"

"Clark's in jail, man. Clark totaled his truck."

Many of the regulars in this game are guys who are either out on bail, returning Viet Nam vets or, in the case of Clark, both. The amazing thing is, in the five plus years I play in this game I never see one serious injury. I see lacerations and stitches and broken noses and knocked out teeth and an occasional broken bone, but not one serious life altering injury and not one fight. The worst injury in the history of the game happens when a former pro NFL player, an Atlanta Falcon free safety shows up and gets in the game and breaks his leg. That's it. This game is the most fun I ever have in my life legally. No one cares who wins or what the final score is in the end. There are no coaches, no referees, no clock and no one to answer to except each other. Everyone plays by the rules and there are no rules. The only point is the camaraderie and the opportunity to, in a socially acceptable way, knock the crap out of each other every Sunday. It's football heaven. I become addicted to playing sand lot tackle football. I'm so into it that sometimes I can't wait until Sunday. I go to various fields in The City and play in pick-up games on Saturdays. Now I'm playing twice a weekend, on Saturdays and Sundays. In some games, I'm the only white guy in the game. It doesn't matter. Guys get to know you. You become a regular. Guys respect you because you play clean and you are not afraid to deliver a hit or take a hit. I spend five plus years throwing my young body into it with complete abandon, without health insurance. It's crazy, but it's fun and a lot of laughs. Dangerous laughs.

THE ZOO REVISITED

Around 1974-75 The Holy City Zoo starts doing comedy again, an open mike one night a week on Wednesday nights. Tony DePaul takes control over running the show. Tony asks me to do it, I'm sure because I am a solid performer and he wants the thing to fly.

At first, I'm somewhat hesitant because the Guinness Stout Incident happened not that long ago and I'm not sure if the statute of limitations has run out on that yet. Tony assures me the Stegers are long gone and a new guy named Pete owns it now. Pete knows nothing about the Guinness Stout Incident, so the coast is clear for me to come back. I do and immediately become a stalwart, working out every Wednesday night. Comedy soon becomes such a hit at the Zoo they decide to add a second night. Now I'm there every Wednesday and Saturday.

After about a year of doing this, I miss one night because I get a paid gig, and that night Tony and Pete and some of the other comedians decide that they are going to start charging a cover charge and split the door. Okay fine. The Zoo never charged cover before, but whatever. It's his club. He can do what he wants. The problem is nobody tells me about any of any of this, and when I show up on Saturday to do my bit, Tony informs me that not only am I not on the bill, but that I have to pay cover to get in. I ask Tony to explain and he says that since The Zoo is small and they're going to do a cover charge now, he is going to decide which comedians are going to perform and split the door; any comedians not on the bill will have to pay the cover to get in, and I am not on the bill. I am dumbfounded. The thing that galls me most is Tony doesn't see a problem with any of this. I do and I make it known to all within earshot. I'm more Ralph Kramden than Clint Eastwood on this one. I say, "Tony, I have been anchoring comedy night for over year now, for no pay, helping turn comedy at The Zoo into what it is and I'm gone one night and you decide to pull this shit?"

Frank Kidder and Ed Turner are standing right there and Tony's just told them the same thing. To add insult to injury, neither Frank nor Ed have any money and I forgot my wallet. I say, "Tony, I forgot my wallet and these guys don't have any money. You know they don't have any money. None of us should have to pay to get in. We paid our dues..."

Tony says, "Sorry, Jimmy. From now on, if you ain't on the bill, you got to pay to get in."

"Tony, I'm a main reason why comedy is a hit here. You don't even bother to tell me or ask my opinion about any of this?"

"Sorry, Jimmy, rules are rules. Me and the other comedians agreed on this."

It's an age-old story. Bring in the Marines to secure the beach and once the pogues can get their hot showers, it's, "Thanks, assholes, but your services are no longer needed."

For a brief moment I think about going home to get my wallet, and it pisses me off even more. I look at Tony and say, "Not this time, you don't! Screw this! This is bullshit! Fuck you guys! Come on Frank, Ed, come with me!"

With Frank and Ed in tow, I storm out of there. At first I don't know what to do, so I decide to head over to the Moonshiner, which is a bar on the next block. But before we get there, I see a large dumpster parked on a side street. I don't know what tells me to look in the dumpster but we do and it's serendipitous. In the dumpster is a full bag of fertilizer labeled COW MANURE, with a picture of a cow on it. There also are brand-new redwood picket fence slats and large perfectly cut square pieces of white cardboard, perfect to make picket signs out of. I retrieve them out of the dumpster. "Come on, let's go."

We head over to the Moonshiner. I ask to borrow a black felt tip marker pen and a heavy-duty stapler gun. They loan me the materials and we make three picket signs, with "Comedy Local Number One" and "Holy City Zoo Unfair to Comedians." We go back to The Zoo and set up a picket line in front and believe me nobody crosses the picket line and now a crowd is starting to gather out front.

Tony and Pete come out, and I make a grand presentation to them of the bag of COW MANURE, telling them it is apropos because what they are doing is bullshit. From that point forward the show is no longer inside The Zoo, it's out in front on the sidewalk. It's total street theater. I have no doubt you can hear me for blocks in every direction giving my union organizing speech. People inside are exiting The Zoo to watch the show outside. Now more people are on the sidewalk in front of the Zoo than can fit in The Zoo.

Tony DePaul is hopping mad, jumping up-and-down like a bandy rooster. Pete has no idea what to do. An SFPD police cruiser rolls up and double-parks in the middle of the street, lights flashing. My buddy, Glenn the Cop gets out with his partner. Glenn says, "What's going on here?"

I announce in my best teamster union organizer voice, "THIS IS A LABOR DISPUTE! THE HOLY CITY ZOO IS UNFAIR TO COMEDIANS!"

The scene is funny to everyone but Tony and Pete and the comedians who are trying to pull the power play. Even the cops think it is funny. Glen the Cop decides to mediate. He says, "Surely you guys can work this out."

"DAMM STRAIGHT!" I tell Pete, " WHY PAY THESE ASS-HOLES WHEN WE'LL WORK FOR FREE?"

Pete sees the logic in this and, anxious to get back to business as usual, agrees to drop the whole cover charge thing. Satisfied that the labor dispute is settled, Glen the Cop gets back in his police cruiser and he and his partner resume their patrol. Tony DePaul is beside himself. He doesn't take a swing at me, but I can tell he's thinking hard about it. People tell me afterwards that once I'm out of earshot, Tony keeps saying, "Goddamn that Jimmy Giovanni! If he wasn't such a tough bastard, I'd kick his ass!"

It was years before they even thought about charging cover at The Zoo.

THE NEW KID

Around this time, I go to the Intersection on a Friday for the open mike. The usual suspects are gathered but there's a guy I haven't seen before. I can tell right off he's different. He looks like a refugee from the Renaissance Faire or like he just came out of some kind of medieval time warp. The minute he spots me, he makes a beeline straight for me. Even the way he moves is different. He reaches me and bows with a theatrical flourish, kneels on one knee, takes my hand and in a Shakespearean actor voice says, "I am glad to finally make your acquaintance, my liege."

I say, " What's this 'my liege' shit? I ain't the King of England."

He says, "I've seen your act."

I say, "Who are you?"

He says, "I'm Robin."

I say, "I'm Jim."

He says, "I know."

Robin's turn comes. Robin does about 10 minutes. It is immediately apparent to me Robin isn't just another run of the mill comic. I can't explain what the magic "it" thing is, but I know "it" when I see "it," and I see "it" that night in Robin. "It" is still in "its" infancy, but "it" is definitely there. I remember one routine where Robin plays a cockroach crawling up a wall. The bit gets big laughs. Come to think of it, everything Robin does that night gets laughs.

Afterwards I say, "That's funny shit, man, really funny! How long have you been doing standup?"

Robin says, "This is it, my first time."

I say, "You're kidding me! Your first time really? How did you get so good so fast?"

Robin says, "I've been doing other things, acting, doing improv..."

"Wow! I can't believe it! It's your first time and you're already as good as you are! Unbelievable! Stick with it, man. You're going to be great! Really great!"

"Thank you. Coming from you, that means a lot..."

I notice a sweet shyness about him. Then suddenly, as if embarrassed by the praise, he says abruptly, "Well, I have to go now..."

And he disappears.

THE COMEDY
COMPETITION

Frank Kidder is now calling himself "The Godfather" of the San Francisco Comedy Scene. Frank is always calling me to talk me into participating in his latest new comedy extravaganza, some cockamamie idea like Comedy Olympics or Comedy Tag Team Wrestling. I like Frank so up until now I always say yes. The trouble is, Frank's brainstorms look great on paper, but in execution always seem to fizzle and topple over on the launch pad. I'm a big supporter of Frank and I generally do whatever he asks but I've been to too many gigs where you get there and nobody's there except Frank and Hilda and maybe Ed Turner and Bob Barry. So these are my expectations when I return Frank's call. I ring him up as the English would say and his wife Hilda, who is from Hull, England and who has a very distinctive English accent, answers. Hilda says "Hello."

I say, "Hi, Hilda!"

"Yes. Who's this?"

"Jim Giovannoni."

"Oh, hi Jim."

"How are you doing, Hilda?"

"Well, not too good, Jim."

"What's wrong?"

"Well, you see, it's my kitty, Winky. Winky has been sick

and I don't know what it is. Frankie and I had to take Winky to the veterinarian."

"Sorry to hear that Hilda. Your other cats are okay though, huh?"

"Oh, yes. All the other kitties are fine. Pinky's fine. It is only Winky who is sick. And we haven't seen Dinky. Dinky has been gone for days now..."

"I'm sorry to hear that..."
"But Dinky always comes back, you know. I think Dinky has a girlfriend."

By now I'm starting to feel like I'm in the middle of a Monty Python routine. "Jolly good for Dinky. And how are Blinky, Binky, and Twinky?"

"Oh, we have no kitties named Blinky, Binky, or Twinky. We had a Stinky, but Stinky passed."

I can't take it anymore. I'm starting to crack like the centurion in the "Biggus Dickus" routine.

Hilda says, "What's so funny...?"
I say, "Nothing, Hilda, I mean, have you ever thought of doing comedy?"

"That's what Frankie says. He says I should be a comedian. Frankie tells me that all the time, but

I don't know what I'm going to do..."

What? Comedy-wise?"

"No, about the vet bill. Veterinarians are very expensive, you know. I suppose I'll have to sell another watercolor."

Uh-oh. I can tell this is going to end up being an expensive phone call. I already own several Hilda watercolors because of conversations like this. I say, "Yeah, I know. Believe me, it's hard making that kind of dough doing comedy."

Hilda says, "Uh, oh! There's the doorbell. It must be my student. I suppose you want to talk to Frankie."

"Yes Hilda, I would like to talk to Frank, please."

"Yes, yes, very well… well, I'll put him on. Frankie! It's a phone call. It's Jim Giovannoni! Oh, yes, well, here he comes. Bye-bye!"
Saved by the bell. Frank comes on. "Hey, Jim!"

"Hey, Frank, How're you doing."

"We had to take Hilda's cat to the vet…"

"I know, Frank. Hilda already told me.

"Those vets are expensive."

"I know Frank. Frank, you called me. I'm returning your call. What's up? You didn't call me to tell me about Hilda's cats…"

"I've been brainstorming and I got an idea…"

"What's it this time, Frank? Don't tell me 'Comedy Mud Wrestling!"

"No, no, nothing like that see I got a great idea it's a Comedy Competition…"
"What?"

"A Comedy Competition, see, it's like this. We're going to have auditions and after that we'll have the competition which will be held at different clubs around town and then after that we'll have the semi-finals and then we'll have the finals…"

"Wait a minute Frank. Hold on, hold on…how many shows?"

"Well, I figure since you're a 'shoe in' for the finals, you'll be in maybe a half a dozen shows. The shows will be spread out over several weeks…"

"I'll pass."

"Pass? I'm counting on you to be in it!"

"Frank, I can't commit to doing a half a dozen shows without knowing when they are or if I am going to get paid when it's over. Most of the time I work for you for nothing as it is. I mean I love doing comedy and I don't mind working for you for nothing but it's starting to get to be a little too much like "work" work, know what I mean? I mean, how many shows have I done for you and even when you pay me, what's the most you've ever paid me, like two bucks or something?"

"Actually, I think it was two seventy-five to be exact..."

"You know, the other thing, Frank is half the time I get to your gigs and nobody's in the audience which is not fun either, know what I mean? I mean, Frank, if it's not fun, why do it?"

"This time is gonna be different. You'll see. I've been brainstorming see? This time it's gonna work..."

Frank is not one to give up easily, so at this point I figure it's best to just cut to the chase and play the ace. I say, "Frank, I got a day job! I never know what time I'm going to get off from work and, seriously, Frank, without my day job, how am I going to be able to afford the water-colors...?"

"There's going to be a cash prize at the end and I figure you have the best chance of winning so you'll probably be the one that gets paid when it's over. It's going to be a big prize too!"

"How big?"

"Like maybe a hundred bucks or so!"

"Frank. Look. Up until now, I've done everything you've asked of me, but half the time I get to the gig and it's some rat hole with nobody in the audience and face it some of your gigs have not been much fun lately. I really would like to skip this one, if you don't mind…"

"What if I grandfather you in, and you don't have to audition and you just go directly to the semi-finals…?"

"That wouldn't be fair to the other comedians. Seriously, Frank, with all due respect, I think I'll do a Paso Robles on this one…"

Frank continues to put the full court press on me, but it's no use. Once I make up my mind, that's it. I finally get Frank off the line and thank God it's a local call because talking to Frank long distance on your dime can run up a big tab quick. So I get rid of Frank and forget about the whole thing, and one day my phone rings. The voice on the other end of the line says, "Hi Jim, this is Frank Kidder."

I say, "Hi Frank. What's up?"

"You know the comedy competition I was telling you about?"

"I already told you I don't want to do that, Frank."

He says, "Don't worry. I don't want you to be in it. We're having the finals next week at Joe Nobrieges' Showcase on Gough Street and the finalists don't think it's fair somebody has to go on first without the crowd being warmed-up so I'd like it if you would come on and be the 'pacer act.'"

I say, "The 'pacer act'? What's that?"

"You know, like in the Indianapolis 500, there's a pacer car that starts off the other cars. You'll be the pacer act and you come out and do ten minutes and warm up the crowd so when the other comedians come on, the crowd will already be warmed up, see?"

"This is a one shot deal? I only have to do the one night,

right?"

"Yes. It's the Finals."

I'm thinking this is going to be another Frank bust, but it's only one night so I say, "Yeah, okay, Frank. I'll do it."

"Really?"

"Yeah, Frank, really. I'll do it. I'll be the 'pacer act.'"

I pick up the Chronicle the day before the show and my name and my picture is in the paper. I can't believe Frank got this much publicity in the Chronicle and I really can't believe they use my picture, the one where I'm Don Corleone, for the promo shot. That night I get to Joe Nobrieges' Showcase expecting a smattering of people at most to be there. The place is small, but it's packed. There's a line outside waiting to get in. I'm starting to think maybe this isn't just another one of Frank's cockamamie ideas after all. I get inside and it's all bright lights. There's even a guy with a TV camera. This is a bigger deal than I thought. Next thing I know I'm up there and it's a hot crowd. By the time I get off they're rolling and it's time to start the competition. I am not going to tell you who wins but I will tell you this: Halfway through Bill Farley's set the sound goes out. Bill improvises brilliantly and gets an enthusiastic response from both the audience and the judges. There's a clue. For the rest of the story, here it is, in its entirety, the review that subsequently appears in the San Francisco Chronicle:

A FUNNY THING HAPPENED...
John L. Wasserman

We all know how comedians start: as class clowns. And we all know where successful comedians finish: with fame and fortune. But what about the period in between?

On Sunday night at Joe Nobriga's Showcase, a nightclub at 900 Franklin that specializes in giving exposure to local singers, musicians and comedians, a small part of the answer surfaced at the First International Open Stand Up Comedy Competition. Five comedians, all unknown to the public but the victors in preliminary trials, which eliminated more than 200 of their colleagues, did 20-minute routines to a standing room only crowd of friends, family and aficionados of the burgeoning local comedy scene.

They were competing for prizes of $100, $50, and $25, but more, for the kind of professional recognition and prestige that comes rarely to those who do it for love.

There were no scouts for Carson or Merv in the audience, no emissaries from the city's big clubs. And none of the five- Bill Farley, Mitch Krug, Mark Miller, Bob Sarlatte, Robin Williams- is in my estimation, yet ready to join the big leagues.

But they were the survivors, the finalists, and they made us laugh.

AMERICAN COMEDY led by Lily Tomlin, Richie Pryor, Robert Klein, Steve Martin and Martin Mull, is having its greatest renaissance since the '50s and this vigor is reflected in San Francisco. The Comedy Scene regularly presents shows at Intersection and the Coffee Gallery, the Holy City Zoo has 'professional' and 'open mike' comedy nights and according to a recent article on this area in Laff Maker News, a New York newsletter, experienced comedians can perform up to seven nights a week if they follow all leads.

Since the remuneration for these gigs 'generally ranges from one dollar to $10 a night,' the gentleman at Joe Nobriga's showcase were looking at the biggest payday of their lives.

The show started about 9:40, after master of ceremonies Jose Simon explained the rules, (points were awarded for stage presence, material, audience response, delivery, technique, audience rapport and presentation) and introduced impressionist Jim Giovanni for a guest set.

Giovanni, called by Laugh Maker "the guy with the obvious

talent-to-make-it" did not enter the competition (a form of comedic noblesse oblige) but started the house roaring with his version of Hamlet as played by George C. Scott, Groucho Marx and Tom Smothers. Giovanni is regarded with respect, if not awe. He has played the Great American music Hall on several occasions.

The big time.

And, in the hot, muggy, densely packed room, a window outlined in flashing lights as their frame, the competitors went to work. Each did 20 minutes, give or take 60 seconds (if they gave or took more than three minutes, they were disqualified), each got laughs, but they had little else in common. They were short and tall, meek and assertive, confident and tentative, good-looking and funny-looking. They used, and did not use, props, voices, sound effects, their bodies, their audience, their wits. They wore (and peeked at) watches on their wrists and in their socks. They were smooth and clumsy and hot. Each was bathed in sweat when he finished, each slumped in exhaustion from the heat and the pressure.

The TV camera and microphone from KGO TV's A.M. Show lurked about, shooting everything that moved. The judges Paul Krasner, Bernie Weiner and Francine Foster regarded their task with appropriate solemnity.

At five minutes to midnight, it was over. The audience had remained remarkably receptive through a long, stifling night. Frank Kidder (a comedian who adopted his wife's last name for obvious reasons and who has been for years a driving force behind San Francisco's comedy workshops) and Bob Barry did a pantomime while the judges tallied their sheets.

Farley won. Williams, Sarlatte, Miller and Krug followed. Not the way I would have picked them, but OK. Except for Krug. Funny man. No way Krug finishes last.

Unless the judge is Robert Mondavi.

A funny business, comedy.

A STAR IS BORN

Not long after the Comedy Competition, I get a call from David Allen at the Boarding House. He says, "I have a date for you..."

I say, "I'll do it!"

David says, "But you need to do two different forty-five minute sets. We're not going to turn the house."

I say, "Two different forty-five minute sets? I can't repeat myself?"

David says, "That's right. We're not going to turn the house. A lot of people are going to be there for the second show that are there for the first."

I hate to say "no" to a gig, but like Dirty Harry says, "A man's got to know his limitations." I say, "David, I can pull off one 45, but two? I'm afraid I'll do great the first set and bomb the second."

Dave says, "I understand. I just thought I'd give you first shot."

"Well, thanks for asking..."

Dave says, "Is there anyone you could recommend? I'd really like to use a comic in that spot. The guy's got to be funny though. I don't want some stiff up there."

I say, "David, to be honest with you there's nobody I know that has that much time and as far as funny goes, well, there is this one guy, he's pretty good, he's real good actually, he's almost as good as me, but I don't think this guy could do two separate forty-five minutes sets. I think he has maybe twenty minutes tops. He's like most of the rest of the guys. They all do the same twenty minutes all the time but I don't know, the guy's good, I could ask him..."

"What's his name?"

"Robin Williams."

Dave says, "Ask him if he's interested and if he is, have him give me a call, I need to find someone as soon as possible."

I go to Robin and say: "David Allen wants someone to open at the Boarding House but you have to do two forty-five minute sets and they have to be two different sets because they are not going to turn the house so you can't do the same material twice and I told David I could pull off maybe one, but no way two separate forty-five minute sets. I told David I can't do it but I told him about you and I told him you were really funny and he asked me to ask you if you were interested so I'm asking you."

I fully expect Robin to say no. Robin says, "Okay, Jimmy."

I say, "Okay, what? Okay, you'll do it?"

"Okay, yes. Jimmy, I'll do it."

Whoa! This in itself blows my mind. I offer him the gig thinking if he's like me, no way in a million years will he take it. Of course, Robin is not like me or anyone else I know in a million years, so take it he does. Now I'm thinking, "This guy has a major set of balls on him, but he'll learn."

Turns out I'm the one who learns. I call David Allen the next day, and David says Robin not only pulled it off, he upstaged the headliner. I am in disbelief. I'm thinking it must be a fluke. I've had nights where I can do no wrong, where even my setups get laughs. Robin must have had one of those nights. It's an aberration! Robin got lucky, that's all. I don't go the first night thinking it's going to be a debacle and I'm going to be at least partly to blame, but this I have to see for myself. No way is Robin going to be able to pull it off twice in a row.

WRONG!

Robin comes out and for the first ten minutes wanders around the stage in an overcoat and Russian fur hat, wearing a University of Moscow T-shirt riffing in a fake Russian accent. He has the audience thoroughly convinced he is some goofy Russian immigrant who just happened to wander in off Bush Street onto the stage. After he's milked that premise for all it's worth, Robin peels off the hat and overcoat and transforms into an impish man/child in rainbow suspenders improvising Shakespeare. "The moon hangs low like a testicle in the sky!" He has a conversation with his penis, pulling his pantaloons open and imitating the sound of an elephant. He tells the audience, "Don't feed him any peanuts!" Then jumps off the stage and starts going through a woman's purse. "Oh, look a condom! No balloon, no party!" He wades into the crowd, randomly observing. "What's that on your lip? Oh, hello, Mr. Herpes! The difference between love and herpes is herpes lasts forever!" He surges through the crowd, randomly grabbing objects and improvising with them. Finally, seemingly at a loss for words, a fleeting moment of panic crosses his face. There is an awkward silence, Robin says, "I've gone too far!" and scurries back to the stage. A moment of apprehension, followed by a moment of tugging on heartstrings, followed by another conversation with his penis and anyone who has peanuts is throwing them on stage. Robin starts imitating an applause meter and the crowd cheers even louder. He can do no wrong. He gets off and the place goes crazy. People are stomping on the floor. "Robin! Robin! Robin…!"

The Pointer Sisters are backstage going, "Oh, my God…!"

Before the second show even starts, the audience is buzzing. Robin comes out and once again is a virtual kaleidoscope of unbridled improvisational brilliance. I'm thinking there goes my gig at the Boarding House! After the show I go up to Robin and say, "Wow, man! Unbelievable! Fucking unbelievable! Congratulations, man, you really pulled it off!"

Robin averts his eyes. I see the painful shyness. Robin seems almost apologetic for what he hath just wrought. He says, "Thank you, Jimmy..."

I say, "Why thank me? You killed, man..."

"Thanks for telling David about me."

"All I did was put the plug in the socket. You supplied the electricity! To tell you the truth, Robin, I didn't think you could do it!"

"To tell you the truth, Jimmy, I wasn't so sure myself..."

"But you did, man, did you ever! You killed, man! How did you come up with so much material?"

Robin says, "Improv, Jimmy, improv!"

LAUGH-IN

After that, things happen fast. Robin moves to LA and is an instant hit, like me five years earlier squared. Before anybody knows it, George Schlatter signs Robin to be a regular on the new *Laugh-In* television show. In turn, Robin being a good scout, tells George to check out talent up North. All of a sudden, folks from *Laugh-In* are coming to San Francisco to audition comedians at clubs around town. I am informed of the development and offered a spot. Given a choice of venues, I choose The Zoo. I remember the good old days there and believe it's time to resurrect the balcony-jump. I'm 27 and I haven't done it in years and I could literally break a leg, but what the hell, anything for a laugh, right? Rose Gramalia is the talent scout I have to impress. I do the bit and Rose is impressed, so impressed I get a coveted call back to perform in front of the man himself, George Schlatter.

The Big Night, The Zoo is packed. Fifteen comics, five minutes each, I have no idea what anybody else does. I only see the inside of the tunnel. I'm number six, a great spot. I've gone over this routine a million times in my head and I'm praying this isn't the night I break my leg. My timing has to be perfect. Slightly off and it's total disaster. I'm nervous to start with, big-time.

My turn comes. Right from the get-go I'm in the zone. I do rapid fire: The Godfather, Columbo, Howard Cosell, John Wayne, Groucho, Redd Foxx, Patton, every punch a direct hit. My pre-recorded voice as HAL the Computer from the movie 2001 comes over the PA system. Now I am Dave the Astronaut, weightless in space, shutting off HAL while HAL insults Dave relentlessly, a la Don Rickles.

HAL winds down, delivers the final insult. "Also Sprach Zarathrustra" comes up over the PA system. I become The Ape from 2001. In slow motion I grab a bottle of Guinness Stout and turn it upward to the ceiling. Guinness foams out of my mouth, rolls off my head. The music blares, I climb the balcony.

Now I'm standing on the edge of the balcony looking down at the crowd, jumping up and down screaming like an ape! I am the Ape Man! The music reaches a crescendo. I jump.

Everything is in slow motion. I see the stage come up. Boom! I feel the stage give like I'm going to go right through it, but both the stage and I survive. It's a perfect stick! I pirouette and bow. The audience jumps to their feet. I leap from the stage, bounding through the crowd to cheers and high fives.

George Schlatter immediately summons me to his table and tells me how crazy and wild and far out I am. "You are something else!" He says. "You'll be hearing from us soon!"

A few minutes later, I am in a daze standing outside The Zoo with my friend, Trevor, who is a large human being I play tackle football with. Trevor is a solid six feet three, two hundred fifty pounds, big-boned with long blonde hair and a beard wearing a "Take a Liking to a Viking" t-shirt. He could easily be mistaken for a pro football lineman or an off duty Viking. Everyone is slapping me on the back, congratulating me. The door opens and out comes Robin, who immediately looks up at Trevor and says, "Whoa, Jimmy, you've only been famous fifteen minutes and you already have a bodyguard!"

A few days later Bill Rafferty, Mark McCollum, and I get the call to meet with George Schlatter. The three of us fly to Burbank and take a cab to Schlatter's office in Beverley Hills. We are escorted into the George's office. I say, "Nice to see you, Mr. Schlatter."

George says, "My father is Mr. Schlatter. Call me George."

I don't know what gets into me that day but once we are in there I take over and George lets me. I'm asking George questions, making him laugh, jumping in and out of my seat, riffing. Nothing is planned, all spontaneous, loose and natural. Rafferty and McCollum just sit there. Rafferty chimes in a few times but I don't recall McCollum saying a word. Finally, George tells me I'm funny and talented and all that and he would like to use me, but I need to lose weight. I tell him, "I'll be 180 lbs. the next time you see me."

George says, "What are you now?"

I say, "205."

He says, "I would guess you at maybe one eighty. You don't look two hundred five."

I say, "That's how I always beat the guys who guess your weight at the County Fair."

George laughs. I feel really positive leaving the meeting. We are in the cab heading back to the airport and Rafferty says, "Man, you got balls, the way you took over in there! Schlatter loves you, Jimmy. You're in."

I say, "You think so?"

Rafferty says, "Shit yeah!"

With that, Rafferty whips out a fatty and fires up. Seeds are popping all over the place. Now I'm paranoid my big break is going to get fucked up by something stupid like getting busted for weed. I say, "I got balls? You fire up a joint in the back of a cab and you say I got balls?"

Rafferty says, "He's a cabbie. He doesn't give a shit."

Rafferty's right. The cabbie doesn't give a shit. I don't need a joint or an airplane. I fly back to San Francisco on a cloud.

THE BIG BREAK

A few days later I get a call from George Sclatter Productions saying I got the gig. A couple of days after that, it's all over San Francisco media. The five *Laugh-In* cast members from San Francisco are: Robin Williams, Nancy Bleiweiss from Beach Blanket Babylon, Antoinette Attel AKA Toad the Mime, Bill Rafferty, and me. I immediately go on a thousand calorie a day diet, start running seven miles a day and doing heavy karate workouts daily. I report to George Schlatter Productions two months later weighing 175. George sees me and says, "Look who got skinny!"

Meanwhile, back in San Francisco, we are suddenly famous. Articles appear on a regular basis in the Chronicle in the Pink Section and the Examiner and we're doing radio interviews and people are calling us the San Francisco Five, hometown heroes who made good in Hollywood and put comedy on the map in San Francisco. There's even an article about us in Playboy and, lo and behold, now the Holy City Zoo is internationally known along with Miss March.

Jim with the cast of Laugh-In, NBC 1977

Jim as Columbo with Richard Garner NBC Laugh-In

NBC COSTUME

We are told to report to NBC on Wednesday, June 15, 1977, for a costume fitting. Some bright bulb decides to give the entire male cast of Laugh-In the same call time, so Robin Williams, Sergio Arrigones, Michael Sklar, Bill Rafferty, Lenny Schultz, Ben Powers, Waylon Flowers, Ed Bluestone, and yours truly all show up at once. We hit NBC like a comedy blithe and immediately overwhelm the costume guys, who we outnumber three to one. The head costumer is a kindly little old guy named Armand who looks like an old school tailor, with the wire-rimmed glasses on the end of the nose and the tape measure hanging around the neck and the foreign accent. His assistants are young gay men.

Robin leads the charge. Two steps in the door, he grabs a woman's red wig and puts it on and says "Oh look. I'm Raggedy Ann sitting on Pinocchio's face going 'lie to me!' Pinocchio's going, 'I must be made out of wood. My hand is on fire…'"

Michael Sklar is a flamboyantly over the top gay guy. Michael takes off like a bottle rocket. "Red slippers! We're not in Kansas anymore Dorothy…!"

Now Robin and Ben Powers are walking around on their knees singing like munchkins, "Follow the yellow brick road. Follow the yellow brick road…"

Lenny Schultz is busy strangling a rubber chicken. "Do you want to see me go crazy? Do you want to see me go crazy?" He's slapping the chicken around. "Huh? Answer me! Answer me, you, you! Do you want to see me go crazy? Huh? Do you want to see me go fucking crazy? Huh?

Huh?"

Waylon Flowers and Madame are: "Forest Tucker, where are you?"

Now Robin is talking down the front of his pants, doing Senior Wences. "Hi Johnny How are you doing? Not so good. Not so good? Not so good. What's wrong? I'm sad. You're sad? Yes. Why are you sad? Nobody likes me. I like you. Do you want to come out and play? No! No, you make me do bad things! It's all right? So right."

The costume guys are in hysterics except Armand who doesn't think it's funny. He is going. "Stop! Stop! Please! Please! You have to stop now! Please...!"

There's no way Armand is reeling this back in. We're in the door two seconds and it's complete pandemonium. They haven't seen this much trouble since the Marx Brothers. Lenny Schultz is stalking around like a deranged PE teacher, Robin is doing Flipper's voice coming out of his shorts, and Michael Sklar is flying around the room with a feather boa going, "Fabulous! Simply fabulous!"

Just as it seems Robin has exhausted every conceivable combination of dick joke and is wrapping it up with a Burns and Allen "Say good night Gracie" routine to Mr. Happy, Lenny decides Robin has had the stage long enough. Lenny says, "FUCK THE CHICKEN!" throws the chicken up in the air. "YOU VANT TO SEE A SHVANTZ? I'LL SHOW YOU A SHVANTZ! THIS IS A SHVANTZ!"

Lenny whips out his dick and starts waving it around. Armand looks like he's going to have a heart attack, the gay guys are screaming, and

Robin says. "OH, LOOK! IT'S THE LOCH NESS MONSTER BUT HE ONLY HAS ONE EYE!"

After that we are only allowed in NBC Costume one at a time.

CULVER CITY

Our first cast picture is taken with Bette Davis on our first day of shooting in June of 1977 at the old Universal Studios in Culver City. I'm dressed in a Keystone Cop uniform. When the time comes to do the Keystone Cop, they take me to an intersection on a back lot. Cameras are set up focused on a guy in the middle of the intersection. The director comes over, says, "Your mark is there, where he's standing. You are going to direct traffic and the cars are going to come down the street and there will be a head on collision and another car is going to then flip and land upside down on the other two and I want you to keep going directing traffic and don't stop until you hear me say 'cut!'"

"How close are they going to be when they crash?

"Close, but not too close."

"How close is close but not too close? Like a few feet away close?"

"Don't worry about it. These guys are professionals. They know what they're doing. As long as you stay on your mark it shouldn't be a problem. Just remember, once you're out there, don't move off your mark. When you hear 'action' do your thing directing traffic and keep going until you hear me say 'cut.' We need to get this in one take because these are all the cars and stunt drivers we have available to wreck today."

In the past I've done live stunts with flying vehicles, but I was always behind the wheel and there weren't any cameras rolling. Now I'm afraid my first day in the big time may turn out to be my last. I go out, stand on my mark. Someone does a last minute touch up of my make-up. I'm thinking, "A lot good that's going to do if a '68 Chevy lands on top of me."

The make-up person leaves. I'm standing there alone. I hear, "Roll camera!"

"Speed!"

"Action!"

I start miming.

Someone cues the stunt guys and a '69 Ford Fairlane and a '68 Chevy Bel Aire come screaming down the street from opposite directions. BAM! They smash into each other in a head on collision. A third car comes flying down the street and hits a ramp. It goes airborne, rolls in mid-air lands upside down on the other two. All this happens a few feet away from me. I hear,

"Cut!"

I stop miming.

"Great! We got it!"

Totaled cars. Total slapstick. Dangerous laughs.
I walk off and the assistant director, otherwise known as the A.D., tells me I'm wrapped for the day. I turn in my costume and I'm ready to go home and Rafferty rolls up in a golf cart. He says, "Get in. I want to show you something." I get in and Rafferty starts driving through the old back lots. It's like a ghost town back in there. There's no one around us except the tumbling tumbleweeds and us. Rafferty pulls out a joint. I say, "What's with you and the weed, Rafferty? Are you trying to get us kicked off this thing before we even get started?"

"Relax, Jimmy. Nobody gives a shit. Look! Check it out. It's the Wall from the old 'King Kong' movie."

Damn! It is!

A couple of minutes later, "Remember the movie *Gone With the Wind*?"

"Yeah."

"There's Tara."

Everything is in disrepair and over grown with weeds and falling apart, but in the late afternoon sun, Tara looks simply magnificent. Rafferty is a little more jaded because he is from New York and has the New York attitude, but for me it's starting to sink in. I look at Rafferty and say, "You know what this means, Billy Boy?"

Rafferty says, "What?"

"We in the big-time now, bubba!"

NBC

June 17, 1977, we begin taping at NBC Burbank. I'm nervous because it's my first day in a big-time television studio. My call time is 8:30 A.M. In addition to Bette Davis and the regular cast, the guest stars scheduled for that day are David Frye, Arnold Schwarzenegger, Kareem Abdul Jabbar, Telly Savalas, and Ralph Nader.

I get to NBC and check in. I am shown to my dressing room, which is downstairs and halfway down a long hallway. On one side of the hallway are *Laugh-In* cast member dressing rooms and on the opposite side are Photoplay Awards dressing rooms. We are taping in studio 4 and the Photoplays are taping in Studio 3. I get to my dressing room, and my name "JIM GIOVANNI" is on the door with a big star. Directly opposite my door is a door with a big star on it and the name "CONNIE STEVENS." Inside my dressing room is where all my costumes are. There is also a large gift-wrapped goody basket and a bottle of Dom Perignon and card that says, "Welcome to NBC."

My first scene is scheduled to shoot at 9:30 in the morning. I change into costume and get to make-up and then to the set. I am wearing boxing trunks. In my first scene I am Rocky getting knocked out by a nun. Typecasting. June Gable is the Nun, which is definitely casting against type. Now's my chance to revive my slow motion boxing routine. We shoot the bit, boom-boom and it's down the stairs to the dressing room for a quick change and back to make-up and Studio 4.

Fifteen minutes later I am a cop in an LAPD uniform. Ben Powers plays a biker. I bop him with a nightstick. It's police brutality Three Stooges style. We hear "Cut!" and it's another lap down and up the stairs.

Ten minutes after that, the cast assembles on stage dressed as union members. We sing "Look For the Union Label" while wildly strewing clothes around.

Another twenty minutes and Lenny Schultz comes out in a tuxedo and does "Dueling Cheeks" to the music of "Dueling Banjos." It's impossible to describe, but I do my best. It starts with what looks like two gerbils having a boxing match in Lenny's mouth and ends with Lenny going crazy and looking like a deranged ostrich. Go on YouTube and type in "Go Crazy Lenny" and you can see for yourself. Ben and I are the men in the white coats. We come out and take Lenny away. George is back to type-casting.

A half an hour later, the entire cast assembles for an ensemble number, with the exception of Ed Bluestone, who reads the script and says,

"I'm not doing this shit."

The sketch is a parody of the Mickey Mouse Club. We are the Moonesketeers, and Robin is The Rev. Moone. Robin immediately starts riffing ad-libs that are way funnier than what is on the page. The NBC Censor goes crazy. It's the first time The Censor has seen Robin and the words coming out of Robin's mouth come nowhere near matching the words on the pages of the script he's been given. George tries to explain to The Censor that Robin is different, we just have to go along with it we just have to let him do his thing, don't worry, we'll get what we want, but The Censor is having a hard time getting Robin, so he's giving George a hard time and the two of them are going around and around and bing! There's the bell ending round one between George vs. The Censor. Meal-break everyone!

We have lunch in the NBC Commissary. It's my first time

in what looks like a regular cafeteria except there are famous people in there whose names I can't remember. After lunch, I go to my dressing room to get ready for our next sketch, and Robert Conrad is there in the hallway, sniffing around Connie Steven's dressing room. I get the feeling he's not here for the Photoplay Awards.

Our next bit is an ensemble piece. The entire cast, dressed in uniforms with the *Laugh-In* logo on them, does a segment titled Naughty Clean Words. Robin is all over the place with naughty clean words, clean naughty words, and just plain naughty words that aren't in the script. Ben, Michael, Lenny, June valiantly try to keep pace with him. The rest of us just stand back and watch in awe. Bing! It's Round Two between George and the Censor. Now they are yelling at each other. "That's not in the script! Do you have to let him do stuff that's not in the script!"

George is going, "Yes, you have to let him do stuff that's not in the script or he won't do what you want him to do that is in the script, and no, his penis doesn't actually talk!"

Next I am standing on a riser in front of a big American flag, dressed in the actual uniform George C. Scott wore in the beginning of the movie *Patton*. I'm wearing the helmet, the pistols, the medals the whole shebang. Standing up there all of a sudden I feel painfully shy. Bette Davis is standing on the floor below, looking up at me, saying, "Magnificent, simply magnificent!"

I want to acknowledge the compliment but instead I stay in character. I have my Patton lines down, but when they put up the cue cards, the lines are different than what I have memorized. That's when I learn the number one rule on *Laugh-In*. Do not memorize anything. Just read the cards. I read the cards. On the last take, the Nun hits Patton in the face with a powder puff followed by a bucket of water, another one-take deal. It's a shame messing up the Patton uniform but anything for a laugh.

Now I am dressed in coveralls. It's my big scene with Bette Davis and I'm bummed because they don't give me any lines. In the scene, Ben, Lenny and I are re-possessing Bette Davis's furniture. Nancy Bleiweiss and June Gable play Bette Davis's daughters. Robin comes out made up like an old man. Robin looks like an old man to start with but now he really looks like an old man. It's a hell of a make-up job. So that's where Robin has been. Robin is walking and talking like an old man, but they don't give him or Ben or Lenny any lines either, so now I don't feel so bad. In the bit Robin is an old grandfather asleep in a chair. We keep repossessing their stuff while Bette, Nancy and June deliver their lines to camera like it's a TV commercial. The last thing we carry out is Robin, still asleep in the chair. Not having any lines doesn't deter Robin. Between takes, old man fart jokes keep coming out of him. The cast and crew are laughing uncontrollably. Bette Davis keeps rolling her eyes going, "Who are you?"

On the first take, I walk off with a coffee table and half way through the take the Director says, "Cut!" I go to put the coffee table back from whence I got it and immediately get a crew guy up my ass. He grabs the thing out of my hand. "You are only allowed to touch this when the cameras are rolling. When the cameras are not rolling I will put it where it needs to be. This is my job. If the cameras are NOT rolling, do NOT touch it!"

My first day at NBC and I'm already in a union beef. We do the next take and the same line gets muffed. I hear the word "Cut!" and drop the coffee table like I just picked it off a hot stove. The guy says, "Now what are you trying to do, break the fucking thing?"

I say, "I'm doing what you told me to do. You said when I hear 'Cut!' don't touch it anymore."

He says, "Never mind what I told you. When you hear 'Cut!' just set it down or hand it to me! You break it, you pay for it!"

Great. Now there's going to be two unions involved. We do several more takes and the same line keeps getting muffed, which means more fart jokes. Everyone is laughing except Mr. Props. I don't want to knock any more apples off this guy's applecart, so I gently hand the coffee table back to him after each take, like it's the crown jewels of England.

Next sketch is a takeoff on *Roots*. Ben is Rhett Butler, Nancy is Scarlett O'Hara, Toad is Butterfly McQueen, Waylon Flowers is a Union General, Michael Sklar is a Samurai, Sergio is a Palace Guard, Ed Bluestone is himself in a suit, Lenny is a Russian, and I am an Eskimo. Robin is a Scottish soldier, which means more jokes that aren't in the script, this time in a Scottish accent. "What's under the kilt? A wee set of pipes, want to give them a blow? Oh, look. A Blue Ribbon! I dinna know where I've been, laddie, but I won first prize. If you like what's under the kilt, I have five more yards of it at home. Aye, it's a quarter-pounder, must be a McDonald! Oh look! It's the smallest airport in the world: Two hangars and a night fighter! Why do Scots wear kilts? The sound of a zipper scares the sheep! Baa! Baa!"

Lenny is going. "YOU WANT TO SEE WHAT I GOT UNDER MY KILT? HUH? HUH? YOU WANT TO SEE WHAT I GOT UNDER MY KILT...?"

Bing! It's George vs. The Censor, Round Three.

DAY TWO

I walk up the stairs from my dressing room and I get to the top and I'm in the lobby between the studios. The lobby is full of famous faces, all dressed in black tie or evening gown and I am wearing a German Luftwaffe officer uniform. Mr. Inconspicuous. I have to cross the lobby to get to Studio 4. "Excuse me. Excuse me…" I am weaving my way through the crowd, past Angie Dickenson, Eliot Gould, Connie Stevens, Bruce Jenner, Alfred Hitchcock. They all stare at me with deadpan expressions on their faces, like it's a normal to see German Luftwaffe officers walking around at NBC. I exit the lobby and enter Studio 4 and as the door closes behind me, I hear Alfred Hitchcock's voice. "He must be one of the *Laugh-In* people."

The set is a military war room and the characters in the sketch are all sitting around a big table, wearing various different countries' military officer uniforms and all holding black boxes of varying sizes. The generals are arguing over who has the biggest "Whopper." George judiciously leaves Lenny out of the sketch. The director says, "Action!" We begin the sketch. Everything is going fine until Robin has a line. He is supposed to say that his nation has developed a "Super Whopper…" Robin says the line and then immediately launches a pre-emptive first strike barrage of dick jokes. "Oh look! Up in the sky, is it a bird? Is it a plane? It's Super Whopper! I step into a phone booth and take off my clothes and out comes my whopper, the Whopper of Steel. My whopper can leap tall buildings in a single bound. My whopper is so big Doug Henning is going to make it disappear in his next television special..."

Lenny is on the sidelines going. "YOU WANT TO SEE A WHOPPER? HUH? HUH? I'LL SHOW YOU A WHOPPER!"

By now it's all-out war between George and the Censor. At the climax (pardon the pun), the Zarathustra music comes up and we turn into apes and scream and jump up and down on the table. I do my best to scream like an ape with a German accent while Robin runs around, picking lint off the other apes, yelling, "Make-up! The baboon's anus needs more rouge!"

One more costume change, and I'm Henry Kissinger introducing the news.

DAY THREE

It's the Disco scene and I am Patton again. My uniform has been cleaned. I am informed there is a missing medal and it is an expensive one. I didn't take it, but the bastards insist I am the one responsible. If there's one thing I hate, it is being falsely accused. I tell them that if they don't want a size 11 riding boot up their ass, they'd better get the hell out of my dressing room. They back out of there like crap out of the back end of a goose. By God, I am Patton and I am on a mission. "Alright you sons of bitches, time to kick ass. When you put your hand into a bunch of goo that a moment before was a pie in your best friend's face, you'll know what to do! Thirty years from now, when you're sitting around your fireside on your grandson's knee and he asks you what you did on the great *Laugh-In* television show of 1977, you will be able to say, 'I told gay jokes in a disco with Roddy McDowell.'"

"I hear Governor Maddox is going to do something."

"Governor Maddox? You mean Lester Maddox?
That Governor Maddox?"

"That's the guy."

"What's he going to do?"

"I don't know. I hear he does some kind of accordion act."

"Lester Maddox does an accordion act? What's next, the Pope on a trapeze?"

"It's a Wacky World."

"You can say that again."

"It's a 'Wacky World,' then we break for dinner. 'Pope on a Trapeze' is after that."

That night they bring in a live audience. George lets me do my own material in the warmup. My jokes are clean and get laughs. Then George cuts Robin loose. Robin gets bigger laughs with jokes I could never get away with. "...Oops! I can't say that on television, can I George?"

"No, Robin. You can't say that on television..."

Lenny is waving around a rubber chicken. "YOU WANT TO SEE ME GO CRAZY? HUH? HUH? YOU WANT TO SEE ME GO CRAZY?"

Laugh-In #1-77, that's a wrap.

ON SECOND THOUGHT

On *Laugh-In*, nothing is ever really wrapped. Bits can be taped anytime and edited anywhere in any episode. Many times George will schedule a taping according to the availability of the guest star. Regular cast members can be called to shoot whenever, wherever. One day I receive a call to go over to NBC costume and get fitted to do Columbo. At the time Columbo is an NBC series and since I wore the real Patton uniform on *Laugh-In* #1-77, I assume they'll give me the real Columbo coat for this. When I get to NBC, there is only one guy in Costume that day and he's a guy I haven't seen before. I tell him why I am there and he brings out a black trench coat with epaulets and a belt. I say, "That's not Columbo's coat."

He says, "What do you mean it's not Columbo's coat? They told me to get Columbo's raincoat and this is Columbo's raincoat."

I say, "No way. Columbo would never wear a coat like that. Columbo wears a London Fog. And Columbo's coat is not black. It's a tan color. And it doesn't have epaulets or a belt."

The costume guy is very gay, and now he's becoming very indignant. "All I know is it says 'Columbo's coat' on the tag. Look at the tag. This is Columbo's coat!"

I say, "Have you ever seen Columbo?"

The guy says, "I don't watch television."

Great. A costume guy at a major television network who doesn't watch television. What is this, a bad Fellini movie? I say to the guy, "Forget about it, I will bring my own costume."

He says, "Do whatever you want, but this is Columbo's coat!"

The day of the shoot, the guest star is Rich Little. I show up wearing my own Colombo coat. At first people think I really am Peter Falk. I scrunch my face up like him and have a bushy head of unruly black hair and a couple days stubble and one eye is like it's off on its own and the coat looks like I've been sleeping in it, and I walk through the lobby and people are doing double takes. "Is that...?"

I get backstage and everyone thinks my costume is perfect except the costume guy. He spots me and announces in a loud voice, "I'm not responsible for this!"

The only guy who hasn't seen me yet is Rich Little. I get to the set and he is out in front of a flat doing one-liners in his various voices. I am waiting in the wings. Finally, Rich Little finishes with the cue cards. George sends me out.

"Excuse me, Mr. Little. Gee, I hate to bother you, but my wife is a big fan of yours. Wait 'til I tell my wife I met you, I mean, she'll be thrilled. Do you think I could get your autograph? For my wife, I mean, she's not gonna believe it..."

Rich Little does not look happy. If there is one thing an impressionist hates it's an impressionist who does an impression better than he does. He looks at me with utter disdain and says, "Why don't I play Lassie and you can be the tree."

This is what ends up in the final cut.

Afterwards the head costumer comes over and thanks me for what a great job I did putting my costume together. He says, "I would have had to go out and buy a London Fog and then drag it around the parking lot and run over it a bunch of times with my car and spend a whole day distressing it to get it to look like that. It's perfect. Whatever you do, don't lose it."

ADDENDUM

One day I am watching an episode of Columbo and Columbo is wearing a raincoat exactly like the one the other costume guy had brought out. The gag is that Columbo's wife gives it to him as a present and he hates the coat, and throughout the entire episode he is trying to get rid of the coat. He finally gets rid of the coat and puts on his regular Columbo raincoat. Now he can think again, and he solves the murder. The costume guy is right. It really is Columbo's raincoat.

Jim as Columbo | Romaine Photography

LAUGH-IN #2-77

Our regular schedule is two weeks off and two weeks on. After each episode it is two weeks before we are back for a script reading, followed by a week of rehearsals and a costume fitting, followed by another three days of taping at NBC. We come back to read for episode #2 and already I smell trouble. We get our script, and it weighs less than our script for episode one. This makes sense. Episode one will serve as a library for the rest of the season. Bette Davis will be saying "Sock it to me" in episode six or whatever.

The problem starts when we all actually sit down and read the script. Several cast members are unhappy about the quantity and/or quality of the material they are given. I open the script and get to a page with my name on it and all it says is "Jim: [line to come]." I am paranoid because after episode #2 is the first round of cuts. Everyone has different contracts. My contract is for two shows with options for four more. This is #2, so it's crunch time for me. Other cast members have options for four and two. Robin is signed for all six. Robin has nothing to lose, which makes him even more dangerous.

THE WRITERS

Over on the writer's side it's, "Did they use any of my material in the script?" There are fifteen staff writers and they are all subject to being cut after episode #2, with the exception of Digby, who is the head writer, and George, who is the Capo Di Tout Di Capo. It's like being a cast member of *The Sopranos* and showing up for the script reading to see if you get whacked.

If I know I won't be doing anything for a while, I go over to the other side and hang out with the writers. Fraternization is highly discouraged between cast and writers, but I do it anyway. If I think we are nuts on our side, I get over there and it's worse. Mike Kagan, a funny writer and a great guy, is going crazy. "I can't believe this. Digby just told me I have two hours to come up with ten Kareem Abdul Jabbar jokes and I can't mention height or basketball."

I like hanging out with Mike. He shows me material he wrote for me way better than what I'm getting in the script. Mike is as frustrated as I am. He says, "If I write 10 jokes on a subject, three will be great, five will be so-so, and a couple of them will be awful but they count as jokes. Inevitably, George will use the worst jokes in the script."

According to my contract, all material is the property of George Schlatter. I honor that, but man, am I tempted to walk off with some of the stuff Mike wrote for me, especially one bit. A parody of the opening speech in Patton, Mike's take is brilliant, hilarious. He tells me he'll look the other way if I take the pages George has already rejected.

I don't, dang it. I could have made good use of that material. With George it ends up in the circular file. I guess that's why they don't want writers and performers fraternizing. The less we know the better.

Another writer I like to fraternize with is Merrill Markoe. I also know Merrill from the Comedy Store. We are both regulars there. I like Merrill. Merrill is cool, funny in a droll kind of way. I can tell she is really smart. Merrill makes it known she does not need the *Laugh-In* gig. She and Mike are the only two writers I know who don't want their contracts renewed. Merrill knows I am into martial arts and encourages me to make Kung Fu movies. A year later, Raymond Ma, the highest-ranking White Crane Kung Fu master in the United States, tells me the same thing, which shows you Merrill is tuned in to the same wavelength as some heavy-duty people.

I love fraternizing with Ernie Glucksman. Hanging out with Ernie is like taking a post-graduate course in comedy. "You want to know about Vaudeville? Let me tell you. They would have loved you in Vaudeville. American audiences are a sucker for two things, impersonations and parody. Impersonations and parody, keep doing what you're doing, you can't go wrong, I don't care what anyone tells you. And you work clean. I like that. A lot of comics today think you have to be filthy to be funny. The funniest comedians I know work clean. Look at Jack Benny. Benny works clean and he can have you laughing all day long at one joke!"

I ask Ernie. "What do you do when hecklers give you a hard time on stage? I do Redd Foxx. I'm not always so clean when I have to deal with hecklers."

"Redd Foxx? Don't get me started about Redd Foxx. Redd Foxx is the filthiest man alive, but is he funny! You do a very good impersonation of Redd Foxx by the way. Impersonations and parody, you can't go wrong. Where were we? Oh, yes. Hecklers. Best thing you can do is to ignore them. Don't respond too quickly. Ignore them a couple of times and if they keep it up, the audience will start to feel sorry for you. This is good. This is what you want. Now when you lower the boom on them, the audience is on your side. Do you understand what I am saying? Let me tell you a story about a heckler and Al Jolson. One time Jolson is playing Carnegie Hall. Jolson is the best there is but what an ego. The man is full of himself. So the concert starts and there is one empty seat in the first row. Jolson comes out and does his opening number and when he finishes the audience is applauding, and a man comes down the aisle and sits down in the empty seat, doesn't say a word, just sits down. Jolson should have just ignored him and gone on to his next number but instead he looks down at this man, this late arriver, and he starts berating him for coming in late. 'How dare you walk in late to my show, who do you think you are?' And he goes on and on berating this man in front of the entire audience. Big mistake. Jolson's ego gets the better of him, you see. Finally, Jolson finishes and when he stops, the man looks up at Jolson and he says, 'Entertain me.'

Well now you can see the fire in Jolson's eyes. Jolson is really mad, you see. He goes into his next number and he finishes and the audience is applauding, but instead of acknowledging the audience, Jolson just stands there glaring at this man who is not applauding. The audience finishes and there is silence and the man looks up at Jolson and he says, 'Entertain me.' Well, now Jolson is out of his mind he is so angry. He goes into the next song, and the whole time he is glaring at this man as if looks could kill. He finishes and, when the applause dies down, the man says, 'Entertain me.'

That's it. Jolson goes crazy and he starts screaming and cursing at the man and now the audience is totally on the side of the heckler and is booing Jolson. Jolson is fercockt. He can't finish the show. The audience boos him off the stage. So you see, it doesn't matter if you're Al Jolson, who is the greatest of them all in my book; if you lose your temper on stage, you lose."

It turns out my paranoia is for naught. All regular cast member options are picked up. Unfortunately, for the writers, they are not so fortunate. Over on their side, the axe falls heavily. Merrill and Mike don't want their options picked up, so of course, George picks up their options. I never see Ernie after that. I am bummed. How many people do you know who can tell you Al Jolson stories? Then again, how many people do you know who can tell you Ernie Glucksman stories?

LAUGH-IN #2-77

We begin shooting *Laugh-In* #2-77 in July. It is 105 degrees outside in Burbank, but we are at NBC Burbank in an air-conditioned studio shooting the Christmas segment. I play Santa falling off a roof. It is an inverted V-shaped roof and we do lots of takes of me falling off the roof. There is a pad on the floor for me to land on, but it is a big roof and a long slide down and I do some pretty wild fall takes, back-sliding flips and flops and head over heels and other crazy stuff that's hard to describe because I have no idea what I'm doing other than just letting it happen. I figure gravity being what it is, relax and let Nature take her course. One thing about Nature, she's consistent in that regard. Ol' Isaac Newton figured that one out. On some of the takes it looks like Santa accidently killed himself. People are going, "Are you alright? Are you alright?"

I'm gasping. "I'm fine. It knocked the wind out of me, but I'm fine, I'm fine…"

Someone says, "Are you a professional stuntman?"

I say, "What? I'm not in trouble with the stunt man union now, am I?"

"Where did you learn to fall like that?"

I say, "Football, although in football, usually I get hit before I fall down. Why? Do I need to be a professional stunt man to do this?"

"It's okay for actors to do their own stunts, as long as the actor is expendable, and you are expendable, so don't worry about it. I would worry about breaking my neck if I was you…"

So if you ever see the *Laugh-In* '77 Christmas show, that's me falling off the roof in the Santa suit.

SCRIPT READING

We are sitting around a big table with our new scripts. Everyone is reading his or her lines. Everything is going fine until it's Bluestone's turn to read. Bluestone looks at the line he's given and goes, "Oh, I'm not doing this. This is shit. Since when do they allow monkeys into the writer's union?"

George looks pissed. Digby turns about ten shades of red. I am desperate to get more material for myself, so I say, "I'm not proud, George. I'll do the 'shit'!"

They look at me like they're not thrilled with me either. Then it dawns on me. These are the guys that wrote the 'shit'!

Oops!

JOKE WALL

Robin is even more emphatic than Bluestone about not wanting to do certain material. One day we are taping and they bring in a live audience. A bunch of us are behind the Joke Wall. One by one we pop out of the Wall and deliver our lines. I pop out and deliver my line and don't get much of a reaction. Robin pops out and ad-libs a line. I can't hear what he says, but I hear people laughing on the other side of the Wall. Then I hear George's voice over the PA. "Please deliver the line as written, Robin." But Robin won't say the line as written because Robin doesn't want to say the line as written. Instead, Robin pops out with variation after variation that is not in the script but is way funnier than what is in the script. The audience is roaring. George says, "Damn it, Robin. Tighten it up! Deliver the line!"

Robin pops out. "Give me a decent line, George, and my delivery will be tighter than a hawk's ass in a power dive."

The audience roars. George flips out. "GODDAMN IT, ROBIN! DELIVER THE FUCKING LINE!"

Robin pops out. "Don't fuck with me George and I will give you fucking ART!"

The crowd roars.

I pop out. "I'll do the line, George."

I pop back in and look over at Robin. They are laughing out there. Robin is giving me the look.

THE RACE TO BE
THE HUNDRED
MILLIONTH SPERM

Robin is already way ahead of the pack, but he is not about to slow the pace. The rest of us go crazy trying to keep up with him, with the exception of Lenny, who is already certifiable. "DO YOU WANT TO SEE ME GO CRAZY? HUH? HUH? DO YOU WANT TO SEE ME GO CRAZY?"

I know impressionists who learn impressions by watching other people do the impression. I prefer to go directly to the source, so that I'm not doing a carbon copy of someone else's version of someone else's version. That being said, for me, Lenny Schultz is a slam-dunk. After hanging out with him for five minutes, I AM Lenny. "DO YOU WANT TO SEE ME GO CRAZY? HUH? HUH? DO YOU WANT TO SEE ME GO CRAZY?" DO YOU DO YOU WANT TO SEE ME GO CRAZY?"

I start doing Lenny and now everybody is doing Lenny, except Bluestone of course, who refuses to play with the other children. The rest of the cast is walking around, "DO YOU WANT TO SEE ME GO CRAZY? HUH? HUH? DO YOU WANT TO SEE ME GO CRAZY?" DO YOU DO YOU WANT TO SEE ME GO CRAZY?"

Bluestone looks at us and says, "I think you are all a bunch of lunatics."

Bluestone is right. Rehearsal hall is a lunatic asylum. The

cast of *One Flew Over The Cuckoo's Nest* has nothing on us. Fortunately, not everyone is "on" all the time. There are long tedious hours of sitting around waiting for someone to tell us what to do. It's a weird feeling, hanging out with Waylon Flowers and Madame and suddenly realizing for the last hour and a half you've been talking to a puppet. Or try to carry on a conversation with Robin. One minute he's all over the place and the next, you go to say something to him and, good night sweet prince, the guy is snoring, which, of course, is Lenny's cue. "I wish I could sleep like that. I can't sleep. Can you sleep? How many times do you have to jack off before you can get to sleep? I have to jack off twelve, maybe fifteen times…"

Which gets June Gable going. "Twelve inches is perfect. I need twelve inches. I can get by with ten. Anything less than ten inches, forget about it…"

Lenny, "TWELVE INCHES? I'LL HAVE TO CUT OFF THREE! CALL THE MOYL!"

Dee Dee Wood, the choreographer, makes her entrance. "Okay children. Time to rehearse the junk food number."

"Is this the one where I play a dancing bag of potato chips?"

WHITE HOUSE CHEFS

Not so fast, Lenny. Wait until you see what Robin does with food. The scene is, it's the White House kitchen and Robin and Michael Sklar play White House chefs. The set looks like the real White House kitchen. It is fully stocked with various pastries including several pies, all kinds of fruit, dozens upon dozens of real eggs, all the cooking utensils and anything and everything else that you would find in the real White House kitchen. Robin and Michael look authentic dressed in White House chef's uniforms. All George cares about is that he gets one good take out of them. The cameras roll and Robin and Michael begin going back and forth as two fey chefs in a cat fight over who's job it is to make the President, Jimmy Carter's lunch and who's job it is to make Amy's lunch. The gag is the president's lunch is a peanut butter sandwich on white bread with no jelly, and Amy's lunch is a peanut butter sandwich on white bread with jelly. They finish the bit and Don the Director says, "Cut!"

George says, "Did we get it?"

Don says, "We got it."

"Okay, Robin, Michael, go for it."

Robin immediately pulls apart a peanut butter sandwich and, in a voice that sounds like a gay inspector Clouseau, slaps a slice onto each of Michael's face cheeks and challenges him to a duel. Michael responds in kind, pulling a sandwich apart and slapping Robin on each cheek. Now the bread is moving around on each of their faces as they speak. The comedic carnage escalates exponentially, both verbally and physically with wild adlibs and with the sundry food items readily available. It's a slapstick tour de force of comedy mayhem that would do Laurel and Hardy proud. Pies fly... fruit... you name it. Peanut butter is smeared. For me the highlight is: Robin takes a dozen eggs and one by one breaks them into a large stainless steel bowl. He then beats the eggs with a manual eggbeater, the whole time chattering away non-stop in his ridiculous gay French accent. Robin finishes whipping the eggs, opens Michael's pants and with great ceremonial flourish dumps the entire contents of the bowl down the front of Michael's crotch. Robin then sticks the eggbeater in, pulls it back out, holds it up and says, "You are still a quart low!"

Finally, after every joke, pie, cake, jar of peanut butter, jelly every last egg has been exhausted, Robin and Michael and Robin are standing there covered in gunk, looking at each other like a couple of spent fighters at the end of a fifteen rounder, and George says, "You missed two pies."

Robin says, "Where?"

George says, "On the bottom shelf. There are two left. There they are!"

Robin says, "And there's the producer!"

Thus begins the chase. There is no studio audience, so the stands are empty except for cast and crew. Robin and Michael each grab a pie and take off after George. Don the director, immediately picks up on the scene that's unfolding and says, "Turn the cameras around and light the stands!" They keep shooting as Robin and Michael chase George through the stands. George is wearing an expensive silk shirt and doesn't want to get pie on it, so he really does try to get away from them. George is a big guy, but he's able to pull off some pretty fancy defensive maneuvers as Robin and Michael chase him through the stands. They corner him at the top. Michael throws.

George ducks and Michael misses but Robin is right there and Robin doesn't miss. He scores a direct hit on George and his silk shirt.

George is not happy as I recall. George's wife, Jolene, is not happy either. She's the one who gave him the shirt. I am sitting there with Alan Sues watching the whole thing. Like everyone else, he is in awe of Robin. When it's over, he tells me a story about an improvisation he and Orson Wells did on the original *Laugh-In*. He says the entire thing lasted about four to five minutes, and afterwards Orson Wells told him that it was the best improvisation he had ever done. After all that nothing but the original joke in the script makes it on the air. I often wonder why George doesn't repackage some of this material, title it "*Laugh-In* Outtakes" and put it on HBO. Just think, George, The Censor can't say shit.

Part of George's MO is he likes to have regular cast members improvise with the special guests. The drill is, writers write lines, usually about fifteen or so nonsequiturs, for the guest star. Most of the guest stars don't rehearse. They just show up the day of the shoot and read the lines off cue cards. Once George has what he wants "in the can," he sends out individual cast members to improvise with the current guest star. It's partly a practical joke on the guest star but the spots are also designed to mine potential *Laugh-In* gold out of what are basically spontaneous improvisational bits.

One night the special guest is Gore Vidal. He is dressed in an Italian suit and a silk tie and expensive shoes and he is impeccable. He is reading his lines off the cards, unaware that Lenny Schultz is lurking nearby. "Can I go now George, huh? Huh? Can I go now?"

"Not yet, Lenny. Not yet."

Gore Vidal reads a few more lines.

"Now, George, huh, huh? Can I go now, George?"

"Not now, Lenny. Just a couple of more lines…"

Gore Vidal finishes reading the cards.
George says, "Have we got it?"

Don says, "We got it."

George says, "Okay, go now, Lenny. Go!"

Both Gore Vidal and Lenny are big guys, about six two. Lenny stalks onto the set. Behind his back he has a couple of pounds of hamburger in each hand. He immediately violates Gore Vidal's personal space, standing toe-to-toe, nose-to-nose with Gore Vidal, who has no idea who Lenny is or what is concealed behind his back.

"Mr. vVidal…?"
Gore Vidal remains on his mark, but leans back with a distinct look of trepidation on face.

"Yes…"

"Have you ever been on the show, *Meet the Press*?"

"Yes, I have…"

"How would you like to come on my show, *Press the Meat*?"

POW! Lenny slaps his hands together splattering meat all over Gore Vidal and his expensive Italian suit.

Without missing a beat, Gore Vidal does a perfect Lenny take back at Lenny. He brushes the hamburger off his suit and he says, "What? No onions?"

THE CHAIRMAN
OF THE BOARD

We are on the set at NBC. It's Saturday morning about 10 A.M. The studio is pretty much empty except cast and crew. We are shooting our first scene. I play a cop escorting prisoners in a lineup and am wearing an LAPD police uniform. We are just getting started and all of a sudden, Don the director says, "Strike the set!"

I say, "What's going on? We haven't finished…"
The AD walks up to me and says, "Go change into a suit and get to makeup and get back here ASAP." He hands me a page and says, "Here's your line. Memorize this, you're on with Frank in twenty minutes."

I say, "Frank…?"

"Sinatra! He's here. Go! You've got twenty minutes!"

I run down the stairs, and I've got the page in my hand, and I'm memorizing the script. Now I'm in my dressing room, and the dresser is helping me dress, and I have the script in my hand, and I'm memorizing. Now I'm in makeup and they are fixing my hat hair, and I'm still memorizing and I'm thinking, it's Frank Sinatra! Now they tell me to memorize! But I'm memorizing. I've got it memorized. It's memorized.

I run back up the stairs to the studio and before there were only cast and crew in there, but where did all these people come from? They are packed to the rafters. The lights seem brighter than usual. I hear: "Quiet on the set."

Cameras are rolling and Frank Sinatra is standing in front of a flat doing a bit with the English girls, Kim Braden and Claire Faulconbridge, and I'm watching this, telling myself: "I got it memorized, I got it memorized!"

The AD looks at me and says, "You're next."

"No problem. I've got it memorized."

George Schlatter is standing there like the head coach telling players when to run on and off the field.

Claire and Kim finish with Frank. They exit and George looks at me, says, "Go, Jim! Go!"

I walk out but, to get to where Frank is standing, I have to walk past Jilly Rizzo, who is standing about ten feet to the right of Frank just off camera. The best way to describe Jilly Rizzo is he looks like an upright double door freezer with a head. And this guy is a freezer alright. Jilly's job is to make sure nobody messes with Frank. Mess with Frank and you're dead. Capiche? So I walk past Jilly and he's giving me the eyeball, and I get to Frank and… here is where it gets hard to describe. Frank Sinatra has a palpable aura around him, like a force field. I can't describe it, but I can feel it. Whatever it is, Frank Sinatra has it. I get to Frank, George says, "Jim, Frank. Frank, Jim."

I reach to shake Frank's hand and hit the force field. I try to say in my own voice the line I have memorized, but what comes out is pure Ralph Kramden: "Hamana hamana hamana…"

The audience laughs, which is good for me, and better yet Frank laughs, which means Jilly laughs, which is better yet. Now everybody's laughing and Frank says, "Relax kid. We'll get this."

The next take, I say the line, "Us Italians have a great heritage. Have you ever had your roots traced?"

Here comes the curve. Frank is the pitcher. He says, "You

don't look Italian to me."

I say, "Well, actually I'm Italian, Irish, Portugese..."

The crowd laughs again.

George yells out, "Nobody cares what you are!"

I say, "They laughed, didn't they, George?"

That gets a laugh. George says, "Just say the line."

I say the line: "Us Italians have a great heritage. Have you ever had your roots traced?"

Frank says, "Yeah, by the FBI in 1958, the CIA in 1963..."

The audience laughs. Don the Director says, "Cut! We got it!"

I thank Frank, shake his hand, and walk off relieved to have it over with. Robin is cued up right behind me. George says, "Go Robin."

Robin comes out wearing his trademark rainbow suspenders and a beat up old straw cowboy hat, gets about a foot from Sinatra, and bounces back like he's bouncing off a force field. He says, "Whoa! Your aura is intense! I'm so excited I could drop a log!"

Sinatra says, "Drop a log?"

Frank Sinatra doesn't come across as the type who is easily impressed, but watching Frank watch Robin, I'd say Frank is definitely impressed. The crowd roars at everything Robin does. Robin leaves and it's like in *Butch Cassidy and The Sundance Kid*. Frank is going, "Who is that guy?"

Afterwards, Rose Gramalia says to me, "When I saw you earlier in the police uniform I thought you were a real police officer. I thought Frank must be here because the police are here. I didn't recognize you. No matter what they put you in, you look authentic. When they put you in a white coat you look like a real psychiatric attendant."

I say, "Only because I'm taking Lenny away."

Once Frank is gone, George starts talking about how glad he is Frank is in a good mood today, how when Frank is not in a good mood, dealing with him is like pulling the pin on a hand grenade and then walking around trying to hold the spoon on with your knees to keep it from exploding. Then he looks at me and says, "And you! Normally, screw up like you did, you're out of here after one take, but with you Frank did three takes. Frank loved you!"

"If Frank loves me, I guess that means I'm okay with Jilly, huh?"

Jim with Frank Sinatra NBC Laugh-In

ENOUGH WITH THE CENSOR ALREADY

One day I pull into NBC. Is that Orson Welles taking up the entire back seat of that Rolls Royce? It is indeed Orson Welles taking up the entire back seat of that Rolls Royce. Now we are in the studio and George and the Censor are going at it again, this time over something that is in the script.

"She can't say, 'I'm pregnant,' George. Have her say, 'with child.'"

"She already says, 'with child.' That's not the joke. The joke is, 'I'm pregnant.'"

"She can't say, 'I'm pregnant.'"

"'I'm pregnant' is the joke! You let them get away with worse on Peyton fucking Place and from me you expect Guiding Fucking Light...?"

We break for dinner in the NBC Commissary. Just as I'm sitting down to eat, I hear George yelling again. I cringe. I'm thinking, "Enough with the censor!" Then I hear the voice yelling back. "George, you hockey puck...!" It's Don Rickles! Everybody's laughing. I'm relieved. It's CPO Sharkey, not the Censor.

SPINNING OFF

During the next several months, I appear in two other George Schlatter productions on NBC. One is The Great American Laugh Off, a movie for television shot in San Francisco at the Great American Music Hall. It is an evening of standup comedy with the cast of Laugh-In. Nancy Bleiweiss is the host. We all do our standup acts: Ed Bluestone, Waylon Flowers and Madame, Toad the Mime, Ben Powers, Bill Rafferty, Lenny Schultz, Michael Sklar, me.

George gives Robin full rein to let the genie out of the bottle. Robin does, and everything he does is pure magic. It's a love affair, plain and simple. The audience adores Robin. He gets a standing ovation, but it's more than that, much, much more. Robin is a phenomenon, like a force of nature. The only way I can describe the feeling as I witness this go down is: Did you ever get the feeling the Queen Mary just passed and you are in a rowboat?

WHERE ARE
THE JOKES?

I am obsessed with trying to come up with new material. When I first get on *Laugh-In*, I mistakenly think that there will be writers to collaborate with, but I soon find out that's not the way it works. The first clue is half the time my script says, "Jim: [Line to come]." I keep waiting for the line to come and waiting and waiting...Meanwhile, Robin is a seemingly endless stream of non-stop improvisational brilliance. Bluestone does his own stuff, mainly because he refuses to do anyone else's. Of course, Bluestone's stuff is very funny and wildly original, so he gets away with it. As far as Lenny is concerned, as long as he can find a supermarket he hasn't been kicked out of, he will never run out of material, rotten as it may be.

One day I get to NBC and in the parking lot I see Fred Sanford's pickup truck. It's just parked there, an old beat up faded red 1951 Ford F1 with "Sanford and Son" on the side. I don't see Fred Sanford or Lamont anywhere, but that's the truck all right. That's when I get the idea to do Fred Sanford. Not a mere vocal impersonation, mind you, but a full on dead ringer look alike and sound alike. I'm doing it with Columbo and Patton and the Godfather, why not Fred Sanford? I have the voice and delivery and timing down. I am pretty close to the size and build and have similar facial bone structure as Redd Foxx. I scrunch my face up like him and look in the mirror and I can see it. Build up the nose and forehead a little, match the skin tone and I'm there.

FLASHBACK

It's Halloween, 1959. I'm ten years old. I don't want to scare anyone with my costume. I just want to get laughs. I decide to go with topical humor. I'm thinking, instead of going as a monster or a super hero or a ghost, why not go as a real-life person, someone in the news? I let Mom, who is always game, in on the deal. She tailors my uncle's Army fatigues to fit me and my dad has a theatrical make up kit that has ropes of real hair that you can pull apart and apply with spirit gum and I do that and with my bushy black hair and patchy fake beard made out of real hair and cap and combat boots and cigar, I'm a miniature Fidel Castro. My phony Spanish accent gets laughs. I win first place in the neighborhood Halloween costume contest. Good thing I don't know what I know now, thanks to the Freedom of Information Act, or I would have been worried about the kid in the CIA getup and the one in the Sam Giancana outfit with the exploding cigars.

FLASH FORWARD

I still have the makeup kit. All I need is putty to build my nose and forehead up and makeup to match Redd Foxx's skin tone. I take a color headshot of Redd Foxx as Fred Sanford to a theatrical makeup supply store. A trip to Goodwill for costume, we're in business. Now we are shooting at NBC and my next bit isn't scheduled to shoot until 4:00 P.M., which gives me a several hour window to pull off the ruse. I don't say anything to anyone. I just disappear into my dressing room and begin my transformation by liberally applying a watery liquid hair whitener to my real hair, which is naturally curly to start with. Once the liquid hair whitener dries, it causes my hair to frizz, exactly the effect I want. I then begin the process of building up my nose and forehead with putty, matching it as closely as possible to the picture I have of Redd Foxx. You never really finish, because with putty things have a tendency to shift around and you constantly have to readjust, especially once you start talking; but when I finish the preliminary putty job, I apply the makeup, first a base and then a second makeup to match Redd Foxx's skin tone.

The patchy beard I apply with spirit gum. The hair is real hair, coarse and a reddish brown color. Once the beard is on, I apply hair whitener to the beard and now I'm really starting to look like Fred Sanford. I adjust the putty and blend the makeup and a trim here and there on the beard and now it's time for costume. A pair of old grey wool pants and a flannel shirt and faded green suspenders with stripes, and a cap like Fred Sanford's, and damn! The illusion is complete. It's Fred Sanford!

Now it's my turn to steal the show. I head up the stairs to Studio 4. They are shooting and don't expect to see me for a couple hours in the studio. I walk in, or should I say waddle in like Fred Sanford. People are doing double takes. Schlatter is up there directing traffic as usual. I announce my presence. "George, you big dummy. Man, are you ugly. You so ugly you could put your face in some dough and make gorilla cookies."

People are laughing and applauding. They think I really am Redd Foxx! George says, "Redd, you old shit eating dog, how the hell are you?"

I say, "You know how to get rid of a peeping Tom? Leave your shades up!"

"Redd, you're a beauty..."

"Not only you ugly, you dumb. You so dumb, if bird doo-doo was brains, you'd have a clean cage!"

We go back and forth a couple more times and now I'm feeling guilty for actually pulling it off. For a split second I drop character and George says, "Wait a minute! That's not Redd Foxx! Who the hell is that?"

There's a pause. Someone says, "Fucking Giovanni!"

Jim as Redd Foxx | Romine Photography

THE JOKE FLOOR

Another time we are shooting the Joke Floor, which is like the Joke Wall except instead of popping out of The Wall we pop up out of The Floor. We have a studio audience in that day, and Robin and I are under the floor on our hands and knees. I have a new gag I'm going to try out that nobody knows I'm going to do. It's an Irish Spring soap commercial parody. I've never done the gag before and I don't tell anyone I am going to do it. I don't know if it's going to work, but my instincts tell me I should get a good response. In the actual commercial there's an Irish guy in the shower. He lathers up, sings an Irish ditty. "Di-dee di dee-di dee-dee-dee-dee di!" He finishes lathering, holds up the soap and says, "Aye, it does have a manly scent!"

We are under the Joke Floor and I have on a grey wool coat and green wool sweater, both Goodwill issues. I am wearing the same wool cap I use for Fred Sanford. I pull out a can of shaving cream and lather up on the outside of my coat and sweater. I look over at Robin and he has got a quizzical look on his face as if to say, "What the hell?" My cue comes. I pop up out of the floor and continue lathering as I sing. "Di-dee di dee-di dee-dee-dee-dee di!" I finish lathering, hold up the soap and say, "Aye, it does have a manly scent!"

The place explodes in laughter. I pop back under the floor and look over at Robin. He has a stunned look on his face. I know what he's thinking: "Fucking Giovanni!"

THE BEST LAID EGGS OF MICE AND MEN

All through that long hot smoggy miserable Burbank Summer I work on a standup comedy routine I believe will be my masterpiece, a comedy tour de force showcasing my best impersonations. The premise is that Boris Karloff and Peter Lorre pay a visit to Fred Sanford's junkyard to get parts for a monster they are building. Sounds good on paper, right? Problem is I don't just stick to the premise. Pretty soon I'm trying to fit every character I don't have a line for into the piece. I even have President Jimmy Carter make an appearance with Grouch Marx as a member of his cabinet. The result is a muddled mess. A muddled mess I decide to debut at the *Laugh-In* Cast Showcase at the Comedy Store.

The Showcase is a big deal. It's a major media event. All the top agents and managers are there. George Schlatter takes over the Comedy Store for the night and personally introduces each member of the new cast of *Laugh-In*. We each have fifteen minutes. George and Rose and Digby have all seen my stuff, so I decide to try out my new material mainly to impress them. It's a ballsy move. The problem with ballsy moves is if they don't work, you look like a real idiot, and that night I end up looking like a real idiot. It's so bad I can't finish the bit. I try to bail halfway through and go to my "A" material but it's too late. I can't pull out of the nosedive. I apologize to the audience for my fuck-up, another giant no-no. The whole spectacle has got to be painful for them as well. I slink off the stage to mercy applause and now I'm sitting in the back by the bar, beating myself up for having so thoroughly misjudged the situation. I'm telling myself over and over, "You're an idiot. You're an idiot..."

Ed Bluestone is there. It's the first time Bluestone has seen me do my act. He says, "What's wrong?"

I look at Bluestone thinking maybe I'll get a little sympathy out of the guy. I know better, but it's worth a try. I say, "I want you to know I don't always suck that bad. That wasn't my "A" material. See, I was trying out this new material I thought would work..."

Bluestone says, "This is a major media event. Don't you know you always do your "A" material at a major media event? You tried out new material? Oh, you are an idiot."

What do you expect from the guy that came up with the National Lampoon magazine cover. "Buy this magazine or we'll shoot this dog."

None of it matters. After all is said and done, all anybody remembers is Robin.

Right before our first episode airs in September of 1977, George gives us the good news. *Laugh-In* #1-77 will air in the same time slot as the original *Laugh-In*, Monday night at 8:00 P.M. on NBC. The bad news is we are up against ABC's Monday Night Football regular season opener: San Francisco 49ers vs. the Pittsburg Steelers. A week before the show airs, our cast picture with Bette Davis appears on the cover of *TV Guide*. We look like the crew of the Titanic right before it hits the iceberg. The big night arrives. The show airs three hours earlier on the East Coast, so at six o'clock West Coast time I call my father-in-law in Virginia to find out if I'm even in it. I say, "Hi John. This is Jim..."

He says, "I saw the show, boy. Where the hell were you?"

I say, "Wasn't my Colombo bit on there?"

He says, "Peter Falk was on there."

I say, "That was me!"

He says, "No, that was Peter Falk...!

I can't convince my own father-in-law it's me on the show. Now I'm paranoid maybe they did bring in Peter Falk and tape something without me knowing. By the time the show airs, I'm a nervous wreck. At eight PM West Coast time, the show comes on and there I am doing Columbo with Rich Little. No wonder I fooled my father-in-law. On camera, I look just like Peter Falk. My Patton getting hit in the face with a powder puff bit is there as well as other numbers I'm in. Of course, it's *Laugh-In*, so everything goes by fast. It's 1977 broadcast television so there is no pause and rewind button. It's there I see me there I went. It goes by so fast I miss myself in bits I know I am in and I still can't find me. The next time I'm in Schlatter's office, George asks me what I thought of the show.

I say, "I don't know George. I didn't see it. I was watching the game."

George says, "You asshole...!"

A month later we come full circle and hit the same iceberg, at which point, someone decides a change is needed. So they give us a new time slot, Wednesdays at 9 PM. This time it's opposite ABC's number one rated show, *Charlie's Angels*. Ironically, the day they give us the news we are going up against *Charlie's Angels*, my wife comes home with a Farrah Fawcett haircut. That's when I realize I'm not on the Titanic. I'm on the Hindenburg. Speaking of which, as a bonus for being good listeners, here's my favorite Pat McCormick joke: "Who said this? 'Is it warm in here or is it just me?' –The Captain of the Hindenburg!"

The rest is history. Like Davy Crockett said to Sam Houston as they looked out at Santa Ana's army at the Alamo. "Are we pouring cement today?"

Speaking of cement, I don't want to mix too many metaphors here, but we disappear like Jimmy Hoffa.

CARRION

Meanwhile, back at the ranch-style house in Burbank, it's 105 degrees, and the little terrier dog my wife brought back from a recent shopping trip to the supermarket accidently unplugs the upright freezer in the garage, which contains a recently purchased side of beef. I mean a whole side of beef! We eat maybe one package of hamburger! So it's 105 degrees and the dog unplugs the freezer, and we don't figure it out for two days. All of a sudden there's this smell and I go out into the garage and it's coming from the freezer. And yes we know it's the dog because he already unplugged the freezer. He jumped on the cord and unplugged the freezer before this. He is definitely the culprit. This is what he does this is his MO; he is a jumper. He jumps on everything. He makes me jumpy he jumps so much. Just having the dog around my eye is starting to twitch like inspector Dreyfus in the *Pink Panther*. In this whole scenario I am Dreyfus to this dog's Clouseau.

This dog is not my friend. I know he doesn't mean to screw up, but like Clouseau, he screws up and I'm the guy who has to suffer the consequences. And the current consequence is an upright freezer, which is now a cool 105 degrees full of rotten steer meat.

So I have no choice but to stuff the disaster into large green garbage bags and load it into the trunk of my car. Of course once I get in the car, it's even worse, especially when you're driving around the San Fernando Valley at 105 degrees in an air-cooled Volkswagen with no air conditioning and a trunk full of rotting flesh. And of course, it's a Volkswagen Beetle, so the trunk is up front, which means I can't even put the smell behind me. To make matters worse, this is when the whole Hillside Strangler thing is going down and here I am driving around LA, smelling like a prime suspect, looking for a dumpster. If someone smells me and gets my license plate number, the cops are going to be showing up at my door.

All these paranoid flashes are going through my head until I see a dumpster covered with flies and I figure, perfect. Unfortunately the minute I start to unload a guy shows up and tells me to get the hell out of there and not dump it there. So I load it back into the trunk and up I go into Griffith Park. Thank God Volkswagens are good in the dirt. I get on up the mountain way up there and I open the trunk and take one last look at my investment and say, "Oh, well, at least I hope the coyotes enjoy this shit."

A LUMP IN THE STOCKING

Christmas, '77 is the worst ever. The show's cancelled. There is no official notification. There are no goodbyes. Rafferty takes off for New York with his wife and kids and leaves his dog with me. He doesn't want to put the dog in a kennel because he says the dog is like a member of the family. The problem is Rafferty takes the family to New York and leaves a member behind and that member is pissed. He's a big old shaggy mutt-looking dog, and it's December and it's cold by Southern California standards, and he doesn't want to be outside. So we let him in the house and all he does is walk around whining and smelling up the house.

Finally, we can't stand it anymore, so we stick him outside and he lets the whole neighborhood know how righteously indignant he is. He is howling and carrying on and now I've got neighbors at my door saying they know it's Christmas, but can I please get the dog to stop caroling? I bring him back inside, and now he's out for blood. He's in the house walking around grumbling and whining and bitching and smelling bad and we've also got a two-year-old human baby running around in there and the dog starts shitting in the shag carpet.

And I mean everywhere in the shag carpet. It's dark brown and it's soft diarrhea shit, and now there are little piles of it settling in and camouflaging into the rug and, by the time I smell it, it is too late. It is everywhere in our dark brown shag carpet, and the two-year-old is running through it. So I'm trying to corral the two year old and she's running through the shit, and the dog won't shut up. He's barking and howling and shitting everywhere and that's when I go Ralph Kramden on his ass. "THAT'S IT! GET OUT! GET OUT! GET OUUUT!!!"

Now the dog is freaking out for good reason. He thinks I am ready to kill him and he's right.

"OUT!!!"

"Howl!"

"OUUUTTT!!!"

So it is Christmas Eve and I'm driving Rafferty's dog to the kennel, and the dog's whining and complaining and trying to talk me out of it and I'm telling him, "Too late, pal. I hate playing Scrooge on Christmas, but you give me no choice. You had your chance." I check the dog into the kennel and get back home, and now my wife is mad about the carpet, and Rafferty is mad I banished his dog, and I'm mad everybody's mad at me, and the only one who is happy is the two-year-old. She is having a great time running through shit. In fact, she has more fun running through shit than she does playing with her toys. My Christmas present from George is a hoodie with a *Laugh-In* logo on it. It's obvious Rafferty isn't going to forgive, and my wife isn't going to let me forget, at least not until we get the carpet cleaned. It is hands down my shittiest Christmas ever. No shit.

THE UNEMPLOYMENT OFFICE

I'm working out regularly at the Comedy Store, but the problem with the Comedy Store is you don't get paid, and I need money. I'm not complaining, mind you. Like most everybody else, I look at The Comedy Store as a place to showcase and try out new stuff. Actually, it's better to try out new material elsewhere and make sure it works before you try it at the Comedy Store. Guys like Robin can get away with winging it but, for most of us mortals, it's best to be prepared, especially at a time when there is a steady influx of new comedians, and the competition is getting stronger by the day.

I am doing my best to keep up with the herd, but unlike a lot of my contemporaries, I am not married to the Comedy Store. I have an actual wife and a two year old and a mortgage and no job. So I do what every other unemployed actor/comedian in my situation does. I head over to the North Hollywood unemployment office.

Here's my tip to anyone who wants to visit Hollywood and see someone famous in the flesh. Go to the North Hollywood unemployment office. I guarantee you will see someone famous in there. You might not know their name, but you will recognize their face.

The first time I walk in there's a guy sitting there. I say to myself, "I know this guy from somewhere." And then it dawns on me. I've seen this guy get killed a thousand times. You'd recognize him if you saw him. He's a skinny rat faced guy with stringy blonde hair. He looks like a poor man's Richard Widmark. In a typical scenario he always plays the slimy little twerp who challenges the lead character, a famous gunfighter who just rode into town and is trying to swear off gun fighting and doesn't want trouble, but his reputation precedes him and now he's got to face down a punk like this in every town. The dialogue always goes something like, the twerp says, "Let's see whose fastest, Ringo! What's the matter? Are you yellow?" And then all the extras clear away from the bar and the twerp reaches for his twin revolvers, he always has two and they're always fancy, and the hero blows the twerp away in the first scene.

Of course, this always happens right before the love of the hero's life, who happens to be a beautiful blonde and the schoolmarm, gets wind of the hero being in town. Next thing you know, she is trying to save him from the bad guys whose brother the hero killed ten years earlier...

Anyhow, the twerp guy who gets killed all the time in the first scene is sitting in the unemployment office at ten in the morning looking like he's still alive but just barely. I hate to mix clichés, but this guy looks like he's been rode hard down a thousand miles of bad road and then put away wet.

So just about the time I'm thinking I don't want to be him in ten years, they call my name. The lady at the unemployment office tells me I may be laid off from my job as an actor, but since I made more money in the previous six months as a truck driver, I am hereby classified as a truck driver. To get unemployment I have to come back every other week and prove that I am actively seeking employment as a truck driver. So now I'm applying at moving companies up and down the San Fernando Valley, doing the same thing I did in San Francisco, only in a much shittier environment. The unemployment people know the whole thing is an exercise in futility. Moving companies lay off in January. This time of year, the unemployment people probably have half the movers in North Hollywood as clients. But I go through the motions and go around filling out the applications so I can honestly say, "I went here and there and here and there. Nobody's hiring. Now can I have my check, please?"

I get a few checks, but I start getting the occasional paid gig and being the honest sort that I am, I declare what I make, which bumps me out of range of getting an unemployment check. It's just as well. I hate the degradation of going down there and being made to feel like a parasite. It's the only time I ever get unemployment. The last time I'm in there, a guy is sitting there who looks familiar. I say, "Didn't I see you on *The Untouchables*?"

He says, "Yeah, and *Dragnet* and *Perry Mason* and *Gunsmoke*..."

WESTWOOD

One day I call the Comedy Store to get my times for the week and they tell me that I am booked Friday and Saturday night at the new club out in Westwood called the Comedy Store Westwood, which is located near the UCLA campus. My first time in the Comedy Store Westwood I immediately notice what a bright room it is compared to the Comedy Store Sunset, which definitely has a much darker feel to it. The Comedy Store Sunset, formerly known as Ciro's, a night club owned by a famous gangster, Mickey Cohen, is said to be haunted by evil spirits, presumably mob guys who got whacked in there. Check out the book, *The Last Mafiosi* by famous mob rat, Jimmy "The Weasel" Frattiano. A lot of it is about that whole scene back in the fifties. As dark as the material is, once they start trying to whack Mickey Cohen, the thing reads like a roadrunner cartoon.

I know comics who say they've been in the Sunset Store after hours and been scared by ghosts. And according to my comic friends, these aren't Abbot and Costello ghosts, unless you're talking Frank Costello. Apparently, these ghosts were good at scaring people before they are ghosts. So compared to Sunset, Westwood is sweetness and light.

Friday night I get there and it is full of bright young faces, most of them UCLA students. I have a good spot in the lineup. I'm number five. As usual there are fifteen or so comics and each comic gets fifteen minutes. Mitzi puts Robin on last because she knows he can't be contained within fifteen-minute parameters the rest of us are given. Robin is a phenomenon, like a force of nature, and unless you're Richard Pryor, nobody wants to follow him.

I can't remember who all are on the bill, but everyone is an excellent comedian. I remember for sure the guy in front of me is David Letterman and the guy behind me is Michael Keaton. It's the first time I've ever seen either of them. The evening goes like clockwork. Every fifteen minutes, a new comic gets up and kills.

Letterman's turn comes. He looks like a frat boy, with long shaggy hair wearing a rugby shirt. Right away he gets into it with a table full of drunken UCLA football players stage left. The whole time he spends going back and forth with these guys. Like Robin, everything seems to be improvisational. It doesn't look like he even has an act, and yet he is very funny. Letterman gets off to a nice ovation. I'm thinking this guy's a genius.

Now it's my turn. I get up and I do fifteen minutes. I get off to a big applause, and then Michael Keaton gets up and does the same. I'm thinking, "Whoa! These guys are all just as good as me!" It goes like that all night. One by one, comics get up, everyone kills.

Finally, Robin gets up and blows the place completely away. He's all over the room, improvising, running into the kitchen and coming back out two seconds later with a tray in his hand, speaking like a gay Spanish guy. People are peeing their pants they are laughing so hard. I go home thinking, "What do I have to do to compete?"

The next night it's the same lineup, only this time Letterman doesn't have a table full of drunken UCLA football players to use as foils, so he starts picking on different tables at random around the room. The night before I'm thinking this guy is a genius. He has no act, and he is able to wing it, totally off the cuff. Now I realize this is his act! He does the same jokes he did the night before only instead of confining his remarks to one table he goes after the whole room.

Letterman gets the whole crowd heckling, which, of course, for Letterman, is great. The problem is, by the time he leaves the stage, the audience thinks it's their job to heckle whoever is up there, and I'm the next guy up.

I am ill prepared to deal with the aftermath of Dave. My act is theatrical. I do strong impersonations and good clean original material and am used to holding the audience's rapt attention, but not this time. I try doing my bits, but the crowd won't let me finish anything.

At least Michael Keaton has a chance to see what is happening and load the ammunition belts. When Michael's turn comes he does a good job dealing with the hecklers. I give him credit for getting the show back on track. After Keaton the show goes on pretty much like the night before. I'll be the first to admit I am the weak link that night. My only solace is the fact that, as usual, in the end, all anybody remembers is Robin, Robin, and Robin.

RETURN TO THE MUSIC HALL

My next big booking up in San Francisco is with Robin at the Great American Music Hall. They give Robin and I equal billing but in reality Robin is the headliner and everybody knows it. I am supposed to do 30-35 minutes and then Robin is going to come out and do whatever he wants on the backend. I want to do my best, especially since it's the Music Hall, and it's with Robin, so I spend a lot of time writing new material and organizing it into an act.

I am focused. I come up with the idea of doing a quick change bit, which hearkens back to my old act during the Nixon era (or should I say "error?") This time, instead of Nixon jokes, I am The Godfather in an American Express commercial. The night of the show, the MC introduces me. I enter as the Don Corleone, wearing a tuxedo with a fake moustache. I have hair whitener in my hair and napkins in my cheeks. I am the Godfather. The audience responds enthusiastically to the visual before I ever say a word.

"Do you know me? A lot of people don't recognize me. At least the smart ones don't.

That's why I carry this…"

I pull out a large realistic looking revolver.

"Sicilian Express. Don't leave home without it!"

Jim as The Godfather | Romine Photography

Part my hair, add glasses and a cigar, I'm Groucho as the priest in *The Exorcist*. "I'm speaking to the person inside of Regan. Say the secret word and you win a hundred dollars."

"Wablezableablezabbleaaaggghhh!!!"

"Congratulations, you just said the secret word!"

Wipe off the moustache, muss my hair and put on the raincoat, do the eye thing looking around fumbling and Columbo is the priest trying to find matches to light my cigar and the crowd is going wild. I milk it as long as possible before I deliver the line. "Excuse me, Mr. Devil. Gee, I hate to bother you I know you're very busy. You know this is a big thrill for me. To tell you the truth, I really didn't think you existed. Gee, how do you make the smoke come out of your ears like that? Do you think you could teach me to do that? I mean I know they'd listen to my sermons if I could make smoke come out of my ears. My brother-in-law is a magician and even he can't make smoke come out of his ears. Wait till I tell him. He's not going to believe it…"

Everything works. I am getting big laughs and applause, I take off the raincoat and tuxedo coat and shirt, add a vest and beat up fedora, and I am Ed Norton, Art Carney's character from *The Honeymooners*, rolling a joint. I'm doing all the Norton moves with the rolling paper, taking forever to accomplish the task.

"WILL YOU HURRY UP AND ROLL THAT JOINT, NORTON!"

Norton finishes rolling the joint, hands it to Ralph. "Here you go Ralph. Wait 'till you try this weed. One hit and you're on the moon!"
Ralph takes the joint. "This better be good, Norton!" Ralph takes a hit, is immediately all over the stage with a coughing fit. He finally feels the effect. "Ooh, how sweet it is! You're right Norton. One hit and I'm on the moon…I feel weightless…!"

"I wouldn't go that far, Ralph!"

The Honeymooners smoking dope kills. Next I do a Japanese light beer commercial. I know it sounds crazy, but I never practice it to see if it will work. I know it will work! Right before we go on, I preset the stage with a full can of Miller Lite sitting on top of a wooden bar stool. I

leave the tab un-pulled and carefully puncture the top with an ice pick so as not to disturb the contents. About halfway through my act I'm rolling right along, and I grab the stool and can and place them center stage facing the audience. I go into my Torishiro Mifune impersonation. "When I drink beer I like to drink light beer. Great taste, less filling.
"

I turn the can over sideways on the stool and strike the can with a simultaneous knife hand strike and "ki-ai!" A still photographer with a fancy big lens camera is stage right standing on the floor next to the stage taking pictures, and the beer shoots straight out of the can sideways like turning on a miniature hire pressure fire hose hitting the guy right in the camera lens before he has a chance to react. He just stands there frozen in place getting hosed for several seconds, not knowing which way to turn. I didn't plan it to work out that way, but timing is everything. The crowd goes crazy. My new material all comes off without a single misfire. I get a tremendous ovation at the end.

Robin comes out and does his patented freewheeling off the top of his head routine, and somehow it doesn't quite work for him that night. For whatever reason, Robin's timing is off and he starts going out on limbs, and either he can't get back down, or the limb breaks off altogether. People start yelling, "Bring back Giovanni!" When I come back out to join Robin for a final curtain call, the crowd goes crazy. I get a bigger ovation than Robin. It's a bush league move, and I regret doing it afterwards, but I do a little Billy "White Shoes" Johnson dance and the crowd cheers. Robin gives me the look. He doesn't say anything, but I can tell he is pissed. I have delusions of grandeur thinking I can compete with Robin after all.

My new material works so well on Friday, I get cocky and decide to try even more new material out on Saturday. Unfortunately for me, Saturday is when roles get reversed. On Saturday, I'm the one with the miscues. My newest new stuff doesn't work, which knocks my timing off. The karate beer thing misfires. Even my tried and true bits go flat. It's a huge letdown from the night before.

Robin comes out and is over the top loaded for bear. He does over an hour and absolutely destroys. After several encores, Robin finishes and the ovation is like an earthquake. You can literally feel the building shake. We get up for the final curtain call and once again the crowd is on their feet, only this time it's Robin who is doing the Billy "White Shoes" Johnson dance.

Jim and Robin Williams
at The Great American
Music Hall SF

IMPRESSONIST VS. IMPRESSIONIST

I go back to LA and now it's time to try out my new act at the Sunset Comedy Store. I am scheduled to go on after Roger & Roger, a comedy team that specializes in impersonations. Normally, it's the kiss of death to follow impersonations with impersonations, especially if they're the same impersonations. I do a lot of the same ones as Roger & Roger, so I am apprehensive as to how well my act will go over following them, but it turns out my apprehensions are unwarranted. Roger & Roger do their act and do well.

The MC introduces me. I enter as the Godfather and do a streamlined version of my quick-change act. Instead of the thirty-five I do at the Music Hall with Robin, I do my absolute best fifteen minutes of "A" material and it kills.

I get a standing ovation and Letterman has to follow me. Letterman can't buy a laugh. He tries everything to get a response out of the crowd, but they are not buying any of his stuff that night. About eight minutes into it, Letterman looks around and says, "This is like walking into a void."

MERV

The next day I get a call from The Merv Griffin people. They ask me to perform the following day on the show. I agree. They ask me what I am going to do. I tell them an abbreviated version of my quick-change act. They tell me I can't do "The Honeymooners Smoking Dope" and a lot of material I do in my nightclub act, not because it is off color per se, but because it is not acceptable by television standards. I know I have material for least one show and I have a good idea of what they want, so I tell them what I plan on doing. They okay my material and book me. The next day I'm in the green room before the show. I meet Jack Sheldon, a hilarious character and a great trumpet player. Jack is one of those funny jazz musicians I keep telling you about. One of my favorite Jack Sheldon lines is: "I like to date women who wear leather because when they take off their pants they smell like a new car."

Mort Lindsey is there. He is the music director and leader of the band. I ask Mort if they can play me on with the Godfather theme and Mort says, "No problem."

I'm backstage in make-up and costume, ready to go on, looking like Don Corleone on his daughter's wedding day. I am watching a monitor and can see what is happening out in the theater in front of the live studio audience. A band called "Brooklyn Dreams" is performing. I am next and I am waiting for my cue. The band finishes playing and Merv walks over to interview the leader of the band, who has long brown shaggy hair and a beard and is wearing an earring. Earrings are not that common on men in 1978. Even though it is obscured by the guy's long hair,

Merv spots the earring right away and says, "Oh, I see you're wearing an earring."

The guy, who is from Brooklyn, says, "You would have to say that. Now my old man is going to give me a hard time about the earring."

Merv gets the cue to wrap up the interview and he says, "We'll be right back..."

The music plays for exactly one minute. Merv has never seen me. He has no idea what I am going to do. The music stops. I hear Merv's voice: "Here's a young man we're all waiting to see. A bright new impressionist on the horizon. He made his television debut on the new *Laugh-In* specials. And that looks just like the beginning of a fine career working out new impressions at the Comedy Store here in Hollywood. Give a nice warm welcome to the many voices of Jim Giovanni...Jim Giovanni!"

One of the musicians plays *The Godfather* theme on a mandolin. I enter as Don Corleone. The crowd goes nuts. The response finally dies down. I say, "I'm the father of the kid with the earring!"
Boom! From then on I can do no wrong.

Everything works as if I just thought it up on the spot. I finish my set, and Merv invites me over to the panel. Now I'm sitting there with Merv and Kay Ballard and another guy whose name I can't remember. I tell Merv I'm from San Francisco and Merv says, "San Francisco, did you play a lot of clubs there?"

I say, "Oh yeah, I played the Boarding House and the Great American Music Hall. The Holy City Zoo is the place where George Schlatter came..."

Merv says, "Good. I'm so glad San Francisco is really spawning a whole lot of new talent."

I say, "Yeah, there's a lot of guys coming up, Robin Williams, I don't know if you've seen him yet. He's really marvelous.

Merv has no idea who Robin is. He asks if I do any other impersonations, so I do Paul Newman, Senator Sam Ervin and this guy: "Hey yo! This is Sylvester Stallone. You know, it's not easy staying in shape, especially with the high cost of meat nowadays. You know what I mean? That's why I use Hamburger Helper. It only costs seventy-five cents a box and I still get a good workout…"

I punch the box of Hamburger Helper. It flies into Kaye Ballard's drink and knocks the drink directly into her lap. An obvious screw-up, my immediate reaction is to recoil in horror at my little faux pas, but the laughs go on and on, and sometimes some of the biggest laughs are the unplanned ones. Like the pie in the face routine I don't know what it is about someone getting doused that is funny but everyone in the place thinks it is hilarious, including the recipient of the dousing, Kaye Ballard herself. Kaye is totally cool with it and in the end says, "I'm very proud of him. He's an adorable young Italian! He's got it!" Which is indeed high praise coming from someone whose real name is Catherine Balotta. After the show everyone is telling me how great I did. I'm leaving the studio, and Mrs. Miller asks for my autograph. Mrs. Miller wants my autograph? I have arrived! I know this much, I am in Comedy Heaven.

The next day I'm in San Francisco at the Boarding House opening for some thrasher punk band whose name I can't remember at a media event from hell. I've literally gone from Comedy Heaven to Comedy Hell in less than twenty-four hours. And little do I know, the worst is still ahead of me.

VEGAS

Merv Griffin immediately re-books me. This time the show is in Las Vegas. It is great they like me so much, but it creates a dilemma. I did all my best TV material in the first show. Now what do I do? I have three weeks to come up with a new act. Last time I did a quick change from the Godfather to Colombo. What if this time General Patton becomes Sergeant Bilko? I hire a couple of writers, Richard Marcus and Terry Hamburg to help me write a whole new act. The next three weeks if I'm not brainstorming with these guys I am working on my own. It's like cramming for a PhD dissertation. I work around the clock, literally, and when I do sleep, I sleep dreaming it. The pressure is on and I am the one putting it on myself.

Not only am I under the gun to come up with new material and organize it and memorize it and get the timing down, I also need to score a Patton uniform somewhere. I call Western Costume and they tell me it is $200 a day to rent Patton. Since my trip to Vegas is going to take three days and $600 is more than I'm going to make for doing the show, I'm thinking screw that. I already have an old World War II Army Officers uniform jacket and some WW I cavalry riding pants. For $600 I can do a hell of a lot of accessorizing.

Now I'm running all over the San Fernando Valley to surplus stores, flea markets, wherever, to get medals, insignia, etc. to put on the uniform. I get general stars and a Third Army patch for the jacket. I get an old World War II helmet liner at a surplus store, spray paint it black and mount stars on the front. I take an old replica Colt .45 BB gun and spray-paint the handles white. I call mom and tell her what I'm doing and next thing I know she makes a sash she says I can wear across the front of the uniform. She says she's going to send it to me along with a medal she found at a garage sale. She says, "It will be great for your costume. It's real too!"

"Gee, that's great mom! Do you know what kind of medal it is?"

Mom says, "I'm not sure, but it says 1917 on it, so I think it's from the First World War."

I say, "Great! That's what I'm looking for! Gee, thanks, mom!"

Now I'm like a kid at Christmas, anxious to get the package from mom, especially since I'm having such a difficult time finding authentic medals for the costume. Patton was in WW I. He led charges alongside Douglas MacArthur. This is perfect! I can't wait to see the medal. The package arrives, I open it and call mom. I say, "Mom, the sash is great, but I hate to tell you, I don't think you'll ever catch Patton wearing an Iron Cross!"

Compared to Patton, Bilko is easy. A trip to the corner drug store and I have Bilko's horn rimmed black glasses. The Army uniform hat and blouse I pick up at the surplus store along with the shoulder patch. Sew that and a pair of Master Sergeant's stripes onto the sleeves and I'm Bilko. The big day comes and now all I have to do is go try out new material on The Merv Griffin Show on the main stage at Caesars Palace in Las Vegas. I'm on the bill with Eddy Arnold, Harry James, Shields and Yarnell, Jack Sheldon, Mort Lindsey and the band. No pressure here. It's either soar with the eagles or crash and burn spectacularly. Finally, the big moment arrives. Merv gives me the big introduction: "As I told you in the beginning of the show, we recently brought a young impressionist to our show from the Hollywood studio and he left the whole audience just roaring and amazed at his hilarious impressions. We've been looking forward to bringing him back and particularly before the Caesars Palace audience because this is the true test of everything but he doesn't need it. You will love him the minute he walks out on the stage. We're crazy about him. Here's Jim Giovanni!"

Jim as General Patton | Romine Photography

The band plays me on with a military march. It's a big stage and a long walk out and the crowd loves that it's Patton. I get to center stage and immediately go into a tirade about how tough it was to get through the metal detector at the airport. I point to the medals on my chest. "A lot of you know this is fruit salad. This is a plum. This is an orange. These two are cherries. When I arrived here at Caesars Palace, some clown pinned a third cherry on my chest and coins fell out of my fly."

A raincoat over the uniform and Columbo becomes Patton. "Excuse me, I hate to bother you, but is the war being held here this afternoon? Say if you capture any Germans, do you think you could get them to help me push my tank and get it started...?

Adrenaline is pumping like crazy, my right leg is shaking so bad I feel like I'm ready to levitate. I take off Patton's jacket, gun, and helmet, put on a hat and glasses and presto voilà: Sergeant Bilko, The Fortuneteller. Las Vegas is gambling and Bilko's whole schtick is gambling. "As the great mystical spinning wheel goes around and around, there you are, Colonel sir, Leo the Lion, fulfilling your destiny at 12 to 1...!"

The crowd loves it. Best of all, Merv loves it. Afterwards Merv comes up and says what a great job I did. I say, "Merv, my right leg was shaking so bad I was afraid everybody could see it. Could you see it...?"

Merv says, "No, but that's a great sign when your right leg shakes. My right leg used to shake all the time. That means you're going to be a big star...!"

AN OFFER I MUST REFUSE

No sooner do I get back from Vegas, I get a call to meet with Merv in his office. Merv wants me to sign a thirteen show one-year exclusive contract, which means I can do anything except another syndicated daytime talk show, specifically *Mike Douglas* or *Dinah Shore*. Strangely enough, I am allowed to go on Carson, but since word has come down from on high that Johnny has banned impressionists from the Tonight Show, it is moot. Merv thinks I could be a game show host. I still have fantasies about winning an Academy Award. Anything is possible. Just sign the contract.

I say, "Merv, I can't sign the contract."

"Why not?"

"I'm going to be honest with you. I'm out of material. I barely came up with material for two shows. I mean, I have material, but not TV material. I'll do your show exclusively. I won't do any of those other shows, but it takes me a year to come up with fifteen minutes of 'A' TV material on my own. To come up with a fifteen new minutes every three weeks for thirteen shows? I might do okay at first, but when I bomb it's going to leave a smoldering hole."

"I still want you to perform on my show when you feel you have the material. I also have some people I want you to meet who are interested in handling your career."

Next thing I know Merv introduces me to the legendary "Bullets" Durgom. "Bullets" is the manager immortalized in Lenny Bruce's famous comedy routine: "The Comedian at the Palladium." When Lenny refers to "Bullets," this is the guy. Bullets' great claim to fame is he discovered and managed Jackie Gleason. He also managed Frank Sinatra, Sammy Davis Jr., Merv Griffin, and Jim Stafford. Now he wants to manage me. Merv also introduces me to Debbie Miller, his agent at William Morris. Suddenly, I'm a hot commodity. I meet with Debbie at her office at William Morris. She shows the tapes of my first two Griffin shows to her colleagues. All agree I'm a leading man. Funny. I never thought of myself as a leading man. I always thought of myself as a character actor. Now Debbie wants me to sign a contract. She wants to manage three comedians. The other two are David Letterman and Michael Keaton.

"Hey! I know those guys!"

I tell Debbie I'll think about it, but I have to talk to Bullets first. I walk out of William Morris and, as I'm walking out, in the front door here comes Jack Lemmon with a script under his arm. It must be a good script too because Jack has a big happy Jack Lemmon smile on his face. Now I have a real dilemma. I have to choose between Debbie and Bullets, who is the quintessential old school manager: Short, round, bald, gruff no nonsense. I tell the deal and Bullets says, "Let's get this straight. If I'm managing you, I call the shots."

I say, "Sure, Bullets. Are you going to want me to sign a contract?"

"Bullets" says, "We'll worry about that after you're a hit."

"Is it okay if you are my manager and Debbie is my agent?"

"As long as you remember I call the shots."

CHARLIE VAN SLAM

Meanwhile the mortgage payment is due and what I'm making doing The Merv Griffin Show isn't covering it, so I go to my fallback. I leave a message with Charlie Van Slam's dispatcher. Charlie is a long-haul furniture mover pal of mine. Charlie likes using me as a helper. We get along, and I know how to load a truck. If you ever meet an old trucker who looks like Jackie Gleason and sounds like Wolf Man Jack with a cigarette in one hand and a Bud in the other, there's a good chance it's Charlie Van Slam. A lot of people know him by "Charlie Budweiser" because, it's no secret, when Charlie ain't driving, Charlie's drinking Bud. Charlie is adamant about drinking and driving, though. "Jim, you know me, I'm a professional truck driver. I never drink and drive. As far as drinking and driving goes, I'm against it. But you know me, Jim. I like my Budweiser. And I drink plenty of it when I ain't drivin', but you'll never catch me drunk behind the wheel, Jim. I'm a professional truck driver."

Charlie does keep drinking and driving separate, but going on a run with him can be plenty scary nevertheless. For instance one time we are headed up a long stretch of Interstate, I look over at Charlie and he's got a cigarette dangling from his lip but I swear looking at him he's asleep. He's making snorting sounds and his fat belly is up against the steering wheel like some sort of automatic pilot steering the truck. No little truck either this is a Kenworth tractor hauling a fully loaded forty foot trailer. Looking at Charlie I can't help but think about all those sad Red Sovine truck-driving songs about jackknifed trucks and busloads of school kids and teddy bears and

167

little boys who lost their trucker daddy and I go, "Charlie!"
"What?"

"I thought you were asleep."

"I ain't sleepin', Jim. I'm just resting my eyes."

EL CAJON

One day I'm home wondering how I'm going to pay the mortgage, and I turn on the TV watch Robin make his debut as Mork from Ork on *Happy Days*. It's official. Robin is in the stratosphere. No sooner does the show end, my phone rings. It's Charlie Van Slam. "I'm makin' a run to So Cal, Jim. If you want to help me pack and load, I'll pay you top dollar."

"Thanks, Charlie. Just say when."

My first Merv Griffin appearance airs, the one where I'm the Godfather. The next day I'm in El Cajon packing household goods with Charlie Van Slam. Not just Charlie, he's got his Mexican nephew, Jerry along. I don't know if the two are kin or what, but Charlie always refers to Jerry as "my Mexican nephew," and Jerry runs with Charlie a lot, so there it is. Now the three of us are in El Cajon packing this lady's stuff and Charlie tells the lady that I am a big TV star and the lady asks what I've done, and I say I was on *Laugh-In*. She asks what it's like working with Goldie Hawn, and I say I was on the second *Laugh-In* with Robin Williams and she goes crazy and says, "We just saw him on *Happy Days*. He is so wonderful. I hear he is going to have a new show in September, and we can't wait for his new show..."

"Well, it's plain to see Robin ain't going to have to worry about making no mortgage payment."

It's a hot day in El Cajon and we finish packing the lady's stuff and Charlie decides it's time to hoist a few, so being the big time professional truck driver he is and not wanting to drink and drive, Charlie leaves his rig parked in front of the lady's house and calls a cab for the three of us to go to one of Charlie's on the road hang outs. This time it's a strip joint in San Diego featuring topless coeds. So we are sitting in the biggest titty bar in San Diego and Jerry tells our waitress, herself an exceptionally cute topless co-ed, that I'm a big TV star and that I'm on the Merv Griffin Show and she immediately goes, "Oh my God I saw you. I saw you on the Merv Griffin show yesterday. Omigod, it is you...!"

Next thing I know, we're surrounded. Topless coeds encircle our table asking for autographs. Jerry looks at Charlie and says, "Charlie, we got to take this guy everywhere we go!"

Finally, Charlie says it's time to go back to the hotel so we get a cab back to the hotel and of course there is a bar next to the hotel and now it's 1:30 in the morning we are in the bar and Jerry is still riled up about the topless coed scene so now he wants to go where it's happening 24/7. "Come on, Charlie, let's go to TJ's, let's go to TJ's...!" He looks at me and says, "Come on, you want to go to TJ's with us, you want to go to TJ's?

I say, "Guys, we're supposed to move this lady's stuff first thing in the morning and we told her we would be there at 8:00 A.M. and it's almost 2:00 A.M. I don't want to go to Tijuana."

Now Jerry is going, "You better come to TJ's with us or I'm gonna kick your ass."

I don't want to get in a drunken brawl with Jerry so I just say, "Okay. Fine."

Charlie calls a cab and when the cab rolls up, I get in first and I slide all the way across the back seat of the cab and get out the other side just as Charlie and Jerry are sliding in behind me. The cab takes off without me and I'm thinking when Jerry figures out that I'm not there, he's going to be really pissed. I'm afraid when they do show up Jerry's going to start swinging at me, so when I get back to the room I push all the furniture up against the door so I can lay down without having to worry about getting pummeled in my sleep.

Turns out, my worry is for naught. Charlie and Jerry stumble in at the break of dawn, looking like the aftermath of a bad Junior Brown song. I've been asleep since about two-thirty and I am relatively refreshed. So there they are at 6:00 A.M., banging on the door for me to let them in. I push the furniture away from the door and open it a crack and look out and it's plain to Jerry's in no condition to kick anybody's ass, so I let them in and they both do simultaneous face plants onto their bunks. Me, being the nice guy I am, give them a full half hour beauty rest before I start kicking their box springs. "Alright, assholes! Let's go! Up and at 'em! We got a truck to load!"

Neither one of them is worth a shit all day. Charlie sleeps on the pad pile in the back of the trailer the whole time. He gets up to take an occasional leak and smoke a cigarette, and then it's back to the pad pile. Thank God the lady's not there because you can hear him snoring all the way in the house. Jerry is next to worthless. I load the truck pretty much by myself, which takes almost twelve hours. By then Charlie's in good enough shape to drive, by big time professional truck driving standards, according to him, so we pull out of El Cajon and no sooner are we on the road, Jerry starts in. "We got to take this guy on the road with us all the time, Charlie. You got to come with us all the time, Columbo!"

"Why? So I can do all the work?"

Charlie says, "That ain't it, Jim. Jerry thinks you're a pussy magnet."

Two hours later, we are in Burbank. Charlie pays me top dollar. "Thanks, Jim. See you next time."

I hear the hiss of airbrakes, Charlie waves goodbye and hits the air horn as he pulls out. I wave back. I get in the house and my wife tells me the Merv Griffin folks called today, and they want me to go on again in three weeks. Okay. I was the Godfather the first time and Patton the second, which hasn't even aired yet. How do I top myself? This time I figure I'll play the ace. I'll have Columbo come out and sing a parody of "My Way" as a farewell to his raincoat. I run it by the censor and get the thumbs up. Everything is copasetic until the day before the show when I get a call from the Merv Griffin people who tell me I can't do the bit. I ask why and they say, "Because Frank says no."

"Frank...?

"Sinatra. If Frank says, no, it means no. You can't do it."

God knows I don't want to piss off Frank or Jilly, so now I have less than twenty-four hours to come up with a new routine. So instead of going on with a killer piece, I go on with Columbo doing a cheap store-bought magic trick, which would be fine if the trick worked. Unfortunately, the trick doesn't work and now I feel like a real schmuck sitting on the panel next to George Peppard, who assures me it ain't as bad as I think. He asks who my manager is and I say Bullets, and now he's telling me how great Bullets is and how I can't go wrong with Bullets. The other guy on the panel is Herve Villachaise, the diminutive co-star of Fantasy Island. In the Green Room Herve shows me a dagger he carries in his boot that's bigger than he is. Apparently, Merv Griffin doesn't think my performance is all that bad either because I am immediately re-booked. On my next appearance I come out and do the Irish Spring parody with the soap on the outside of the coat. My routine gets big laughs and puts me back in the catbird seat temporarily. Riding shotgun in the seat next to me is Mr. Slapstick himself, Soupy Sales. Soupy says, "I love your stuff, man. Brilliant, man, simply brilliant!"

"Gee, thanks, Soupy. I stole it from you."

"That's what I'm saying, I love it man, brilliant, simply brilliant."

THE OLD WALDORF

One day I get a call from a guy who says his name is Jon Fox and who shall hereby be referred to as "Jon Fox the promoter" (as opposed to John Fox the comedian). So Jon Fox the promoter asks me if I've ever heard of the old Waldorf in San Francisco. I say, "Yeah, it used to be on California Street, now it's out on Battery. They book headline acts there."

Fox asks if I would like to do a show at the old Waldorf with Robin Williams and Bill Rafferty. Of course I say, "Yes." The Old Waldorf is a great venue. Besides, it's an excuse to get out of LA and up to San Francisco and a chance to make some money. Fox tells me the lineup will be: Rafferty opens and does fifteen minutes. I do the middle spot and do thirty. Robin closes the show and does forty-five. Fox offers me $150 for the middle spot and without even attempting to negotiate, I say yes. Now all I have to do is figure out how to get up to San Francisco for the show. My car is a Chevy Vega with a cracked aluminum block and I've got too much stuff to hitchhike. Just as I'm thinking I'm going to have to spring for a ticket for a flight on the airplane with a smile on its face, I get a call from Charlie Van Slam. Turns out he's running a load up from Van Nuys to San Francisco and wants to know if I want to help him load. The timing couldn't be better. It coincides perfectly with my show at the Old Waldorf. "Not only will I help you load, it would be great if I hitch a ride back up to the SF with you, Charlie."

"You got it, Jim."

I help Charlie load the truck and spend a sleepless night

watching his fat gut steer the truck. He's making snorting sounds the whole time, looking like he's going to have a heart attack any minute. I keep telling myself as long as the cigarette is still dangling from his lip, we're okay. Next morning, thanks to God and Saint Christopher, we're in San Francisco.

THE RELUCTANT
HEADLINER

I get to the Old Waldorf that night and Jon Fox is there with his wife, Anne. I have all my costumes with me and tell Fox I need a place to change. Fox takes Rafferty and me to an empty office space next door to the Old Waldorf and tells us this is our dressing room. I take a peek over next door at the house. The capacity is around four hundred fifty seats and the place is jammed. The energy in the room is electric. Everyone is anticipating Robin. Fox comes backstage and informs us that Robin is a no-show. He's doesn't tell us the reason why Robin doesn't show, and I never ask Robin about it, so I can't tell you for sure why Robin isn't there that night. All I know is Fox is in a panic because he has a full house and no Robin. I say, "Here's what I suggest we do. Rafferty go out and do the opening spot for ten to fifteen, then bring me on as Patton. I'll do ten to twelve, something like that, then I'll split, Rafferty come back and do another twenty or so..."

Rafferty says, "I can do twenty-five my second set."

I say, "Great! That'll give me more time to do the costume change. So, Rafferty, do your twenty-five, thirty if you want..."

Rafferty laughs. He says, "We'll see how it goes, Jimmy."

"The point is do whatever time you want, and when you're done, introduce me and I'll come back as the Godfather and close the show. How's that for a plan, Jon?"

Fox agrees. He has little choice, which turns out to be a good thing. Everything works beautifully, better than anyone could imagine. Rafferty goes out and opens, does fifteen, gets the crowd going. He brings me on. I come out as Patton and kill. The crowd is hot. I do close to fifteen. Rafferty comes back out and keeps them rolling for another twenty-five or so and introduces me. I come out as the Godfather. Everything works. I do my quick-change act, but I don't stop. I keep going dredging up every old bit I can think of. Even the Nixon stuff destroys again. This crowd wants to laugh big time. Now I'm kibitzing with the crowd, ad-libbing, improvising with props, telling funny true stories, singing songs they won't let me sing on The Merv Griffin show. I'm a regular Shecky Green that night. No concept of time, I'm in the riff zone, everything works.

Afterwards Anne tells me my second set was an hour twenty. And I wasn't just treading water. I killed. Anne is telling me how I saved the day. Then Jon comes to me to settle up and gives me $150. I say, "Jon, I just did my time and Robin's and then some. Aren't you going to give me a little extra?"

Fox says, "You agreed on one-fifty, and that's what you're getting."

A hundred fifty is what Fox gives me. I could go on with stories, there's plenty more where that came from but that's pretty much all I am going to say about Jon Fox, the promoter. It's like with John Fox the comedian. Get a bunch of comics in a room someone mentions Fox and the stories go on and on and on...

WHEN YOU SLEEP WITH DOGS

After the Old Waldorf show I stay with Rick and Ruby and their manager, Bob Lacy in a house at Fulton and Park Presidio. Bob tells me I can crash on the couch in the living room. What Bob fails to tell me is two large canines normally sleep on the couch. No wonder these guys keep eye-balling me. I wake up eaten alive by fleas. I guess the old adage is true about sleeping with dogs. Later that morning Charlie picks me up and I help him load another truckload of household goods headed to So Cal. The day after that I'm back home in Burbank, enough cash in my pocket to make another month's mortgage payment. I'm still making more moving furniture than I am in show business. As Waylon Jennings says, "Are you sure Hank done it this-a-way?"

MTM

Debbie Miller tells me I am third in line to be a regular on the *Mary Tyler Moore* summer replacement show. Like *Laugh-In*, it is six specials to start, basically the same format as the *Carol Burnett Show*, sketch comedy, starring Mary Tyler Moore and four unknown actors. There are parts for two male and two female cast members and I am third in line for one of the male parts. Ahead of me are Debbie's other two comedian clients, Michael Keaton, who is a definite, and David Letterman, who is a maybe. Debbie's negotiating for a talk show for Dave and if Dave gets his talk show, I'm in.

I hope and pray Dave gets his talk show. I desperately need the gig. I'm really starting to feel the pressure financially. I need a score just to keep going. This ratchets up on my degree of desperation, which is the kiss of death in Hollywood, the basic rule being: The more desperate you are, the less chance you have of scoring. It's like women. Once you get to the point they smell desperation on you, forget about it. You're never going to get laid.

So I am pretty much at the peak of desperation, standing in front of the Westwood Comedy Store. The late afternoon sun is bright, there are a bunch of comics standing around, Letterman is there, and I spot Dave. One thing about Dave, if Dave is desperate, it sure doesn't show. I am tired of sitting around waiting for the phone to ring, anxious to hear of any word, anything to give me an inkling of hope, so I go up to Dave and say, "So what do you think, Dave? Does it look like you'll be doing the *Mary Tyler Moore Show*?"

The response is typical Letterman: "Well, gee, I don't know. I'm still waiting to hear from Lou Grant. Gee, what's that scent I detect? Could it be: Desperation?"

Dave doesn't get his talk show. I'm the odd man out. In the end, it's not a big loss, since the show goes nowhere, although being on it would have bought me time. Like *Laugh-In*, the MTM variety show lasts six episodes and disappears into oblivion, a fate I am desperately trying to avoid.

TAKE THIS JOB
AND SHOVE IT

It seems like Burbank is nothing but an endless stream of 105 degree days. I can't see the mountain, which is a half a mile away, for the smog. I'm in Comedy Hell, sitting by the air conditioner, waiting for the phone to ring. It finally does, but it's not good news. Debbie Miller tells me she can't work with Bullets. Now I have to choose between Debbie and Bullets and that's a spot you don't want to be in. My gut instinct tells me to go with Debbie. I like Debbie. She's young and cool, not old and gruff like Bullets. But the name Bullets is synonymous with Jackie Gleason and Frank Sinatra and all those other big name guys. Besides, who in their right mind would want to piss off a guy whose name is Bullets?

Not that he would have me whacked or anything, but would turning my back on him be the kiss of death for me as far as my show business career is concerned? I am tormented by the dilemma. On top of it all, the pressure of not having a steady paycheck has become unbearable. I'm driving down the Hollywood freeway one afternoon praying out loud, "Dear God, I feel like Job. My show's been cancelled; my wife has just had major back surgery. We're out of money with a mortgage and a two-year-old. What am I going to do? What am I going to do...?"

I turn my radio on and it's tuned to the Country station. The first voice I hear is Johnny Paycheck's: "Take this job and shove it. I ain't workin' here no more..."

"It's an omen!"

I go home that night and I get a message Charlie Van Slam called. He left a number to call him back. I dial the number and sure enough it's the number I think it is. Voice on the other end of the line says, "Castle Lanes."

It's the bartender at Castle Lanes Bowling Alley in San Francisco, Charlie's home away from home. I say, "Is Charlie Budweiser there?"

"Hey Charlie, it's for you!"

Charlie comes on, says, "This is Charlie…"

I say, "Hey, Charlie. It's Jim. I got a message you called."

Charlie says, "Hey, Jim!"

"What's up?"

"To tell you the truth, Jim, I know what kind a bind you been in lately, hard up for cash and all, so I talked to a couple guys up here in San Francisco who can get you in Teamsters local 85 delivering wholesale groceries. The job pays top dollar and benefits and the best part is you're home every night!"

It's an offer I can't refuse.

It's also a decision I have spent the rest of my life second-guessing. At the time I did what I thought was right. I had to make steady money to keep my family together. But what if I had stuck it out in LA? What if I had a stake or backers where I could have gone out and taken my shots without all the financial pressure? Would I have made it? Would I have had my day in the sun? Would my name be on a star on the Hollywood walk of fame? As they say hindsight is 20/40, and that's if you're lucky.

How am I supposed to know that Debbie is going to take on David Letterman and Michael Keaton as clients, and they are both going to become huge stars? All I know is at the time I'm afraid to piss off Bullets, and I don't want to say no to Debbie because I like Debbie and I don't want to say no to her. So I decide to take a powder, thinking, if I'm nowhere to be found, how can anyone be mad at me? In my naïveté I fail to realize how ridiculous this is. No one gives shit if I throw away a potentially life-changing career opportunity, especially if it's my own. As far as anyone else is concerned, my loss is my loss. That's one thing. Another factor in my decision is the comedian strike at the Comedy Store is just starting. I don't want to get in the middle of that debacle either, so why not just split, disappear, go MIA and come back after the smoke clears. Oh, of course it's ridiculous to think this. It's LA! The smoke never clears. Oh, and by the way, in case you haven't heard, comebacks ain't that easy to come by.

COMEDY HELL

It's fall 1978. I'm humping hundred pound sacks of flour and sugar down narrow cobblestone alleyways in China-town with Chinese guys yelling at me in Cantonese and hanging cooked ducks hitting me in the face. No matter where I look I see Robin staring at me. Magazines with Chinese writing on them have his picture on the cover. I look down at a filthy sidewalk full of grime and spit and pigeon shit, and Robin's face is staring up at me from a bubble gum card. Chinese guys are walking around going, "Nanu nanu!"

I'm in Comedy Hell! If I still think of my post-Nixon reentry to the San Francisco comedy scene as being pain-ful, I am soon to find out Nixon is nothing compared to this. I have been to the top of the mountain. This time it's a much bigger fall. Looking back on it, I inflict the pain on myself. To my way of thinking, there is no way I can compete with Robin and, if I cannot compete with Robin, I am unworthy to compete. Bullshit, of course, but I man-age to convince myself of this. I have lost my comedic sense of self-worth. My name still has cachet in the Bay Area and I get calls for gigs, but I am jaded by the whole LA experience, which has left me with a decidedly bitter aftertaste. To make matters worse, Robin is everywhere. He's down there. He's up here. One night they do a benefit for the Boarding House. I'm not on the bill but I go over there anyway and there is a line of limos double-parked in front on Bush Street. It is Robin's entourage. I can't even get in the door.

The lowest of lows for me comes one night at the Holy

City Zoo. I'm on stage doing my act, which now includes several prop gags. In one bit, I do a mime of a little kid starting a Cox model airplane engine, using a kazoo for sound effects. The bit always gets laughs, but this night my heart isn't in it, and the audience knows it. The kazoo bit and pretty much everything else I do fall flat. I do about ten minutes and get off to tepid applause, leaving my props behind.

Robin, who is now a superstar, explodes from out of nowhere onto the stage, appropriates my props, and proceeds to launch into 45 minutes of improvisational brilliance with my props while I'm standing there, watching it all go down like Salieri watching Mozart. All I want to do is get the hell out of there, but I can't until Robin finishes and I can get my stuff back. The second he's off, I gather my props and head for the door. I get about two steps outside and a drunken woman, who is a Zoo regular and who used to be a fan of mine back in the old days with the Strands, comes up to me and says, "You used to be big around here, but you're nothing now. Robin is king! You ain't shit!"

"Oh, yeah? Well, you don't look like the freshest daisy in the vase either, sweetheart."

She continues to blather on about how great Robin is and how un-great I am. I leave not in the best of spirits.

"Knock Knock."

"Who's there?"

"'The Ape Man'!"

"'The Ape Man' who?"

"How quickly they forget."

I don't know it at the time but I am suffering from PRSD, Post-Robin Stress Disorder. I'm still doing comedy, but my heart is not in it. I spend way too much time on the pity pot beating myself up for not being Robin. I desperately need an outlet, something that is not comedy. I find it in a traditional Japanese karate dojo. For the next several years, I train relentlessly, driving truck by day, running twenty-eight four forties (seven miles of sprints) after work and then going to the dojo. After that, if I have a gig, I go do comedy. Since it is an old-school Japanese karate dojo, we fight with no protective equipment whatsoever including cups. It's bare knuckles and bare feet and many times I show up at work or at a gig with a broken nose or stitches on my face or worse. My new act quickly wears thin with both my employers at the trucking company and the comedy club owners I work for.

THE OTHER

The Other Café has picture windows and is on the corner of Cole and Carl in San Francisco. You can look out the windows and see the people on the street. Often there is a crowd out on the sidewalk looking in. One night I get up at the Other Café with a butterfly holding the cut over my eye closed. I intend to do my set and then go to SF General emergency afterwards, but halfway through my set the cut opens up and blood starts running down my face. The audience is aghast. Someone says, "You're bleeding!"

I say, "Earlier this evening I was standing outside The Other, and Michael Pritchard told a group of lesbians I was Bobby Slayton."

This gets a laugh, but the management of The Other is not happy. Besides comedy they are trying to sell soup and sandwiches, and a comic on stage with blood running down his face into his mouth is not conducive to selling either. My run at The Other comes to a bitter end one night when I get there and discover my sandwich has been removed from the menu board. I am informed there will no longer be a "Giovanni," a veggie burger billed as a "meat impersonator" on the bill of fare. You know it's over when they take away your sandwich.

THE NIGHT I OPEN FOR JAMES BROWN

In 1979 I get a phone call from a producer. He says, "Is this Jim Giovanni?"

I say, "Yes."

He says, "You are on *Laugh-In*."

I say, "I'm on *Laugh-In*, the *Great American Laugh Off*, *Just For Laughs*. Anything with 'Laugh' in the title, I'm in it."

He says, "Great! Here's the deal. I got a gig for you, it'll be opening for James Brown, and it's going to be taped live for a cable TV special we're doing."

It's 1979. I say, "What's cable TV?"

The guy explains it to me and I still don't know what cable TV is, but I agree to do the gig. The guy tells me to dress nice and keep it clean and I agree. Hey! I don't give a shit about the TV part of it— it's James fucking Brown! So the night of the show I get to the Monterey Convention Center at seven-fifteen and the show starts at eight, and already there's a crowd lined up outside waiting to get in. They should have opened the doors fifteen minutes ago, but instead they are making the crowd wait outside in a drizzle, and believe me, no one looks happy when I walk right up to the front of the line and tell the door man the magic words, "I am the opening act," and he lets me right in.

I get inside–and I can see why they're not letting the

crowd in. Guys are running around yelling and setting up scaffolding and lighting and cameras and now I know why they call it cable because guys are dragging cables everywhere, and I'm standing there holding my garment bag with my John Travolta *Saturday Night Fever* stage outfit in it watching guys drag cables around. A guy comes to me and asks me who I am. I tell him and he says, "Come with me," and he takes me to the stage manager, who says, "I don't have a dressing room for you. You're going to have to change in the bathroom."

I say, "How soon do you think we will get started?"

He says, "Are you kidding? Look at this. It won't be for a while. Hang tight. I will give you heads up when we are ready to start."

He disappears and now I'm standing there and someone comes up and asks if I'd like to meet James. I say, "Sure."

So he takes me to meet James and he says, "James, this is your opening act, Jim Giovanni."

I say, "Nice to meet you, Mr. Brown.'"

James sticks out his hand. "Heh, heh, heh…"

That's it, just, "Heh, heh, heh…"

This is before he gets arrested for driving through three states with his tires shot out.

Now they are letting in the people who have been outside waiting in the rainy drizzle, and this is not a happy bunch. I hear them as they are coming in: "The show was supposed to start at eight! Motherfucker, it's already after eight!"

Now the theater is full of grumbling people, we're still nowhere near ready to go, and a chant starts: "James Brown! James Brown! James Brown!"

The MC comes up to me. He is a DJ on the local Soul

station there and a celebrity on the Monterey Peninsula. He's wearing a lime green leisure suit and he's got a big Sly Stone natural and the Soul Train announcer voice. He says, "I'm going to go out and do my thing."

I say, "Go for it."

He walks out and starts talking and the crowd is waiting for him to introduce James Brown, but instead he pulls out a turntable and starts spinning records, doing his DJ thing. So now the crowd is screaming, "Get off the stage. We want James Brown! James Brown! James Brown! James Brown...!"

So now the MC is yelling at the crowd: "Fuck you mother-fuckers! Fuck you motherfuckers! Fuck you mother-fuckers!"

So the crowd starts booing and throwing shit at him, and now he's dragging his turntable off amidst the flying debris. His parting words are: "Fuck you motherfuckin' motherfuckers...!"

He's looking at me the whole time as he walks off, aside from the times he looks at the crowd to call them motherfuckers. His eyes are fixed on me as he walks straight towards me. He gets to me and says, "You ready to go on, man?"

"Now that you got 'em all warmed up for me!"

So the MC picks up the off-stage mike and goes into his announcer voice. "AND NOW IT'S SHOWTIME! *LAUGH-IN* SUPERSTAR. YOU'VE SEEN HIM ON STAGE, SCREEN, AND TELEVISION! HERE HE IS THE GODFATHER OF COMEDY, JIM GIOVANNI!"

I never change into my stage clothes. I'm still dressed in sneakers, blue jeans, and a t-shirt. I look like a roadie coming out to fix the mike. As I'm walking out I hear, "I came to see James Brown. Why's his funky white ass up there?"

I get about ten feet from the mike and a guy who is sitting about eighteen rows back stage left yells out, "YOU BETTER BE FUNNY, MAN!"

I get to the mike and say, "I'll get to it."

I start doing Columbo. "You know, you probably are wondering who I am. You are saying, 'We never heard of this guy.' Well, if you saw the TV show *Laugh-In* you might have seen me on there playing Columbo. You might have even thought I was Columbo. My own father in law saw me on there, and he thought I was Columbo. I called him after the show and he said, "I saw the show. Where the hell were you?"

This gets a laugh. The heckler says, "Well, it's about time!"

I say, "What's the matter, brother? Don't you believe in foreplay?"

Boom! Another laugh.

I try to go into my next bit, John Wayne, the Duke, but the heckler won't let me do the bit, so I switch gears and become Jackie Gleason. "And now I would like to do my impression of 'The Honeymooners' smoking dope." I point to the heckler and say, "And if you want to know why they call it 'dope', get a load a Norton!"

This gets a laugh. The heckler yells, "James Brown!"

I say, "You want James Brown?"

"Yeah!"

So I start doing James Brown. "Ha! I feel good! Ha! Good God! Ugh...!"

This gets a big laugh. The crowd is into it.

Someone yells out, "Do Richard Pryor!"

"What? You crazy motherfucker! We are gathered here

today to say goodbye to our dearly departed, this crazy motherfucker whose ass is about to be thrown out by the bouncers and when it is, his ass will be dearly and it will be departed. Do I get an amen?"

I hear: "Amen" and "Hallelujah!" The crowd is talking to me like in church, going, "Yeah! That's right! Uh-huh! You know it...!"

But the heckler won't stop. The audience has no idea what he is saying half the time and neither do I, but I do know this much. I have a huge advantage over him. I have a mike and he doesn't and who better to work a mike than Howard Cosell? "And this young lad, an amateur before he became professional, coming on strong during the latter half of the season despite a nagging groin injury which has hampered his performance both on and off the field. And now here he is, the greatest heavyweight champion of all time, Muhammed Ali!"

"Now don't you be goin' and messin' with me. I am The Greatest, Muhammed Ali. I float like a butterfly, sting like a bee. A chump like you, I knock out in three!"

The crowd roars. You think the heckler would get the message, but this guy is persistent if nothing else. He yells out something else unintelligible and I flash on the fact I haven't done Redd Foxx yet. So the guy yells out whatever it is he yells out and I say, "Lamont, you big dummy! I told you wait in the truck! Shut up wait in the truck and for god's sakes change them funky drawers you got on! How do you expect to get a date smelling like that? They got a washroom here. Wash up! You got to wash your ass! Not your whole ass, your asshole! You may think no one knows but the nose knows! You'd be surprised the amount of pollution you'll find in a spot the size of a dime, or a quarter or a fifty cent piece. Hell you know your own ass better than I do. You may have a silver dollar! You got to wash your ass! How do you expect to get a date when you ain't washed? Oh, I forgot! Your date, she don't care. Hardest part about your date is blowing her up!"

The heckler doesn't have a chance. He tries to say something else but I have the mike and I ain't stoppin' now. "Don't look at me. I didn't start this shit. I'm going to ride this horse to the finish line just like that famous jockey, Jockey Strap! That's right. Tonight, Jockey Strap will ride My Dick. Oh wait a minute! Scratch that! Jockey Strap has been scratched. A Crabbe will ride My Dick. You may know A. Crabbe, Arthur Crabbe, a member of the Crabbe family. Some of you sporting men may have seen A. Crabbe ride. In fact, the entire Crabbe family is here with us and they are all riding tonight. Stand up, Lamont, and let the Crabbes take a bow!"

I see people writhing around in their seats. It looks like they are pissing their pants they are laughing so hard. "And now a word from our sponsor: This portion of our show has been brought to you by Fugg Soap spelled F-U-G-G! If you want a clean can, wash your can with Fugg Soap. No one likes a dirty can. Wash your can with Fugg . That way, when your loved one comes home and smells your can, they'll say, "Baby, it smells like your can been Fugged!"

The crowd is hysterical. I am laughing at them laughing at me, and they're laughing at me laughing at them, and the whole thing is one big laugh fest. I am in Comedy Heaven, just bobbing on the waves. It doesn't get any better. Comics reading this know of whence I speak. It doesn't always work out so well. It works out this time though, in fact it works out so well even the heckler is impressed. He yells out: "Man, you are funny!"

I say, "You too, man!"
It's the biggest rise I get out of any crowd anytime anywhere! I know there's no way I'm going to top that and now's a good time to leave them wanting more, so I say, "Thank you. Good night!"

The place goes nuts! I get to the wings and Macio Parker, the sax player, is standing there. He's all duded up, he's got his axe and he's ready to go. He's slapping me five, going, "Damn, brother that was cold! You out there naked, brother, you naked! I go out with a horn and the band, but you out there naked, brother, you out there naked!"

THE GODFATHER OF SOUL

By the time James comes out, the crowd is more than ready. Now James is moving and the crowd is grooving. Funk is in the air. I'm walking down the aisle and I see a dude coming up the aisle in my direction. And I mean when I say "dude," I mean this dude is a "dude." He's got on a purple zoot suit with matching fedora and shoes and looking straight ahead moving real slow like he's gliding. This guy is "Super Fly." I'm gliding toward him like a reflection of him minus the purple zoot suit. I know he knows I know we both know we both cool. It's hard to explain the perfection of the timing of this, call it mental telepathy or whatever, but it comes off perfectly synchronized like it's been choreographed: Look straight ahead, you cool, here it comes, the handshake, slide, don't break stride, oh yeah, baby, we definitely cool now. All the rest of the night it's like that. I'm Cinderella at the ball.

The next morning in the coffee shop next to the hotel a bunch of folks who saw me at the show are in there when I walk in, and everyone starts clapping. People are coming up telling me how great I am, how everyone was bummed before the show but I made everybody laugh. I was hilarious and James came out and he was on fire and it turned into a great night after all. I'm signing autographs on napkins and a woman comes up and says, "Baby, give me a hug."

I give her hug. She looks at me and says, "Baby, we love you. You the blackest white boy we ever saw."

Screw fame and fortune. Nights like this are what it's all about.

DEMOTED

Now I'm middling at The Punchline, and a lot of head-liners don't like it because I push them. It's not like I'm trying to. They just don't like it because my act is strong. I get a big reaction from the crowd. I'm not going to mention names, but some so called big-name comics complain to management or tell me to cut bits because they have a hard time following me. I've always thought of that as chickenshit. In my experience, you should be able to follow damn near anybody if you put a little brain-power into it. If I'm headlining and the middle pushes me, I do my best to figure out how to follow the guy. It's not up to me to tell him or her to change their act; it's up to me to rise to the occasion.

Most of the time I think of stuff I would've never thought of if I weren't being pushed. Inevitably, I end up being a better comedian because of it. The night I upstage Robin at the Music Hall look how he responds. He never says a word. He comes back the next night and blows the doors off the joint. That's how it's done. Get off your ass and do the work.

Unfortunately there are a lot of comics out there who don't want to work that hard. They would rather pull rank and tell the middle guy or opener what to do or not to do and to me that's chicken shit. There it is. I will touch again on this subject later in greater detail. I have a great story on this subject, but I'm doing my best to keep this in chronological order, so I'll save it for later.

Now look where we are. Robin is a superstar, and I am busting my ass by day on the truck trying to raise a family and do comedy at night. And you want me to enter the Comedy Competition, which is a whole other grind with no guarantee of anything except maybe a chance to win first place and still be a distant second to Robin?"

One headliner at the Punchline who has no problem following me is an eminently likeable comic and a great guy named Jerry Seinfeld. One time in the early eighties Jerry says to me, "I love working with you man. It's non-neurotic comedy week."

"I love working with you too, Jerry."

The saying "Nice guys finish last" is bullshit. Jerry is as nice of a guy as they come, and I can't think of anyone more successful. Congrats, Jerry!

THE CORPORATE MIND

Oh, irony of ironies, now that I have a steady job in the Teamsters, I start getting calls to do corporate gigs for several thousand dollars a pop. It's 1982. The Japanese are riding high and money is no object. A production company offers me $4,000 to play "Patton" in front of 1,500 truck dealers at a convention in Orlando Florida. It's an offer I can't refuse. I am an honest guy. I tell my boss the truth. I need three days off to go to Orlando Florida to make four grand. He is not happy about it and he makes known he is not happy about it. He says, "Jesus Christ! Make up your mind! What do you want to be, a truck driver or an actor?"

Don't make me answer that.

After a great deal of pissing and moaning he agrees to let me do the gig. He says, "I'll cover for you this time, but this is it! Make up your mind what you want to do!"

"Gee, thanks boss."

Now comes the hard part. I have less than three weeks to memorize a twenty-page speech and it is a dog, eighteen and a half minutes of humorless redundancy, the message: "Sell trucks, sell trucks, sell trucks..."

The original George C. Scott "Patton" speech in the movie is three and a half minutes. Anytime you parody a famous speech, it's best to use the famous speech as the template. Get your message across in three and a half minutes, punch it up with humor and you have a hit every time. I am unable to get this basic principle across to the geniuses in charge. Being corporate minds and not entertainment minds, they don't get it. They act like Moses brought their script down off the mountain written on stone tablets.

"We're paying you four thousand dollars to memorize the speech. Memorize the goddamn speech!"

I have no choice. They already paid me half the money upfront and the check is deposited in my bank account and I don't want to have to give them their money back, so I memorize the speech. I carry it with me everywhere I go. I make a tape of it to listen to while I'm driving. I fall asleep listening to it.

Finally, comes the big event. The day before the show I fly to Florida. A driver picks me up and takes me to the hotel in Orlando. I'm extremely apprehensive about the gig, barely sleep that night. I run my lines over and over in my room. I finally get to sleep and I'm dreaming it and they aren't pleasant dreams. Call it a premonition if you will, I already know what is going to happen.

The next morning it's drizzling outside. I don't say anything to anyone. I just leave the hotel and go for a run. Rehearsal is not until 1:00 P.M., and I don't have to be available until then, so I do about ten miles. I get back and I'm walking through the hotel lobby, I'm soaking wet and people are looking at me like I'm crazy. Someone says, "You weren't running in that, were you?"

I say, "Yeah. A little rain ain't gonna hurt me. I ain't made out of sugar!"

He says, "Are you out of your mind? Forget about the rain. There's a tornado watch on. A tornado just knocked down the Disney World sign and you're out there running in that? What are you, nuts?"

Don't make me answer that.

That afternoon the tornado watch lifts and I go over to the convention center, a giant quonset hut shaped building, located right next to another giant quonset hut shaped building. I get inside and immediately see the magnitude of the situation. The first thing I notice is there are bars everywhere set up like MASH units. The booze is in what looks like IV bottles. There are stretchers everywhere too, as if they are expecting lots of casualties. From the looks of things, this could be worse than I thought.

On stage rehearsing is the Lawrence Welk Band with the Lawrence Welk Dancers and a several Lawrence Welk regulars. I ask where Lawrence is and they say, "Lawrence isn't here, just his show is here."

"I don't get to meet Lawrence?"

"Lawrence is not going to be here."

I'm thinking, Lawrence probably read the script and told them to fuck off. I can hear it right now. "Are you out of your fucking minds? You expect me to do this shit? Take your fucking script and shove it up your ass!"

Oh. Wait a minute. My bad. For a minute there, I had Lawrence Welk confused with Buddy Rich.

So I'm in the Convention Center, and the band is on stage rehearsing and the dancers are going through their moves, and everywhere else in the joint people are running around pounding nails and slapping together risers. They still haven't finished building the runway which is half the length of a football field leading up to the main stage, and I'm thinking, "Why are they building a runway?"

No sooner does this thought go through my head, when in walk the "Bathing Beauties," twelve scantily attired superhot eighteen to twenty-something year old runway models. I immediately get a sinking feeling in the pit of my stomach. I look at the guy in charge and say, "When do I go on in the show?"

He says, "You follow the Bathing Beauties."

"I follow hard body strippers in butt floss bikinis? Teleprompter! I need a Teleprompter!"

"We paid you to have the script memorized!"

"I do have it memorized, but that's not the problem! Three minutes into my speech, drunks are going to be yelling 'Bring back the broads' and 'Take your clothes off!' Look at the bars you got set up in this place! I'm going to have to deal with a bunch of drunken hecklers and then try to find my way back to the script and for that I'm going to need a Teleprompter!"

It's last minute and he's not happy about it, and I'm sure it costs them a fortune, but ultimately they see the logic in my argument and agree to arrange for a Teleprompter. The bad news is I never actually see the Teleprompter until I am on stage for the performance, so I don't get even a single run through with it. There is no chance to practice my entrance either since the riser that I am supposed to climb up to get to the runway isn't built yet. They are still pounding nails as they let in the crowd.

THE INVASION

Inside the convention center, just before I'm to go on, the troops are a-hootin' and a-hollerin' stomping and yelling for the "Bathing Beauties" to come back. By God, I hope I have enough ammunition. I get the sign to make my entrance. The cue guy says, "Go!"

The door opens, a spotlight hits me, the sound effects are deafening, helicopters landing, bugles blowing. The spot follows me as I weave through the crowd like a broken field runner, zigzagging between banquet tables full of drunken truck salesmen. I make my way to the riser, climb the stairs and make the forty-five degree right turn from the riser to the runway, and boom!

My head explodes! Not literally of course but the effect is such that it looks like it has. Unbeknownst to me, there is a half-step from the riser onto the runway. Since we haven't rehearsed, I don't know the step is there and, even if I did know, I can't see the floor. The floor on both the riser and the runway is black. All the lights are off except for the spotlight focused on my head, which captures everything: The Dick Van Dyke trip take, simultaneous helmet sidewise/explosion of dry powdered hair whitener which follows me down the runway like a vapor trail coming off the back of a fighter jet.

The crowd is hysterical, roaring with laughter. I could not have planned a more hilarious opening. I reach the main stage, turn around, and salute as a halo of dry hair whitener swirls around my head. The contrail just hangs there extending the full length of the runway.

The troops are still laughing as I launch into my Patton speech. As great as my entrance is comedy-wise, three minutes into it, the dust has settled literally, and the crowd's not laughing anymore. Precisely three minutes to the gnat's ass into "Sell trucks! Sell trucks! Sell trucks...!" I hear: "Take off your clothes!" and "Bring back the broads!"

You could have set an egg timer by it!
"Okay, boys and girls! Time for: General George S. Patton, insult comic!"

"You, you shoddy-looking drunk bastard, you look like the son of a bitch I slapped in World War II...!"

I do twenty-three minutes total, which by my reckoning works out to a two to one ratio of: "Sell trucks" to insults. Thank God for insults. Other than the exploding head routine, they are the only things that get laughs. And thank God for the Teleprompter. Without it, I could have never found my way out of the minefield. The production company is aghast, horrified by the turn of events. Immediately after the show, the head honcho comes up to me and says, "I want Patton and you give me Inspector Clouseau!"

This story has a happy ending. Turns out the big bosses from Japan love Patton. They love him so much they want the general to do a meet and greet afterwards. I get there and the bastards can't stop bowing. They treat me like a goddamn rock star. They all want their picture taken with me.

There is one thing I am able to say, and I thank God for it. Someday I'll be sitting around my fireside with my grandson on my knee and he'll ask what I did at the great Japanese truck convention of 1982 and I'll be able to say, 'By God, I made the bastards laugh!'"

EVERYBODY WANTS TO GET INTO THE ACT

The eighties comedy boom is on. Every neighborhood bar, restaurant and 24-hour laundromat has comedy night. I can't escape it if I try. Half the time the phone rings and it's a comedy gig. Now I'm juggling my schedule between driving a truck and doing comedy. Weeknights I limit gigs to ones within a couple hours drive of the house. Weekends I do overnighters in Reno or Redding or Fresno or Chico or and anywhere and everywhere between. Many times I stay in dumps that look like the Bates Motel or worse. Come Monday morning, I am back on the truck. By the mid-eighties, after years of literally spinning my wheels and getting nowhere, my level of frustration is at an all-time high. Other drivers are ribbing me. "Hey, Columbo? How come you're driving a truck when you could be famous on TV like your buddy, Robin Williams?"

It hurts but they're right. Not just Robin, plenty of guys I know have made it or are making it, and where am I? "Oh, Lord, stuck in Lodi again…"

I need the freedom to go whenever and wherever the call arises. If I'm going to make a serious run at the comedy brass ring again, something's got to give. That something has to be the day job. It's scary to think of having to make ends meet on comedy alone. I remember the last time. The difference is back then there weren't the coast-to-coast comedy clubs there are now. I know I can get work, more work than I can handle as long as I'm willing to stay on the road. Work is not the issue. The issue is having the freedom to capitalize on opportunities if they arises, and for that I have to lose the day job. This is not to say there aren't naysayers, some of them so-called "experts" who tell me I don't have a snowball's chance in hell of making it.

"It's already too late for you. If you haven't made it by the time you're thirty, forget about it!"

"You're telling me thirty-five's too old?"

"Thirty-five's ancient! Nowadays you've got to young. You've got to be hip!"

"Hip? I'm an original hippie comedian. I rode the first post-sixties comedy wave!"

"Yeah? That wave has long since passed!"

"There will be more waves. The sea is full of waves."

"You're not cutting edge! You've got to be cutting edge…!"

"I'm better than 'cutting edge'! I'm actually funny…"

"Funny's not enough…!"

"I get more laughs than cutting edge guys…"

"You're a museum piece…a dinosaur!"

"More standing O's…"

 "Forget about it! You're never going to make it."

In the words of the great theologian, W.C. Fields: "Oh ye of little faith…!"

Jim with comedians featured in Comedy Tonight 1982: Barry Sobel, Darryl Henriques, Bobby Slaton, Bob Sarlatte, Dana Garvey, Ronn Lucas, Jane Dornacker. SF Examiner Photography by Ted Betz

INTO THE ABYSS

This is my life, not theirs. I must admit naysayers do have a way of planting seeds of doubt. It is with a good deal of trepidation I quit the day job. I quickly discover the only thing that changes really, other than the security of knowing where my next paycheck is coming from, is now I'm doing gigs in places like Dallas and Anchorage and New Orleans and Las Vegas and Cincinnati and Portland and Boston and Seattle and Oradell and Atlanta and Buffalo and Houston and Phoenix and Fairbanks and Chicago and Honolulu and Hartford and El Paso and Couer d' Alene. I don't have anyone managing me or doing my bookings so I do the gigs in the order they come up and a lot of times the order is literally all over the map. Now instead of bouncing like a pong ball all over California I'm bouncing like a pong ball all over the country.

And through it all, the streak lives! Everywhere the ball bounces I run ten miles. I run in snowstorms in Buffalo and freezing rain in a Louisiana bayou. I run in the Arizona desert where sweat dries faster than you can sweat it. I run in Fairbanks where sweat freezes on you the second it hits the outside air. At forty-five degrees below zero everything flash freezes. If your hair is wet and you step outside don't touch your hair or it will break off. You can imagine what happens if you pee. I am in Fairbanks, it is fifty degrees below zero, and I run ten miles barefoot.

"Ten miles barefoot, you say, in fifty degrees below zero weather? This is preposterous! I don't believe it for a minute!"

Ten miles barefoot on an indoor track in the Fairbanks athletic center, eleven laps to the mile one hundred, and ten laps the streak lives on!

BLOWING IT

Some of the joints I play are "A" rooms. Some are not. Many are lucky if they're "C" rooms. None have actual chicken wire in front of the stage, which is not to say some of them wouldn't benefit from it. I've had stuff thrown at me, guys jump up and try to kick me, drunken women hecklers arrested in my show. I believe every comic should be required to play rooms like these, at least in the beginning. They toughen you up get you ready for the big leagues should the opportunity arise. The experience is invaluable. Time and time again I see comics get a big break and then blow it because they don't have experience playing the tough rooms. Michael Richards is a case in point. I bring this up because when the subject of hecklers is breached, Michael Richards's name inevitably comes up. I don't know Michael Richards, but here's my take on Michael Richards. Michael Richards is an improv actor who gets his big break and lands on Seinfeld's show. He's not used to being on stage by himself. He's used to being up there with other actors. Now he's famous and he decides to capitalize on his fame by doing standup. But he's never paid his dues, played the toilets, so someone tells him he's not funny and he goes up like a bottle rocket, starts spewing racial epithets because that's all his little under-developed comedy pea brain can think of. This is a rookie error. Not just that he ranted out derogatory racial shit, but the fact he lost it on stage in the first place.

I've seen it time and time again. An inexperienced comic goes ballistic because someone tells him he's not funny, he becomes temporarily insane and loses all judgment. I make this mistake myself in an "A" room of all places, the Punch Line in San Francisco. One night an overflow crowd for a punk show at the old Waldorf invades the Punchline. I'm on stage trying to do my act, and all of a sudden one of the punk assholes is standing in front of me yelling, "You suck!" and "You're not funny!"

My reaction is classic: "Fuck you motherfucker I'll kick your motherfucking ass!"

For me it's no longer about being funny, it's about kicking motherfucking ass. I come off the stage and the motherfucker backs out of there real quick. He knows I'm serious. The bad part is the audience knows I'm serious too. Try getting laughs after that one. Good thing they didn't have YouTube back then.

So in Michael Richard's defense: How can Michael Richards learn from mistakes he has never made? How can anyone expect him to be funny dealing with people who tell him he's not funny when he's never developed the thick skin, not to mention the jokes required to deal with the people who tell him he's not funny?

Please note: I'm giving Michael Richards the benefit of the doubt here. Bottom line: I don't think Michael Richards is a racist. I think Michael Richards is an inexperienced standup who ended up on YouTube screwing up in front of millions of people. That's my theory. I may be wrong. If I am wrong and Michael Richards is an experienced road comic, and he still screwed up the way he did, then Michael, if you're listening, as Ed Bluestone once told me, "Oh, you are an idiot!"

THE LAST MAGAZINE SHOW

It's 1984 and I'm cast as an ensemble player on a TV pilot named *The Last Magazine Show*. It is a take-off on magazine shows and is mostly sketch comedy filmed on location. One of the other cast members is an unknown comedian/actress named Whoopi Goldberg. Whoopi is a bone fide tie-dyed hippie chick. She drives a dilapidated Volkswagen bug, which reeks of patchouli oil and is piled in the backseat to the shoulders with old fast-food wrappers and other sundry debris. She's got the little rainbow colored yarn hippie whatchamacallit hanging from her car mirror. Whoopi is my kind of person-a freak.

I notice right away she's very talented doing character voices. We are at a location up in North Beach, standing outside on the street and a carload of valley girl types drive by in a BMW, windows up, checking us out. Their mouths are moving, and we can't hear what they're saying, so Whoopi starts doing their voices, supplying the dialogue. She has the Valley girl thing down. Her take is hilarious. I'm thinking, "Hey, this chick's good!"

We finish at that location and need to drive our own vehicles to the next one. We're getting ready to leave and Whoopi says, "Hey man do you think you guys could help me push my car and help me get it started…?"

The next location is by the Fairmont Hotel up on Nob Hill in San Francisco. Whoopi and I have a scene together. We dance in a crosswalk. She is dressed as a Lithuanian peasant. I never do get the gag on this one. Hey, I didn't write the shit! We finish and Whoopi goes: "Hey man, do you think you could help me push my car...?"

Every location we go to, we have to push Whoopi's Volkswagen to get her jumpstarted. We finish shooting the pilot. I say, "It's been great, Whoopi. You know you and I ought to do something together. You do great characters and character voices, and I do characters and character voices. And I'm a writer, and you're a writer, and we could write sketches we could do together and do our solo acts, and maybe we could do a thing together at the Great American Music Hall?"

Whoopi says, "Sounds great man, cool man, why don't you call me? Here's my number. Call me February 14, I'll be back from New York, man, I'll be at Blake Street in Berkeley, we'll do something, call me!"

February 14 rolls around, and I call the number at Blake Street in Berkeley. The guy who answers the phone tells me Whoopi is still in New York and won't be back for a couple of more weeks. A couple of more weeks go by, I read in the San Francisco Chronicle Mike Nichols has discovered Whoopi in New York and is directing her one woman show on Broadway. Shortly after that I read where she is being directed by Steven Spielberg in *The Color Purple*. An Academy award nomination later, Whoopi is a superstar. A couple years later, I pick up the Chronicle and read in Herb Caen's column that Whoopi's been spotted in Berkeley behind the wheel of a red Porsche with two guys pushing her to get her jumpstarted. I bet the Porsche reeks of patchouli oil and had a yarn hippie doohickey hanging from the mirror and a backseat filled with old McDonald's wrappers. Am I right, Whoopi?

The pilot? Let's just say that's another one that landed in the dud pile.

PLAYING THE TOILETS

So now I'm back to playing tiny little off the beaten track hole in the walls. It's the eighties. Chinese takeout joints are doing standup night. One night I'm in the Happy Family restaurant headlining the comedy show there. "Hi, I'm Jim Giovanni. Some of you may have seen me on *Laugh-In*. Chances are you did not see me on *Laugh-In*. Chances are I wouldn't be here tonight if you had. Speaking of chance, it's amazing how accurate these fortune cookies are. I just opened my mine. It says, 'Success eludes you.' No dung, I Ching. " A guy gets up to use the restroom, and now I'm doing Redd Foxx. "Confucius say: 'Man who read handwriting on wall is in toilet…'" I do forty-five for people eating noodles and close with my big finish: "That's it for me, good night folks, don't forget to tip the waitress. Let's hear it for Ma Jong!"

Not exactly the kind of material that gets you on at Carnegie Hall. Speaking of Carnegie Hall (how's that for a segue?), my all-time hero comedian is George Burns. George Burns may not be the funniest man who ever roamed the planet. For my money, the title goes to Jonathan Winters. But as a guy who got it together and kept it together for generation after generation over a span of nine decades, no one beats George Burns. Who else books himself at the London Palladium for his hundredth birthday? At his age most guys don't even buy green bananas. I think George himself comes up with that line. Either George or Henny Youngman. Either way, you can count on Milton Berle to steal it. But I don't want to be like Milton. Actually, come to think of it, in one way I'd like to be like Milton, but in every other way I'd rather be like George. So when a financial planner asks me when I want to retire. I say, "Never!"

He looks at me like I'm crazy but I point to George Burns as a role model and I say, "I want to be like George Burns. I want to be booked at the Palladium in London on my hundredth birthday!"

The financial planner doesn't understand because he is not a comedian. He is a financial planner. Comedians understand because comedians are comedians and not financial planners. Bob Hope is both but he has writers. The bottom line: When I take the final bow of all final balance bows, I want to go out with a laugh. Old comedians don't die. They reinvent themselves. I don't think anyone reinvented himself more successfully over more incarnations than George Burns. That's why I want to be like him. I want to be booked at the Palladium in London on my one-hundredth birthday, in a tux, with a martini in one hand, a cigar in the other, a beautiful blonde on each arm, and a boatload of Viagra jokes. I mean, come on. Who wouldn't want that for a finale? There's only one problem as far as making this happen is concerned. Unlike George, no one knows who I am. How do I get on the map? How do I get the big break?

COMIC RELIEF

In 1986, there's big buzz in the comedy world that Robin Williams, Whoopi Goldberg, and Billy Crystal have joined forces to star in Comic Relief, an HBO comedy special to raise money for the homeless. Shortly after I hear about Comic Relief, I get a call from a person who says they represent Comic Relief. Maybe Robin put in a good word for me and I am going to get a shot on HBO! My hopes are quickly dashed when the person on the end of the line explains this is not the case. They want me to participate in a "satellite" Comic Relief show. I think, okay, it's not the main event. It's a "satellite" show. Since it's Comic Relief, surely it will be in a theater or some such venue and there will be cameras to document the proceedings. Wrong again and by the way, since it's for charity and since it is a "satellite" show, not only will I not be getting any publicity or recognition whatsoever out of the deal, I will not be getting paid period, the irony being every day I don't get paid period, I place me one step closer to being homeless myself period. But being the charitable sort that I am, I agree to labor for free in the hopes that if nothing else I will rack up brownie points in heaven or at least knock some time off my sentence in purgatory. Come to think of it, that's where we are right now, isn't it?

They give me an address on Bryant Street in San Francisco. I get to the place and it is not a mere homeless shelter, it is a serious first stop detox center, where the most extreme cases go to literally get hosed off. I arrive there and amassed waiting to go on is a slew of fresh face young San Francisco comedians. As I recall, David Feldman is there, among others. Correct me if I'm wrong on this, David, but I am pretty sure you are one of the guys. So here are all these young comedians, filled with youthful vigor, doing their best to get laughs talking about their fucked up girlfriends or their fucked up roommates or their fucked up parents to a room full of semi-comatose hard cases laying on mattresses on the floor with their faces literally stuck to their pillows. One by one comics get up and eat the big one. I anxiously await my turn in the queue thinking this truly is a hopeless situation, but who knows? If the Buddhists are right, maybe by doing this gig it will help me un-fuck my karma. Finally, after a string of duds, Clark "T Boy" Taylor gets up and doesn't waste any time getting their attention. He says, "Fuck this shit! What say we blow this joint and get drunk?"

The reaction is like telling Italians Italy just won the World Cup. The place goes berserk! Clark doesn't stop. "I'm from Louisiana. Out here you all call yourselves homeless. Where I come from we call ourselves campers…!"

Clark kills. How do I follow Clark? With John Wayne of course. "This week on American Sportsman, Curt Gowdy, Phil Harris and myself are gonna hunt butterflies with a .44 magnum!"

The cheer that goes up, you'd think it was the Duke his self! Now I'm doing Walter Brennan, who looks like half the guys in this room. Walter goes over big. Everything goes over big. As Walter his self would say, "No brag, just fact.

Which goes to show it's true what they say about there being no such thing as a bad audience.

And that's what I call comic relief!

NEWMAN'S GYM

I'm in my mid 30s and people are constantly telling me to give it up, I'm already over the hill. But I don't feel like I'm over the hill. Far from it, between running and martial arts training, I'm in the best physical shape of my life. But it's not getting me anywhere in show business. I need a vehicle. I need a hit! I get the bright idea I could do like Sylvester Stallone and create my own vehicle write my own hit. I decide to dream the impossible dream and write a screenplay. Like Stallone, my goal is to write a boxing movie about a boxer named "Rocky." Only this time, instead of a fictional character, this is about the real life story of the only undefeated heavyweight boxing World Champion in the history of the sport: Rocky Marciano.

Of course I begin writing this with the idea of me playing the lead. I'm the same height and weight as Rocky Marciano, same black curly hair. I do my own stunts. I can look like him sound like him. Like Marciano, I'm not afraid to get hit. Now all I need to do is two things: Come up with a great script and join Newman's gym and start getting this boxing thing down for real. As it turns out, accomplishing the second is a lot easier then accomplishing the first. Newman's Gym all you have to do is walk in off the street, give Stewart fifteen bucks and you're in.

It's a great old boxing gym in the heart of the tenderloin in San Francisco in a seedy neighborhood to start with and then you get inside Newman's and it's a throwback to another era. Practically every famous boxer in the history of the sport trained at Newman's at one time or another including world champs "Gentleman" Jim Corbett, Bobo Olson, and George Foreman. The minute you walk in the door, you know Newman's is for real. Climbing the steps you hear the speed bags, heavy bags thumping, the sound of footwork on the canvas, guys sparring, the ubiquitous bell every three minutes with a minute between rounds. You get to the top of the steps you smell the sweat from a thousand sparring matches going back in history. Once you're in there every Damon Runyon character you can imagine is in there. The first guy I see when I get to the top of the steps has a face you could perfectly fit a boxing glove into so I know he's the right guy to ask.

I say, "Who do I talk to about signing up?"

Manual says. "You got to talk to Stewart. Stewart you got to talk to, you got to talk to Stewart…"

So I say, "Where's Stewart?"

"Stewart's back in the office. You got to talk to Stewart, he's back in the office he's back there you got to go talk to Stewart back there…"

I get to Stewart's office, and it's classic the place is cluttered old boxing photos hanging everywhere off the walls. The desk is cluttered. Stewart himself is classic, a gruff little guy with a bad rug, perfectly typecast as the character in the Jimmy Cagney movie, who runs the boxing gym. Of course, those movies are thirties and this is the eighties. These guys are still in the thirties but then again that is the charm, isn't it? So I introduce myself to Stewart and explain that I want to make a movie about Rocky Marciano, and I want to train at Newman's, and I show him a black and white eight by ten of me as Rocky Marciano in boxing trunks in boxing pose, and Stewart looks at it and says, "You're a light heavyweight and your stance is too wide."

I say, "Oh, can I still sign up for your gym?"

"Give me fifteen dollars and sign a waiver you ain't gonna sue me."

That's it. I give Stuart fifteen dollars in cash, sign the waiver and now I'm officially a member of Newman's Gym. I say to Stewart, "How do I find a sparring partner?"

Stewart says, "Talk to Manuel."

I say, "Who's Manuel?"

"He's out there. You can't miss him."

"Is he the guy with the face that looks like not too many people missed him?"

"That's him. Talk to Manuel, he'll set you up."

"That's what I'm afraid of."

I walk out of Stewart's office and the first guy I see working out on a heavy bag is a black guy about my size with a fair to medium size Afro. This guy's around my age, maybe a little older, maybe a little younger, it's hard to tell. He looks like Archie Moore and it's hard to tell with him too. Anyhow, this guy is perfect Archie Moore if I'm going to play Rocky Marciano. I'm thinking I could get in the ring with this guy, not Archie Moore, but with this guy. I'm in the best shape of my life and this guy ain't no spring chicken neither. We both have a few flecks of grey. Don't get me wrong. I may be crazy but I'm not stupid. I'm not going to pay some 22-year old middleweight contender with the nickname "Cobra" to knock my head off, not unless he looks like Ezzard Charles of course. And then I'm going to want him in the movie too.

In fact I'm going to want everyone in this place in the movie. Which reminds me I still need to write the script. But let's not get ahead of ourselves here. If I am going to play Rocky, I need to think Rocky. I need to train Rocky. I need to be Rocky. Then, if I still have any brains left in my head, maybe I will be able to write the script maybe I will be able to write the script maybe I will be able to write the script... Where was I? Oh, yeah, I want to find a sparring partner. So I go up to the guy with the face that looks like you could perfectly fit a boxing glove into it, and I say, "Are you by any chance Manuel?"

He says, "Yeah I'm Manuel. Who are you?"

I say, "My name's Jim Giovanni. I just joined the gym here and Stewart says I should talk to you…"

He says, "I'll show you where the locker rooms and showers are…"

"Before we do that, can I ask you a question?"
"What? What do you want to know?"

I say, "The guy over there…"

He says, "Who what guy?"
"The guy over there working the heavy bag that

looks like Archie Moore."

"Oh, him? That's Lester what do you want to know about Lester?"

"Do you think he would be interested in sparring with me?"

He says, "You want to spar with Lester?"

I say, "Yes."

He says, "Oh, you better watch out for Lester he'll hook you Lester will, he'll hook you he'll hook you…"

"I'll probably need headgear…"

"Oh, you'll need headgear he'll hook you Lester will, he'll hook you…"

"How do I arrange to spar with Lester?"

"You got to talk to Lester about that he's going to want you to pay him something but if I was you I'd watch out for Lester he'll hook you Lester will, he'll hook you…"

ANY CHUMP WHO'S WILLING TO PAY TO GET HIS HEAD
KNOCKED OFF IS WELCOME HERE

I wait until Lester is done punching the heavy bag and I
say, "Excuse me, are you Lester?"

"I'm Lester."

"Lester, my name is Jim I was wondering if you would be
interested in sparring with me?"

Lester says, "I'll spar which you but it's going to cost you
cash money."

I say, "How much?"

"You pay me $10 a round cash money, I'll spar which
you..."

I say, "When can we do it?"

He says, "We can do it right now if you like it, don't make
no never matter to me."

"Okay, Manuel where do I change?"

"You gonna get in the ring with Lester? You better watch
out for Lester he'll hook you, he'll hook you..."

I bring trunks and boxing shoes old school black high-
tops like Marciano wore but I don't think about gloves and
headgear. Lester is getting his gloves on and I'm standing
there and Manuel says, "Where's your gloves and headgear?"

I say, "Don't you have gloves and headgear here at the
gym?"

Manuel says, "No you're supposed to bring that stuff, personal gloves headgear, you're supposed to bring your own
stuff. It's like your jock, you're supposed to bring your own
stuff..."

Somebody else overhears the conversation and offers to

rent his gloves and headgear to me for five bucks each. I'm in business. The agreement between Lester and I is that I am going to pay him ten dollars a round for three rounds, so it behooves Lester that I remain upright, at least until the start of the third round. And just think I'm writing a screenplay so I get to write it all off on my income tax.

Now, just as I'm standing in my corner in the ring across from Lester wondering if I'm allowed to deduct concussions, there's the bell. Manuel's right. It takes about two seconds before Lester starts bouncing hooks off my head. Here's the scary part. I kind of like it. Lester's bouncing shots off my head and I'm chasing him around the ring. In my mind I am Rocky Marciano, superbly conditioned at approximately 6.2% body fat and 184 pounds with no chance of running out of gas and Lester himself being no dummy knows this, so he stays on his bicycle, and he just keeps circling the ring staying away from my right the whole time bouncing left hooks off my head while guys are yelling at me from the stands to keep my right up and throw the jab. Lester is definitely wary of me getting lucky and connecting. That's how it goes for three rounds. I manage to land a few glancing shots but in the end, it's Lester all the way on points. The bell rings ending the third round and I come out of the ring and Manuel's right there.

"What I tell you he's gonna hook you!"

I pay Lester the thirty dollars I owe him in cash and go home with a feeling of accomplishment and headache that lasts about three days.

Couple weeks go by and the headaches gone, and I'm thinking you know that was fun let's go back and do it again, like I already have too many brain cells what do I need all these for? So I go back to Newman's and Manuel's there and Lester and a Mexican trainer with a little Mexican flyweight who's busy working on a heavy bag and I go up to Lester and I say, "Lester is it possible to do another sparring match?"

He says, "Yeah we can spar, we can spar you pay me fifteen dollars a round I'll spar witch you."

I say, "Fifteen dollars? It was ten last time."

He says, "You make me work too hard, you give me fifteen, now you give me fifteen dollars a round I'll spar witch you."

"Great, that means now I don't have money for headgear. Oh, well screw the headgear. Here's five bucks. Let me borrow your gloves."

I suit up and get my hands wrapped and get the gloves on, and I'm climbing in the ring. Lester's already in there, and the Mexican trainer goes, "Hey man you gonna spar with Lester?"

I say, "Yeah."

He says, "Where your headgear, man?"

I say, "I don't have any."

He says, "What do you mean you don't got no headgear? You got to have headgear, man."

"Why?"

"Sparring with Lester you got to have headgear."

"I sparred with him before. I can handle it without headgear."

He says, "You can't do that man!"

I say, "Why not? Is it illegal?"

He says, "No, it's fucking crazy!"

"Didn't Willie Nelson write that?"

We get in the ring and it's the same as last time. The bell rings, I chase Lester around the ring, he bounces shots off my head. The difference is this time the Mexican trainer is there, and he's stoked. He jumps up on ring apron, and now he's yelling instructions at me: "Double jab double jab, you got to double jab...!"

The bell rings, and now he's in my corner pouring water in my mouth out of a plastic two-liter soda bottle going, "Let me pour it...don't put your mouth on it man! I told you let me pour it! OK spit it out spit it out, not on the floor man, in the bucket! OK you got to cut the ring off you got to cut the ring off you got to double jab man you got to double jab...!"

The bell rings and we're back at it. For three minutes I chase Lester, and he hooks me but I'm strong. The Mexican guy can see that, and he's into it yelling at me the whole time: "Double jab cut him off you got to cut the ring off...!"

We finish the second round and I'm still not breathing hard, I'm breathing through my nose, the Mexican guy is in my corner and he's giving me instructions and pouring water in my mouth, and after a minute there's the bell. Lester and I are back at it. Three minutes later "bing" the bell rings and it's over, and the Mexican guy's jumping up and down crazy excited. "You're going to be good, man, you're going to be good, but you have let me show you what to do! You got to learn how to double jab, you got to learn how to double jab and cut the ring off! Double jab and hook off the jab man, set him up with the jab and hook off the jab then you hit him with the right! You're going to be good, man, you're going to be good, but I got to show you what to do. How old are you man?"

I say, "Thirty-five."

He says, "Oh forget it man! What are you fucking crazy? Thirty-five? Get the fuck out of here! You're fucking crazy man!"

That's it. Just like that he walks away. He's done with me.

He goes back to training his flyweight.

Lester's says, "Where my money at?"

I pay Lester and go in the stands and sit down next to Manuel. The adrenaline is still pumping. I feel strong. I admit I am fishing for a compliment. I say, "Can you believe it, Manuel? That guy actually wanted to train me until he found out how old I am. He actually wanted to train me!"

Manuel says, "Let me tell you something. Yooz kids today, yooz kids, yooz quit too soon, yooz kids. Let me tell you something back in the old days guys was a lot tougher. I used to fight in the twenties and thirties. One time I fought seven rounds wit a compound fracture, I was fightin' wit one hand, I had a compound fracture. Them old time guys was a tougher than yooz kids today. Them old time guys yooz knock 'em down they get back up, yooz knock 'em down, they get back up, yooz knock 'em down they get back up. Yooz kids today, first sign of brain damage yooz want to quit!"

As far as the script goes, I don't get past the research stage. I talk to Rocky's daughter, Marianne, and she sends me Xeroxed copies of her dad's old spiral notebooks with his thoughts, poems. That's right, believe it or not, Rocky Marciano wrote poems. I talk to guys who knew him who used to fly him around in their airplanes who share great stories about him. I'm thinking this could be a terrific movie! Then I talk to his brother, Peter, and tell him what I'm up to and he says, "That's our story! You do that we'll sue the shit out of you!"

That's the end of that. I don't spar with a pro boxer again until my fortieth birthday, but that's another story. Oh, and I find out the reason the Mexican guy is so eager to train me is white chumps like me who are willing to get in the ring and take shots are worth dough are worth dough are worth dough...

THE BEST OF TIMES

Next story best exemplifies the title of this book. This story is about pain. At the time it's not funny. Looking back on it, it's pretty funny. It begins when I run into Robin out in front of the Holy City Zoo. It's 1984 and Robin is a superstar. All I want from Robin is for him to think of me as a friend from before he got famous. I am reluctant to ask him for anything, and I never do. I know everybody is pulling at his coattails all the time wanting him to do this and that, and I don't want to be one of those people. I'm no weaving spider. If I were a weaving spider, my web would have more holes in it than Bonnie and Clyde. I'd be starving, and flies would be taunting me. "You call that a web! Ha! Ha! Ha! You couldn't even catch a sick louse with that!"

So when I run into Robin that night, I have no agenda. Robin spot me and says, "Hey, Jimmy…"

"Hey, Robin…"

It's an awkward moment. Neither one of us says anything. Now that I think about it, I've shared a lot of awkward moments over the years with Robin. Finally I say, "So Robin how are you doing these days? What's up? What's happening?"
Robin says, "I am working on a new film."

I say, "Oh? What is the film about?"

Robin says, "It is about a football game between Bakersfield and Taft."

"Bakersfield and Taft? Taft JC?"

225

Robin says, "Taft High versus Bakersfield. It's about an alumni game between Bakersfield and Taft..."

That's all I need to hear. I am reluctant to ask Robin for anything but this time is different. I say, "Robin, I played with eight guys from Taft JC in college! These guys were National Junior College Champs the year before! The next year, my freshman year, the Taft guys came to USF. These guys beat the crap out of me every day on the practice field, and later on a bunch of us played on the alumni team against the USF Varsity! We almost beat them too! This is my life you're talking about here!"

Long story short: Robin gets me in the movie, not as an extra, but as a principal. One day I get a call to go to Los Angeles to meet the director Roger Spottiswood. There is another guy there with long hair wearing a T-shirt and a work jacket and jeans, average looking. At first I think he's one of the crew guys. Robin says, "Jim, this is Kurt, Kurt this is my friend Jimmy."

Kurt says, "Hi Jimmy."

I say, "Hi, Kurt."

Just as I'm thinking, "This guy looks familiar," I realize that it's Kurt Russell, Robin's costar in the film. Kurt is a nice guy, real down to earth. The meeting goes well. Afterwards, I head back to San Francisco feeling positive that this is really going to happen.

A couple of weeks later I get a phone call saying that they are going to send me a contract, and please put down who my agent is because they're going to pay him 10% on top of whatever they are paying me. It's a basic SAG contract. I put down Agent Orange as my agent even though Agent Orange didn't get me the gig.

For me it's not about the money. I need the money, but it's not about the money. It's about hope. I still have this crazy idea that somehow I'm going to fuck up and make it.

My part is "Taft Player," but they don't send a script. They tell me the reason they are not sending a script is because I have no lines. This gets me thinking. Since I have no lines, I need to create a memorable character that will stand out without words. Hmmm. I've been to class reunions. There's always a nut there, the oddball who never quite fit in. The quiet psycho in the combat jacket and black T-shirt who just kind of lurks in the shadows with his eyes rolled up in his head and says nothing and scares the shit out of everyone. I'll play that guy!

I get an old Army field jacket, olive green, and a black T-shirt and I've got the faded 501s and a pair of black leather combat boots. Now all I have to do is wait until I get the phone call. They tell me that we are still a few weeks away from shooting and to hang tight until I get the word. I am excited at the prospect of being in a movie, but this is more than just a movie. At age thirty-five, I am going to get to put on pads again. I'm going to get to run around on a football field. I'm going to get to hit people! I double down on the training. I run twenty-eight 440s a day and laps between 440s. I train at the karate dojo six days a week, two-hour sessions, sometimes twice a day. I lift weights on a neck harness to build my neck up. One day the phone rings. It's a production person for the movie. The production person says: "Be at the Field House at Redondo Beach College at nine A.M. tomorrow morning."

INTO THE FOG

It's nine hours from my house to Redondo Beach. It's now 3:00 PM. I consider my options. I can either: Pack and get out of here by 5:00 or 6:00 P.M. and get into Redondo Beach between 2:00 and 3:00 A.M., or I can pack my stuff, try to get some sleep, and leave at midnight which, by my calculations, puts me at the Redondo Beach Field House at precisely 9:00 A.M. I decide on the latter. I get everything I'm going to need together, wash and pack enough clothes for three weeks, and then I lie down and try to sleep until midnight. Of course I'm too excited to sleep so I just lay there and thrash around until about 11:30. Then it's up and out the door. I load up my 1965 Volkswagen bug and off I go.

I pull in, and it is 9:00 A.M. straight up. There is a large semi-trailer parked outside the Field House, and it's a big one, a forty footer. The trailer is loaded with football gear, and there are a couple of guys standing on the back end handing out equipment. Turns out they are trainers for the LA Rams and recently defunct USFL team the LA Express, which is the same team that made Steve Young the highest paid quarterback in history at $32 million. You see where this is going? So I go up to the trainers and tell them I have been told to report to the Redondo Beach Fieldhouse. They say, "Are you one of the players?"

I say, "Yes."

The guy says, "What position?"

I say, "Linebacker."

Both these guys start laughing. One of them says, "Have you seen the linebackers?"

Right on cue a guy comes walking out of the Fieldhouse. He's six foot eight and weighs about 315, has blonde hair and is wearing a grey Tampa Bay Buccaneers sweatshirt and pants. Under one arm he's got about a hundred dollars worth of McDonalds. Under the other, he's got a ghetto blaster about the size of a small refrigerator. He says, "Where's the weight room?"

The trainer looks at me and says, "See what I mean?"

I say, "OK, safety then."

The guy fits me for pads and gear. I like to wear a neck roll so I ask the guy if he has any and he pulls out a box full of used ones. He says, "Take your pick."

I find one that fits me. It has "Dickerson 29" hand written on it. I don't really care that it's Eric Dickerson's neck roll. All I care about is, once the hitting starts, not breaking my neck. Eric Dickerson's is a perfect fit. I say, "Thanks guys. Please put this with my other stuff."

There is a meeting at ten o'clock. By now the meeting room in the field house is filled with football players. Coach Fears walks in. Tom Fears is a former LA Ram Hall of Fame tight end and coach. With the exception of a handful of us, most of the guys there are Fears' guys, NFL pros who he's coached over the years. Mike Douglas of the Green Bay Packers is there and Herman Edwards of the Philadelphia Eagles, Benny Ricardo and Maury Buford from the San Diego Chargers and a whole bunch of other guys from the 49ers and Dolphins and Vikings. Most everybody there has played or is currently playing on one NFL team or another.

Coach Fears tells us they want this to look real so we are going to run sprints, run drills, run plays do calisthenics, practice like it's for real. Once we put on pads, hitting will be live.

I realize I have been naïve all along. I thought that since the movie is about two high school rival alumni teams that the players would all be normal size guys, probably professional stuntmen. I think this because realistically in the sixties every high school football team had mostly normal size guys with maybe one or two big guys. A big guy was maybe six foot five and weighed 250. You didn't have squads of six foot eight 300-plus pounders who run the forty in under five seconds and play in the NFL.

I remind myself of rules number one and two of football: Rule One: Don't think about getting hurt. Rule Two: Always go full-speed. He who does not go full-speed whilst everyone else does gets hurt.

There is only one problem with this theory: Once we get on the field, full speed to me is half speed to them. We run 40-yard sprints. I come in dead last every time. If this were a horse race I'd be shipped to the glue factory. One of the players, a former Miami Dolphin, immediately starts in on me: "Look at this guy! Look at him! He runs like an old lady!"

Now we are running drills and the Dolphin guy is riding me, going, "Look at his stance! What a joke! Look at his stance…!"

I ignore the guy and do my best to do everything everyone else is doing. I try to blend in like I'm one of the pro guys. The whole time we're on the practice field he's the only one who says anything. At the end of practice someone says they're going for pizza and beer and would I like to come along. Hey! Nothing tastes better after football practice then pizza and beer!

Now we're sitting in the pizza parlor eating pizza and drinking beer and pretty soon I'm doing my act and everyone loves it, everyone except for the Dolphin of course. Other guys are slapping me on the back telling me how funny I am and the Dolphin is shaking his head going, "What a joke. This guy's a joke."

The next day at practice it's the same thing and the next day after that. The guy dogs me the whole time I'm down there. I don't say anything but all the while I'm sizing him up. He's 6'4" and 225. I'm 5'11" and 184 the same size Rocky Marciano was when he knocked out Joe Walcott. My Dolphin friend looks like he bends in the middle. I like guys that bend in the middle.

One of the players I get along real good with is John Sanders, a former LA Rams safety and defensive back coach with the Houston Oilers. John has a great sense of humor and appreciates mine, so we hit it off from the get-go. We become instant pals and hang out pretty much the whole time we're down there, whether it's on the set or at the pizza joint afterwards.

After a few days of working out with the pros, I am told to report to the set where they are shooting actual scenes for the movie with the principals. Now I am with the actors running fake workouts and doing calisthenics in the middle of a bunch of oilrigs with cameras rolling. This is the Taft practice you see on the big screen. We basically play a bunch of bumbling idiots. We're supposed to be in Taft, but in reality, Seal Beach is doubling for Taft, since they have oilrigs in Seal Beach as well. I meet R.G. Armstrong in Seal Beach. R.G. is a great old character actor who plays our coach in the movie. He is a big craggy mountain man looking hulk of a guy with a strong Alabama accent. I know R.G.'s face from years of watching him play villains in Westerns. In the movies, he comes off as plenty intimidating. In reality R.G. is a nice guy, a big friendly easy-going good ol' boy.

DUB

Our next location is at Moorpark High School in Simi Valley. It's late January and even during the daytime the weather is freezing. I'm down on the football field with John Sanders and I see an old guy sitting there on the sideline in a director's chair, all bundled up with blankets wrapped around him. He's got a nurse with him. I'm not really thinking about it, he just looks like a little old man to me, and Sanders says, "See that old guy over there?"

I say, "Yeah...?"

He says, "You know who that is?"

I say, "No."

He says, "That's Dub Taylor."

"Dub who?"

"Dub Taylor. Remember Bonnie and Clyde?"

I look at the old man in the chair. John says, "That's CW Moss's daddy, the guy who rats out Bonnie and Clyde and gets them ambushed and killed in the end!"

I say, "I know that guy...!"

John says, "That's him, Dub Taylor. Why don't you go introduce yourself? He's cool."

I go over to the old man in the chair. I say, "You're Dub Taylor."

He says, "That's right. I'm Dub."

I say, "Mr. Taylor, I'm Jim Giovanni. I'm a big fan of yours. I love your movies. I love Bonnie and Clyde. It's one of my favorite movies. I love all the stuff you've been in, all those Westerns and Paul Newman movies..."

I don't realize at the time but Dub has never been in a Paul Newman movie. He doesn't bother to correct me. Instead he says, "Paul Newman, he ain't box office no more! Nowadays you got to be box office. Paul Newman ain't box office no more!"

Talk about Southern accents. Next to Dub Taylor, R.G. sounds like a Yankee.

Dub's nurse is apparently worried about him getting too excited. She says, "Dub just had a quadruple bypass..."

Dub says, "Yeah, and I'm mean, dirty, and I don't wear underwear. That don't mean I don't have artistic value."

I say, "I remember that! That's from that Don Knotts movie...!"

Dub says, "Shakiest gun in the West!"
I say, "That's it!"

Dub says, "You have seen my movie, you cocksucker!"

After that Dub, John, and I are the three amigos. We hang out between takes, on dinner breaks. Dub is a riot. He doesn't care what he says or whom he says it to. In the movies he is often cast as a dirty old man type of character. His movie character pales in comparison to the real deal. I see the twinkle in his eye as John and I laugh our asses off at some of his more outrageous comments. At one point I say to Dub: "You know what my favorite scene of yours is? It's the scene in Bonnie and Clyde when you find out C.W. got a tattoo, and you get mad and throw gravy on him and say, 'Why did you get all jellied up like that, boy?'"

He says, "You like that? Yeah, I come up with that myself.

I slap that gravy on him. He don't know I'm going to do that. That weren't in the script you know. I come up with that one myself. I say, 'Why'd you go get yourself all jellied up like that there for, boy?' And I slap that gravy on him and the director, he like that so he kept it in. He don't know I'm going to do that. 'Why you get yourself all jellied up, boy?' I slap that gravy on him, heh heh heh the director, he like that so he kept it in. Heh heh heh!"

Once cameras are rolling, Dub is All Pro. Talk about energy. I learn more watching him than from any acting teacher. This guy's no method actor. They say "Action!" It's like someone flipped a switch. He instantaneously becomes larger-than-life. A minute before he is a little old man heart patient. "Action!" and suddenly he's the lead bull in the buffalo herd. I'm in awe watching him. He finishes doing his thing and sits back down and just like that he is a little old man heart patient again. I say, "Dub, that's unbelievable! They say 'Action!', and you light up like the scoreboard at Texas Stadium. How do you do it?"

Dub says, "That ain't nothin'. Do it as long as I have, you'll get used to it."

Time comes to shoot the big Homecoming scene in the movie. We shoot in the gymnasium at Moorpark high school. It's the Taft Homecoming Dance and Class Reunion. Everybody's there, the old Homecoming King and Queen and Captain and quarterback of the football team, who is played by Kurt Russell, and Robin's character, who is the goat receiver who dropped the game-winning pass in the big game all those years before. All the lead actors and actresses and principals are on the set and a whole bunch of extras, many of them beautiful young women dressed in low cut evening gowns. Men are wearing coats and ties. I show up in the olive drab Army jacket with the black T-shirt and jeans and combat boots. The director Roger Spottiswoode comes up to me, says, "Is that the costume the costume department gave you?"

I say, "No, this is my own costume I brought myself." I explain to him my theory on how every class has a crazy who shows up for the reunion. Roger hears me out and says, "Okay, you can wear that but no camouflage!"

Roger agrees to this, I don't know why, but he agrees to let me do it. So now I'm on the set lurking in the background looking like a psycho. They say, "Action!" I don't say anything. I quietly turn on the energy like I watched Dub do and become a scary weird guy lurking in the background exuding scary weirdness. We shoot for a while and break for dinner. Cast and crew dine together, so we all grab trays and get in the chow line and who grabs a tray and takes his place in the back of the line behind a couple of crew guys, but Kurt Russell. I'm thinking this guy doesn't have to wait in line. He could just sit in his trailer and have anything he wants brought to him.

I say, "Hey, Kurt."

Kurt says, "Hey, Jimmy."

I say, "I thought you'd have special food delivered to your trailer..."

Kurt smiles, says, "I'd rather have what you guys are having."

See what I mean? What a great guy! So John Sanders and I are sitting there and I overhear one of the principal actors saying, "I can't believe security hasn't thrown out the psycho. Where is security? Why haven't they thrown the psycho out?"

This guy doesn't realize I'm the guy he's talking about and it takes me a minute to figure it out. Now that I'm acting normal, he probably thinks I'm a crew guy, a gaffer or something.

I say, "Maybe he's a cast member. Maybe he's one of the actors..."

He says, "He's not an actor! How did he get past security? How the fuck did he get in here? I know a psycho when I see one. He's a fucking psycho I'm telling you!"

I say, "I know for a fact he's one of the actors."

He says, "Bullshit! I read the script! There's no psycho in the script!"

I can't hold it in any longer. I say, "It's me! I'm the guy playing the psycho and you're right, it's not in the script..."

He says, "What the fuck? Why are they letting you get away with that shit?"

I say, "They didn't give me any lines so I came up with a character. I ran it past Roger and he said 'OK'."

He says, "You are one hell of an actor, my friend!"

I say, "You think so?"

He says, "I fucking know so! You had me convinced! If security didn't do something quick about the psycho I was about to vacate the fucking premises, I shit you not!"

We go back, shoot a few more scenes and wrap for the night. I come back the next day and I know I made an impression because I when I get to the set I am "the buzz" everyone is talking about. Extras are telling me how their agents are all talking about me, asking who I am, crew guys are walking around impersonating me, everyone's calling me "Psycho." All of a sudden I'm a celebrity. I'm no longer anonymous "Taft Player."

You know you've made an impression when they give you a nickname. "Psycho"! Cool! That's even better than "The Ape Man!"

Crew guys are saying stuff like: "Hey Psycho, how you doing? You having fun?"

"Yeah. You guys having fun?"

"Yeah, we're having fun, we're psychos too!"

Then they start impersonating me. Yeah, I would definitely say I made an impression.

PUTTING ON
THE PADS

After a couple of nights of such tomfoolery, we get our call time for the next day, and it's for 8:00 P.M. the following night. This is what I've been waiting for. They are going to start shooting the game. According to the script, which I surreptitiously obtain a copy of, the field is dry for the first half. Bakersfield thoroughly thrashes Taft in the first half, scores three touchdowns to none for Taft. It begins to rain at the end of the half. By half time it's a monsoon and the field turns into instant mud bowl. In the second half, Taft makes a comeback. That's all I need to know. I love mud. I am sure footed in mud. The best thing about mud is it slows down fast guys. All of a sudden here comes a fast guy and you get the angle on him and he can't cut because he's afraid he's going to slip and WHAM! You nail him! So much fun I promise you. So I read the script and my plan is to sandbag the first half and watch these guys knock the crap out of each other at full speed. In the second half when the field's nice and muddy and everyone slows down, I'll make my move.

By 10:00 P.M. we are on the field. It's thirty-two degrees, extreme cold by Southern California standards. I'm standing on the sidelines, Taft number 31. The field is dry, cameras are rolling, the pro guys are moving fast and they're really hitting. Every time someone yells, "Speed!" guys are going "All the way live! All the way live!" meaning: Go full speed and nobody gets hurt. But guys are getting hurt. Guys are getting mad, there are scuffles; it looks like there are going to be fights. Guy's are coming off the field saying stuff like, "If that guy submarines me one more time, I'm going to kick his fucking ass..."

These guys aren't playing. This is the real deal. We shoot till 4:00 A.M.

The next night it's the same and the night after that. I learn a lot watching these guys. One thing I learn is the difference between the active pros and the guys that are no longer active in whatever league they were formerly active in. (There are disgruntled USFL guys there as well.) The difference is: Active pros are cool. They still have careers. They don't want to get hurt making a dumb-ass movie. It's the guys who are no longer active, the guys who have been cut, especially guys who got cut right before they got vested for their NFL pension, these are the dangerous guys. Some of these guys want to hurt people and they do. One former 49er safety blindsides one of the actors and destroys his knee, breaks his tibia and fibula, tears his Achilles tendon, I mean blows this guy's leg up. It's bad. I watch the insanity go down. This is definitely not the time to make my move. I have second thoughts about what I am about to do, but I try to put them out of my mind. I haven't come this far to wimp out.

Every now and then the camera focuses on our sideline. When it does, everybody scrambles to get as close as they can to either Kurt or Robin. The camera is on the two leads and everybody knows it. I'm no different. I'm desperate to get in the shot like the rest of them. We're like a bunch of hogs at the teat. The least aggressive hog gets no teat.

RAIN

One night we get there and there are rain machines on the set. The irony of this is it actually does rain that night. It's a freezing rain but they still need rain machines because water photographs best if it has glycerin in it. Real rain doesn't show up as good on camera as the fake rain, so now they are adding fake rain to the real rain and we are freezing and we are getting rained on by both real freezing rain and fake freezing rain. The cameras are rolling, and the players are running plays and, holy shit, now it's actually snowing for real! It's twenty-nine degrees, and the field is wet and sloppy, and players are slipping and sliding and crashing and splashing in the mud.

They shoot a few plays of this, and pretty soon we're coming up on 4:00 A.M., and we hear the call to wrap for the night. Same call time tomorrow night, 8:00 P.M. when we are going to start shooting the second half. This is what I have been waiting for. I barely get any sleep in anticipation of it. I am going to actually get in there and mix it up with the pros. The next day I run 10 miles like I do every day. I get to the set that night, and I'm psyched like Rocky getting ready to fight Apollo Creed.

In the locker room guys are putting on pads, getting taped up. This is it. Tonight's the night. This is for real. I batten down the hatches: My Erik Dickerson neck roll strapped down tight, Anderson knee braces, ankles, anything I can think of that can conceivably break loose I'm taped like the mummy. We walk out of the locker room, cleats clattering on the asphalt, the big Tampa Bay blonde guy, who doesn't like to be called "Baby Huey," looks down at me and says, "You must be a real motherfucker!"

We get out on the field, the temperature is hovering around thirty degrees. They bring out fire hoses and soak down the field until it's sufficiently pigsty, and they get cameras in position and extras in the stands. Now they are running plays in the mud like it's the end of the first half, and pretty soon everybody is muddy enough to match shots from the night before.

We break for dinner. I don't eat anything because when we come back, we are going to start shooting the second half. This is when I am going to make my move, and I don't want to be puking on the sidelines. So there I am at dinner trying not to think about what happened to the actor who got his leg blown up, all the while watching a bunch of muddy football players try to eat without getting mud in their food. After dinner we head back down to the field. By now both the real rain and the fake rain have stopped. A freezing fog is shimmering up off the field. Both teams are on their respective sidelines. The kickoff and kickoff return teams line up. Time to make my move. I go to Coach Fears and say, "Is it OK if I get in, Coach?"

Coach Fears says: "Be my guest."

I run in and tell one of the guys I am replacing him. He is ecstatic because he is freezing his ass off and all he wants to do is get off the field and go stand by one of the big propane blowers that they have on the sidelines. He emphatically says, "Yes!" and makes a beeline for the heater. I line up for the kickoff in my clean white uniform. It reminds me of the old joke: "What did the brown gerbil say to the white gerbil? New here, huh?"

In other words, my presence does not go unnoticed.

Roger, the director, immediately runs up to me and says, "Get off the field right now! Get off the field! I'm not assuming liability for you! Off! Get off the field right now!"

I say, "Roger I can do this. I've been training for this, I'm in great shape..."

He says, "I don't doubt your ability, but we have already had one actor seriously injured. I am not going to assume liability for you. No actors allowed on the field! Get off now!"

I head to the sideline. They don't give me any lines. They won't let me in the game. I'm nothing but a glorified extra in this thing. I am bummed. Robin comes over and says, "What's wrong, Jimmy?"

I say, "Roger won't let me get in the game. I'm in great shape, Robin. I can do this. He won't even let me on the field..."

Robin says, "I'll see what I can do." And Robin does his patented disappearing Robin thing.

I appreciate Robin's concern, but I'd wager good money no way is Roger going to change his mind. Much to my amazement, Robin comes back a few minutes later and says, "They're going to give you a play."

"Whoa! Thanks, bro!"

Good thing I didn't bet on Robin's lack of influence. Sure enough, here comes Roger. He says, "All right, we're going to give you a play, this is going to be your play: You are going to score a touchdown! You are going to intercept the pass, run into the end zone, and spike the ball! This is your play! Remember, you are going to intercept the pass, run into the end zone and spike the ball!"

I approach this with every ounce of professionalism that I can muster. I have every intention of doing what the director tells me to do. Having the good Catholic school background that I have, I am respectful of authority, provided the authority deserves respect. In this case I fully intend to follow instructions. I am grateful to and respectful of both Roger and Robin and I wouldn't do anything to deliberately undermine their authority or credibility.

However...

Right before we're ready to shoot the play my nemesis, the Miami Dolphin who's been giving me a hard time since the get-go, comes to me and says, "Your ass is mine." That's all he says. But he says it in such a way I know he's fixing to do me like the 49er did that other actor who got his leg blown up. There's no doubt in my mind what he means when he says, "Your ass is mine." I immediately start thinking in terms of self-defense, which is exactly the plea I plan to enter when this is over, either that or not guilty by reason of insanity. My nemesis is wearing number 12. He is the quarterback! He will be throwing the pass I will be intercepting. Nothing I love better than hitting the quarterback!

Roger says: "Alright everybody, listen up! We're going to run the play!"

I am psyched. I'm wearing a white jersey with green number 31. I am no longer Jim Giovanni, actor. I'm Jim Taylor, fullback, Green Bay Packers

.

We line up. I hear Roger's voice. "Alright, everybody ready! Places everyone! Number 31, Remember to spike the ball!"

"Speed...Action!"

Guys on the line are going: "All the way live! All the way live!"

Pads pop! Pop! Pop! Pop! Number 12 drops back. He throws the pass in my direction. I catch the ball and start running. I may not even reach Number 12. Here come a couple of guys who don't follow directions either. I stiff arm one and the other guy barely misses me and slides past. Now I have a head of steam moving in a beeline straight towards the target, Number 12. He thinks I'm going to cut away from him at the last second and he's going to have a free shot at me. Wrong! I lower my head: BOOM! Split the 1 and the 2 on the front of his jersey with my facemask a direct hit like hitting a home run ball! Number 12 explodes backwards and lands in a mud hole in the end zone. I land on top of him. People go crazy cheering!

Now I'm up and guys are slapping me five. I still have the ball in my hands. John Sanders is jumping around. "Jesus! What a hit! What a hit! You lit him up like a Christmas tree! Holy shit! You are a psycho!"

Roger runs over to where we are and says, "That was great! That was great, but you forgot to spike the ball! Let's do it again. Okay, everybody, back to your marks. We're going to do it again!"

Now the pro guys are giving Number 12 a hard time. "You let an actor kick your ass?"

He's going: "I'm going to kill the motherfucker! I'm going to kill the motherfucker!"

Guys are yelling at me from their huddle: "You better run the other way, motherfucker! This motherfucker going to kill you!"

I don't want the next take to be the one where he kicks my ass, so now I'm Rocky Marciano going: "Remember: You need the K.O.! You need the K.O.!"

"Everyone on your marks...Speed...Action!"

Number 12 drops back, throws the ball; I bobble it, drop it and hear groans. Roger says, "All right, let's do it again, everyone back to your marks!"

"Alright everyone, ready...Speed...Action!"

The ball is in the air, damn, I drop it again!

Now guys are booing. Producers aren't happy because

there are a lot of moving parts in this thing, and every time I drop the ball it's time, and time is money, and every time I drop the ball I cost them money. Football players aren't happy because all they want to do is get this over with so they can go stand by the propane blowers and get warm. They're saying stuff like: "C'mon, Psycho, hang on to the damn ball! I'm freezing my nut sack off here!"

I'm not worried about getting hurt. I'm worried about doing right by Robin, who is standing right there watching the whole thing. We line up once again. All eyes, not to mention all cameras, are on me. Talk about pressure.

One of the players yells, "Get it right this time, numb nuts!"

"Speed...Action!"

Pop! Pop! Pop! Number 12 drops back and throws the ball. I bobble it but this time I hold onto it. I tuck it in with both hands and start running. Number 12 is stalking me, moving laterally across the goal line. He doesn't think I have the balls to do it again. He realizes too late his miscalculation. I lower my head and run into him full speed like a torpedo. At the last second he gets his helmet down and we go helmet-to-helmet on the goal line. "BACK" is the sound it makes, appropriate because BACK is where his ass lands in the mud hole. The second hit is bigger than the first. I land in the mud hole on top of him with a gigantic splash, jump up and spike the ball with both hands. Pandemonium ensues! People are jumping around, cheering! The energy is real and the cameras get it all! Roger says, "That was great! That was great...!"

Then he looks at me and says, "Very well. Let him play!"

I scrimmage the rest of the night with the pros. Afterwards I get to my trailer and mud is completely imbedded everywhere in my football uniform. There's so much mud I can't read the number on my jersey. I'm so full of mud I can't find the straps on my shoulder pads. It takes me an hour and a half to get out of my uniform. I'm in no hurry. I breathe a sigh of relief as I take my helmet off. I take a closer look at it. What's this? We have brand-new white helmets and they have brand-new black helmets. I wipe mud off my white helmet and see a black plastic stick mark, the size of a large Band Aid, right smack dab in the middle of the forehead on the helmet. I get to the mirror and start washing my face off and see a raspberry abrasion the size of a large Band Aid smack dab in the middle of my forehead, a perfect match for the one on my helmet. Damn! That hit was bigger than I thought! I sit there for the next forty-five minutes contemplating my helmet. I'm muddy and beat up and freezing and I feel great. I finally change back into my civvies and head back to my room at the Motel 6. They leave the light on for me but I don't get much sleep because within a few hours my body feels like the train after the opening sequence of *The Fugitive*.

In the movie *Rocky* Sylvester Stallone talks about being so beat up "I have to call a cab to take me from the bedroom to the bathroom." This is what it feels like, like Nick Nolte the morning after in North Dallas Forty. I roll out of bed onto my knees and it's 10 in the morning and I'm sitting on the floor of my room putting my running shoes on. As much pain as I'm in, I've got to keep the streak alive. I head out the door. The first mile is pure agony. After a couple of miles I'm starting to loosen up and by the time I finish ten, I feel pretty good. Maybe I wasn't in a train wreck last night after all. When I get to the set I tell John Sanders about it. I say, "Man, I was sure beat up after last night but I ran ten miles and I don't feel so bad now..."

John says, "That's the way we do at Houston. We run them the day after the game and run the soreness out of them and let them have the day off after that."

Well, how about that! I am doing something right after all.

FANTASY FOOTBALL

The next several nights are fantasy camp for me. Not to say there isn't a downside. The average temperature is between twenty-nine and thirty-two degrees. Much of the time we are wet and muddy and miserable. That's where I learn about pantyhose. Turns out a lot of pro guys wear pantyhose underneath their football uniforms to keep them warm. When I say "them" I mean their prize pair. I hear this and buy pantyhose the next day. So now we are muddy, freezing, running around on a football field in our pantyhose slamming into each. The director says, "Cut!" We run to the sidelines and huddle as close as we can get to the propane blowers to get warm. Of course, everyone is trying to huddle around the propane blowers at the same time, so now we're back to the old "hogs at the teat" routine. If you're lucky to get close enough to the heaters, by the time they move the cameras you've hardened into a brick. You are just starting to get nice and toasty and you hear "Back on the field!" and you run back out and immediately get hit in the mug with a high-pressure blast of ice water. Your body is stiff, now you are wet and freezing again, and they are hosing you down with fire hoses. When it's determined you are sufficiently messed up enough to match shots, they say "On your marks!" and then it's: "Speed! Action!" And you run and slam into someone. After a few takes, you hear: "Cut! Move the cameras!" And it's back to the propane blowers. By the third night there isn't a player out there who doesn't have walking pneumonia. Players are on the sidelines shooting B12 into their muddy arms with syringes.

"Hey Psycho, want some B12?"

"No thanks. I think I'll take it orally."

The nickname really stuck because now all the pro guys are calling me "Psycho." They are saying stuff like: "OK, Psycho, be cool. I don't want you to be going and landing on my knee or nothing. Don't be messing up on me now..."

Really? You guys are afraid of me? Then it dawns on me. I'm like "the fish" in poker. "The fish" is the guy that doesn't know what he is doing, which makes him the most dangerous guy in the game. The fish makes moves a pro would never make, causes cards to come up that never would have come up if the fish wasn't in there. The fish can throw the whole game off. And if the fish gets hot, look out! Anything can happen. All of a sudden it dawns on me: I'm the fish.

But I'm not the only fish in the sea.

Okie Joe, the Taft oilrig worker, is a fish and another one is a too-dumb-to-play-in-the-NFL lug whom I'll refer to simply as Clown Face. Joe and Clown Face are the other two nut jobs that try to knock me down the first time we run the interception play. These guys aren't play-acting. They seriously try to knock me down. The shit you see in the movie is real. It doesn't take genius to figure out these guys ain't playin' by the rules either. Along with disgruntled ex-pros, we are the wild cards in the deck. No wonder guys who still have careers are afraid of us.

"Remember what I told you, Psycho, be cool..."

OKIE JOE

Before I go any further, here is a little backstory on Joe, the Okie Taft oil rig worker. Joe is an interesting case. Early in the production schedule, the production company is shooting in Taft and they discover this guy. He looks like a gnarled up version of Kurt Russell, enough so that they have him doubling for Kurt in a lot of the shots. You don't want any close ups of him smiling on camera though because, unlike Kurt, he's got scars. Half of his teeth are missing. It's hard to tell anything in a football uniform, so he doubles for Kurt in the first half when Kurt is getting seriously pounded. As a double for Kurt taking a beating on camera, this guy is perfect.

In the second half Kurt does most of his own stunts, which leaves Okie Joe free to suit up in a Bakersfield uniform. Now Joe thinks it's his turn to inflict the pain. That's exactly what he is trying to do when he and Clown Face decide they are going to knock me down. Thankfully, I am able to avoid them and inflict pain on number 12 instead. But this is just one play. We are out there several nights, and these guys figure that means they're going to have several more shots at me.

Once they say "Action!" it's a free for all. Everyone wants to get the tackle. It's live. The hits are real. Roger the director announces: "Number 27 will get the ball. Number 27 will run with the ball. Whoever gets there first gets the tackle!"

I'm lined up at outside linebacker opposite number 27, Okie Joe. Right before we shoot the play, he comes up to me and says, "Ain't no way you'll ever get me down. You ain't never gonna tackle me. I'm going to run over your ass."

Roger says, "All right rehearsal, everybody, rehearsal, rehearsal..."

I'm thinking: "This time I'll be Ray Nietzsche."

"Everyone, places. We're going for a rehearsal now..."

Even though it's a "rehearsal" cameras are rolling. "Speed..."

Guys on the line are going: "All the way live! All the way live!"

"Action!"

Pop! Pop! Pop! Here comes Joe. He's got a full head of steam running straight at me. I square up and hit him head on face mask to face mask. The hit stops him dead in his tracks. I stand him up, but like me, Joe has a low center of gravity. Now we are locked in a wrestling match as I struggle to pick him up and he struggles not to be picked up. We twist in circles, like we are doing some kind of weird dance in the mud. Getting this guy down is like trying to bulldog a steer. Maybe Ray Nietzsche is the wrong choice. This looks like a job for Walt Garrison. He rodeos in the off-season, doesn't he?

Finally, I get leverage. Just as Roger yells, "Cut!" I get under Okie Joe's pads and flip him, dump him face first into the mud and his head dislocates. Now his head is on backwards and off to the side, cocked off at a weird ninety degree angle. It is grotesque, one of the most frightening things I have ever seen, especially since I am the one responsible. Now the director's yelling at me, "I said, 'Rehearsal! Rehearsal!' You idiot!"

The writer, Ron Shelton is yelling at me: "You fucking idiot! Didn't you hear Roger say rehearsal?"

Some of the pro guys look like they're ready to heave.

They are going, "Look what he did to Joe! Look what he did to Joe! Poor Joe!"

I am in shock. I didn't mean to hurt anyone. Now I'm scared, really scared. People are yelling at me. Joe is lying there with a dislocated head. I'm thinking, "I really fucked up this time..." I start praying, "Dear God, please let Joe be all right please let him be all right...!"

Joe goes, "Ain't no big deal, it happens all the time." He sits up and grabs his own head with both hands, lifts up and starts to chiropractor himself. He twists his own head around SNAP, CRACKLE CRUNCH! He gets it facing front, lets go and POP! It goes back into the socket. I know what you are thinking. Heads don't have sockets. This mutant's did. It's the only way I can describe it. Big linemen look like they're ready to blow chunks. Guys are going: "Nine years in the NFL and I've never seen anything like that! That was disgusting!"

I've had prayers answered quickly before but damn! I breathe a sigh of relief. Thank you Jesus!

Much to my surprise, Roger lets me continue. Nothing more is said. They must like what they're seeing in the dailies.

"Hey, Psycho, watch it, dude! Don't be doing nothing stupid now!"

WRAP PARTY

The wrap party is in Los Angeles. Robin is very gracious. He thanks me for participating in the filming and gives me a gold-plated Cross Pen as a gift. I thank Robin for getting me in the movie. I go over to the bar and my nemesis number 12 is standing there. I sidle up next to him. We both are looking straight ahead. He spots me in the mirror and looks down.

I look up at him and say, "Hi."

He says, "Hi."

He looks up and then he looks down and he looks up and looks down again at me, and I can tell by the quizzical look on his face he is still trying to figure out what happened.

FINAL CUT

Most of my stunts end up in the film. In addition to the touchdown I make several tackles and recover a fumble. The fumble recovery is not in the script but it ends up in the movie. It happens on a play where the ball carrier is supposed to run until he gets knocked down by whoever gets there first. Me and another Taft guy hit the Bakersfield guy at the same time and knock the ball loose and now the ball is spinning around in the mud. I dive on it and thrust the ball up in the air triumphantly. The shot makes it in the final cut.

After 30 years I still get the occasional residual check. I just got one for $0.00, hardly enough to pay for the arthritis medication.

Was it worth it? Hell, yeah! I got this story out of it, didn't I?

Cross one and a half off the bucket list. Scrimmaging live with professional football players is one. I'm in a movie, but I don't have lines, so it counts as a one and a half. When the day comes I'm in a movie with lines, cross two.

TUCKER

I don't have to wait long to get my wish. One night I am home on a Friday night having dinner with my wife and another couple and the phone rings. It's Agent Orange. He says, "What are you doing?"

I say, "What do you mean what am I doing? You mean like right now? I'm having dinner. Why?"

He says, "I've got something for you, but you need to go right now!"

I say, "I don't want to go on a cattle call right now! I'm having dinner with, we have company in our house right now..."

"This is for a Francis Ford Coppola movie and they want you there right now...!"

"A what?"

"Francis Ford Coppola is shooting a movie in Oakland and they want you there right now..."

"What movie?"

"It's called, *Tucker*! The name of the movie is *Tucker*! They want someone to do a scene with Jeff Bridges and they specifically asked for you. They want you over there if you don't get over there they'll get someone else..."

"I'm going, but how do they know about me?"

You auditioned for *Peggy Sue Got Married*, remember? They are calling other guys as well so get your ass over there pronto."

Next thing I know I'm flying across the Bay Bridge to Oakland. It's like the scene from *It's a Mad Mad Mad Mad World* where Dick Shawn is flying low going: "I am coming Mom! I'm coming Mom!"

Old City Hall in Oakland is a big imposing looking building with pillars and big stone steps leading up to it. I get there and there are lights and cameras and crowds of extras in forties period costumes. Real Oakland Police motorcycle officers cordon off the side streets. I walk over to where they are shooting and already I see a guy in a police uniform doing the part that I'm supposed to do. They are doing a live take, and I can see from where I'm standing that it's not working. This guy has no energy. An assistant director approaches me and asks who I am. I tell him and he takes me to where Francis Ford Coppola is standing. The AD says to Coppola:

"This is the guy they sent over to do the police sergeant."

Coppola eyeballs me up and down and says, "Put him in the police uniform and cut his hair."

Now I am in a trailer and they are fitting me for a police sergeant's uniform, and they are zapping off my hair with an electric shaver, giving me a forties style haircut. It's 18 years since one of those things has touched my head, but what the hell, I'll sacrifice anything for art! Hair and makeup finishes with me and I look in the mirror and holy shit I look like Oliver North! The AD is right there on the walkie-talkie and I hear them say, "Get him to the set right now!" So they whisk me to the set, and now I'm standing in front of Francis Ford Coppola. On their marks are about a hundred extras in period costumes.

Coppola says, "OK, this is your scene. I want you to take control. Jeff is going to come around the corner in the Tucker chased by two police cars and he is going to stop in front of City Hall. You're going to come down the steps of City Hall, arrest Jeff and take him to jail. You make up the dialogue. OK, we're going for a live take!"

I say, "Mr. Coppola..."

"Call me Francis, my father is Mr. Coppola."

"What are my lines? What am I supposed to say?"

"You make up the dialogue. This is your scene. Take control."

"Is there a script I could see?"

"It's not in the script. This scene needs something. I'm looking for comic relief. I need you to improvise."

I say, "Do you have any idea what you want me to say?"

"I don't know, say something like, 'What's going on here?' or 'Let's get to the bottom of this!' I don't know. You make up what you want to say. Jeff will answer you and you arrest Jeff and take him up the steps to jail. This is your scene. Take control. We're going for a live take."

Francis walks away. Immediately the director of photography comes up to me. He is the DP who won the Academy award the previous year for *The Last Emperor*. He has a strong Italian accent. He points to an X in gaffer's tape on the ground and says, "This is you mark! All I ask is you hit a you mark!"

He walks away and I go back up the stairs to the spot where I'm supposed to start from. The pressure is on. I have already seen one actor in this part get canned and I'm sure there is a guy queued up right behind me. I'd better get this right. The guy in front of me has no energy. I can see it is a problem watching him. I figure I'll go the opposite. I'll give them over-the-top energy. It is easier to ratchet down then it is to ratchet up. I figure if nothing else, it'll give Francis something to work with. The good news is I have no time to get nervous, no time to even think about it. I hear: "Speed...Action!"

I flip the switch like I watched Dub do. I am no longer Jim Giovanni. I am Jackie Gleason! I march down the steps as Jeff Bridges screams around the corner in a Tucker, police cars chasing, sirens wailing. I hit my mark just as Jeff skids to a halt right in front of City Hall. Jeff gets out of the Tucker and is immediately engulfed by hordes of fedora wearing extras playing old-fashioned reporters. They are snapping light bulbs, yelling questions. I tell the crowd to shut up and they do. Jeff makes his way to where I am standing. I say, "What's going on here?"

Jeff says, "Well Sarge, I just led your cops here on a hundred-mile-an-hour chase. What are you going to do about it? Aren't you going to put the cuffs on me?"

I say, "You're going with me!" And I grab Jeff by the collar and start marching him up the stairs on his tippy toes.

"Cut! Cut!"

Coppola runs up to us. " Put Jeff down. Put Jeff down!"

I put Jeff down.

Coppola says. "Great! It's great, but don't touch Jeff! I don't want any police brutality!"

Just then someone announces that it is time for a meal break. No doubt management doesn't want meal penalties on this big of a cast and crew, so we break for dinner, which gives me extra time I don't need to get nervous. Just like in "The Best of Times" I know they are going to shoot my big scene immediately after dinner. If I eat now it's going to slow me down. This could be my big break. Again, I don't want to be puking on the sidelines, so I don't eat. I don't even drink coffee for fear that is going to make me jittery or make me have to pee at an inopportune moment. All I can do now is worry about getting it right. I tell myself, "Relax. At least this time if you fuck up you don't have to worry about a Baby Huey-sized brute plugging you into a respirator! I am not going to fuck up. I am going to nail this. I am the little engine that could! I think I can I think I can I think I can...!"

We get back on set and everything is like it was before the dinner break. Everyone's in place, we're ready to shoot the scene and Francis says, "Remember! No police brutality!"

"No Police brutality? But that's the fun part of the job!"

Extras laugh. This is good.

Francis says, "I'm serious."

I say, "Don't worry Francis. I won't touch Jeff!"

This is of course Jeff's cue to start touching me, pushing me, poking me, which makes for an interesting dynamic. The more he pokes and prods me, the more I have to restrain myself from reacting. It's Kramden and Norton, the old Gleason slow burn.

We're back to our starting places. I hear: "Speed! Action!"

I start down the steps and here comes Jeff in the Tucker with the cops chasing him and I get down to the sidewalk and hit my mark just as Jeff gets out and camera lights are flashing and extras are going crazy and I yell, "Pipe down!" And the crowd goes silent like someone flipped a switch. I start talking. A few seconds later I hear, "Cut!" Francis comes over and says, "That didn't work."

I say, "I know."

Francis says, "I don't want eighties style acting I want thirties. Do you remember the character actor in the thirties who always played the flustered police sergeant or the exasperated detective, a comic relief type of character...?"

"I think I remember the guy you're talking about..."

"I am looking for comedy. I don't want eighties style acting. I want comedy. Comedy is, comedy is..."

I say, "Timing!"

Francis says, "That's right! Timing!"

I say, "In that case, Francis, can I tell the extras what I need them to do?"

Francis says, "This is your scene! Take control!"

I address the extras: "OK everybody listen up! I'm going to need three beats. The first time I yell, 'Pipe down!' I'm going to look to my left and make an arm gesture like this: the pipe down gesture. On the first 'Pipe down!' do not stop! Keep going! Keep yelling out questions! Keep flashing your cameras. Then I'm going to look to my right and do the same thing. I'm going to make the pipe down gesture and yell, 'Pipe down!' a second time. Do not stop! Keep yelling questions like you never heard me. On the third beat, I'm going to look straight ahead and make a gesture like this, the "cut!" gesture. I'm going to yell, "Quiet! When you see me make the cut gesture and yell "Quiet!" – cut it immediately! Do not make a sound. When you see that, immediately everyone, silence! Remember, three beats: 'Pipe down! Pipe down!' And then 'Quiet!' Everybody got that?"

Extras are going, "Got it!"
"OK, Francis. We're ready now."

The third take works like a charm. Francis says, "Cut it and print it!"

All of a sudden they are striking set to move to the next location. ADs are looking at each other going, "You mean we're through here?"

An AD comes up to me and says, "You're wrapped. Get over to costume and turn in your costume, and get back here to do your paperwork."

Another AD comes up to me and says, "I can't believe we're out of here! We spend two days shooting a piece of falling paper and you nail it in three takes! Unbelievable!"

I turn in my costume and paperwork. By 12:30 AM, I'm back home. The adrenaline is beginning to wear off. I am in a dream state. It's like: Did what just happened just happen? Am I in the Twilight Zone? I get inside, look in the bathroom mirror: "It's for real! You did it! You spoke lines in a movie, a Francis Ford Coppola movie no less!"

The following Monday morning I get a call from Agent Orange. He says, "Fred Roos loves you!"
I say, "What?"
He says, "Fred Roos loves you! You nailed it! How many takes did it take you?"

I say, "Three."

He says, "Do you have any idea how much money you saved the production?"

I say, "No."

He says, "A ton! They're going to give you a bonus, pay you double scale."

Now my imagination is running wild. Fred Roos loves me. Maybe Francis will cast me as Sonny Junior in *Godfather III*!

SPEAKING OF THE GODFATHER

Right after Tucker, I get a booking at the Comedy Cabaret at Caesar's in Lake Tahoe. Across the street at the Horizon, Wayne Newton is doing his tribute to Elvis. Wayne's new schtick is that Wayne is a Native American and Elvis appeared to him in a vision and passed him the mantle, and now he is carrying the mantle for Elvis.

So I'm walking down the sidewalk in front of Harrah's, the baseball playoffs are on, suddenly a door flies open and two guys, the size of NFL linebackers, explode out of Harrah's. One guy is wearing a Giants windbreaker and the other guy is wearing an Astros jersey. They are wailing away, punching each other silly. A crowd gathers to watch the fight. I'm standing there watching along with everyone else and a black dude, who is standing next to me watching the fight says, "Man, ain't that stupid? That's like me wanting to fight you because I wear BVD and you wear Fruit of the Loom!"

I tell the story that night on stage and it gets laughs.

I finish my set and now I am on an in-house phone in Caesar's and I call backstage to the Main Showroom. A couple of comics I know are there, Mitch Walters, who I know from the Comedy Store and Steve Kravitz, who I know from San Francisco. They are one half of "The Outlaws of Comedy" and are the opening act for Sam Kinison.

"Oh hey, yeah Giovanni, hey man we're having an after-hours party in the spa with Sam. Why don't you come by and check out our show, and then we'll hang after the show…"

"I have another show myself, man, I'll come over after that. Is it okay if I bring Jim Samuels?"

"Who?"

"Jim Samuels is at the Cabaret with me. Is it OK if I bring Jim along?"

"Oh yeah, great, sure bring Jim. I'd love to see him!"

"There are a couple other guys if it's OK, the sound guy and the light guy…"

"It's cool man, bring them too."

Originally Jim Samuels and the sound guy and the light guy and myself planned on going to a little bar called the Rusty Duck or some such name in South Lake Tahoe to play darts and drink beer after the show, but this changes everything. I inform the rest of the guys about the invitation and right away the sound guy and the light guy are apprehensive. "I don't feel good about this. I don't think we should be partying where we work…"

"Don't worry about it man. Kinison's the headliner! It's a chance to hang with Sam Kinison! I haven't seen Mitch Walters in years. I haven't seen Mitch since the Comedy Store. I'd love to see Mitch and Steve Kravitz. I haven't seen Steve Kravitz since the time in San Francisco he was a passenger in a car and the driver slammed on the brakes and Kravitz broke his nose flying head first into the windshield…!"

I talk the sound guy and the light guy into it. Samuels knows Mitch and Steve. He's already game.

HOLY BAT SHIT

It's my last set. I'm on stage and there is a good crowd in the cabaret, but I can't see them. The room is dark except for the spotlight shined on my head. "I feel lucky tonight folks. I am on a roll. Earlier this evening I went to make a phone call and stuck a quarter in the phone and got eight quarters back! True story!"

Vah-voom! Something flies by my head!

"Later tonight I'm going to hit the poker tables. I love poker. It's the only game you can win with a losing hand! Don't take my word for it, ask Sergeant Bilko, 'Look alive! Doberman, Paparelli, Fender, platooyaheya...!'"
Vah-voosh! Something flies by my head again!

"In the words of W.C. Fields, 'Never give a sucker an even break!'"

Fah-fwoosh!

"What the hell! Who's throwing shit?"

Somebody in the audience yells out, "It's a bat!"

"A what?"

"A bat! There's a bat flying around the room!"

Turns out, the bat is attracted to the spotlight on my head.

Oh, but the evening gets stranger. I finish my set and get off before the bat has a chance to shit on me. I head to the main showroom. I get there and Kinison is already halfway through his set. He is hunched over an enormous black grand piano, on top of which is a single silver candelabra with lit candles. Kinison is wearing a long dark overcoat and with a beret pulled over his head and long brown hair flowing out from under the beret down his shoulders. The room is dark except for a single spotlight on Kinison, who speaks softly into the microphone, "This song is dedicated to my ex-wife who is the inspiration for this and so many of my other songs. This one's for you dear: 'YOU BITCH! YOU WHORE! YOU WRECKED MY LIFE YOU FUCKING WHORE! AGH! AGH! AGH! AGH! AGH…!'"

Kinison is screaming and pounding on the piano as a young woman escorts a little old lady, who looks like she's about to keel over, down the main aisle out of the theater. This show is obviously not for the faint of heart. Just as I'm thinking, "The wrong guy got the bat!" a voice that sounds like Liberace comes over the PA system. "Sam."

Kinison stops and gets real quiet. "Who's that?"

The voice says, "It's me Sam, Liberace."

"Who? Who is it?"

"Liberace, Sam…"

"Liberace?"

"That's right, Sam."

"So, what's up, Lib?"

"Sam, you know how Elvis influences Wayne?"

"Yeah, Lib, Elvis influences Wayne. So…?"

"So I want to influence you the way Elvis influences Wayne."

"Sorry, Lib, you can't do that."

"Why not, Sam?"

"BECAUSE ELVIS DIDN'T DIE FROM SUCKING BIG DISEASED COCKS! AGH! AGH! AGH! AGH! AGH...!"

Now it is a stampede of little old ladies headed out the door.

After the show, the sound guy and the light guy and Samuels and I go over to the spa. It's after hours so a guard lets us in. We get in the spa and the first thing I see as I come through the door is Kinison baptizing two hookers in the swimming pool. We all sit down on chaise lounges by the pool, and someone hands us bottles of Corona. Kinison finishes with the hookers and gets out of the pool and sits down next to us. I've never met Sam Kinison before. He seems like a nice guy, pleasant, soft-spoken, surprisingly unlike the character I just witnessed on stage.

We're sitting there and "Outlaws" are running around with bottles of Courvoisier jumping into the swimming pool. Kravitz dives into the shallow end and breaks his nose. It's déjà vu all over again. Kravitz had a freshly broken nose the last time I saw him. Now he's staggering around with a new freshly broken nose.

Just when I think it can't get any crazier, Kinison and several of the Outlaws disappear into the dressing room. A little while later they reemerge wearing jumpsuits and are clearly packing heat. Kinison leans over and I see what appears to be a 9 mm automatic in a shoulder holster hanging under his jumpsuit. I don't say anything, but now I'm thinking, to paraphrase Waylon Jennings, "Don't you boys think you done took this outlaw bit a little too far?"

I don't think much else about it other than by the time we leave, I'm glad to be out of there. The next morning at 8 AM I get a call from the sound guy. "We're all in trouble, we're in deep shit. I may lose my job. I have to go in and explain what happened, you have to explain it...!"

I say, "Explain what?

Nothing happened!"

He says, "Kinison and them guys did $20,000 worth of damage to the spa last night and we're all implicated. They found cocaine residues all over the counters in the bathrooms…"

"I never did cocaine in my life! And I never even went to the bathroom in the spa!"

"I never went in there either, but that's not the point! You know those beers we were drinking?"

"Yeah?"

"They broke the locks off the beer coolers, the liquor cabinets, they broke shit, they're saying we did twenty thousand dollars worth of damage to the spa! I'm telling you they're holding all of us responsible! Management's pissed, these guys don't play around we're all in deep shit!"

Later that day I get to the casino and they call me into a back room at Caesar's. A guy who appears not to have any cartilage in his nose says, "What happened?"

Have you ever felt guilty even though you know you're innocent? People are looking at you like no matter what you tell them, they are not going to believe it? I try to explain to the guy with no cartilage in his nose the story and he keeps saying, "Yeah, yeah, right…!"

Finally I say, "Look, you guys got cameras everywhere, you know what happened!"

The guy with the cartilage-free nose gets a smile on his face and says, "Yeah, I know. I'm busting your balls. Okay you can go, but watch your step!"

I find out later Caesar's never gives anyone after hours use of the spa but makes a one-time exception for Kinison.

Apparently the whole thing starts when he slips in the bathroom and tells management he hurt his back and is going to sue them unless they give him after hours use of the spa. It is a total con job and Samuels and I and the light and sound guys get swept up in it. Fortunately they let us all off with warnings. You would think that they would ban the real culprits from ever playing Caesar's again but a few months later Kinison is back headlining, which proves the old adage: If you are a big enough draw to bring in high rollers, you can get away with damn near anything.

HEADLINER

Headliner status means nothing if you don't have the goods to back it up. Credits mean nothing if you are not funny. Earlier in this book-length set I mentioned how one of the perils of being the headliner in a comedy show is finding yourself in the awkward situation of having to follow an act that is stronger than you. As I previously mentioned, I'll never pull rank on a guy. If he's hard to follow, my job is not to complain about it. My job is to figure out how to follow him. It's as simple as that. If he kicks my ass the first night, I'd better figure it out by the second night. Otherwise it's going to be a long week. It's not his job to change his act and it's not my job to tell him to. My job is to meet the challenge no matter how strong it is. Believe me, there is a sense of pride and accomplishment when you do. It's fun having the last laugh. Most fun is seeing the look on their face when they say, "Top that, motherfucker," and you do. Ha!

TREE

One night I'm headlining a place in Santa Rosa called the Sweet River. It's a two-man show. Tree is the other comic. Tree is aptly named, big, rangy, formidable looking, about six foot three, with a shaved head wearing black wrap-around sun glasses black leather motorcycle jacket, black t-shirt, black leather chaps, boots, the works. He looks like a skinhead Mr. Clean. His act is anything but Mr. Clean. Tree does not ease into his act. He takes the stage like the Wehrmacht took Poland. To say he is imposing is an understatement. He immediately commands the audience: "YOU WILL LAUGH!" They do! The next thirty minutes is shock comedy, each line edgier than the line preceding it. I have to admit, it is funny, although this comes with a caveat, a warning if you will: It ain't for church folks or those who are faint of heart. In one bit he talks about resisting the urge to pleasure himself by pulling out his trusty Bible. He then says, "I open to page such and such chapter 12 verse six and I STICK MY COCK IN THE BIBLE AND I SLAM THAT PUPPIE SHUT!"

By now, the audience is in convulsions, the sacrilegious motherfuckers, so Tree pulls out a little Japanese paper fan and now he's fanning himself and carrying on like a gay cocksman at the Folsom Street Fair in San Francisco, regaling the audience with graphic descriptions of what some would call aberrant sexual behavior, visual cornucopias of bizarre and twisted sexually deviant shit, which of course has the crowd convulsed with laughter, the sick fucks. I have to admit I'm laughing too. It is pretty funny, although "pretty" may not be the operative word here. It ain't pretty, but it is funny! Tree destroys.

He leaves utter decimation in his wake. He exits to thunderous applause and I keep waiting for the applause to stop but it doesn't. Now the crowd is pounding on tables: "TREE! TREE! TREE!"

Tree comes back and does another five minutes and is even more outrageous the second time around. I don't think it's possible, but he tops himself! He exits and the process repeats itself, the crowd chanting in unison: "TREE! TREE! TREE!"

How do I follow this? The answer is: I don't, at least not the first night. I give it my best shot. The announcer gives my credits: "You've seen him on: Laugh In, Merv Griffin, Best of Times, Tucker..."

To say it's a struggle is an understatement. I walk out and burn my best 30 minutes in 15 just to get the audience to settle down enough to listen. I finally get them, sort of, but by then it's too little too late. I walk out of there, knowing full well I just got my ass handed to me. As I head to my car I'm hearing stuff like: "I really like the first guy. That first guy, Tree, he's really funny! The last guy, he was okay..."

"I think the last guy kind of sucked to tell you the truth...!"

They look over and see me. "Oops!"

Doesn't matter. I know the score. Tree: 1, me 0. I drive home that night vowing this is not going to happen again. I desperately need to figure out a way to follow this guy. This cannot happen again. I have less than 24 hours to figure it out. I know that tomorrow night is going to be even more intense. The place we played tonight, the Sweet River is a little restaurant/bar type situation. It is not a club per se. Tomorrow night we will be in Santa Cruz at OT Price's, a major Rock & Roll club with a real stage and a big time sound system and a much larger and rowdier crowd. If what happened tonight happens tomorrow night it's going to be a thousand times worse. It's going to devastate my comedy ego, not to mention it will probably be my last headlining gig at OT Price's. Wimping out and asking to go on before Tree is not an option. I have to find a way to follow this guy!

I don't sleep much that night thinking about it. Just as I'm about to drift off, I am jarred back to reality. The nightmare is real! What little sleep I get, I wake up thinking I've got less than twelve hours to figure this out. What am I going to do? I get up and my OCD kicks in. I have to run ten miles. If my streak gets broken I will really be bummed. At that point I won't give a shit about not being able to follow Tree. To break my streak six plus years into it, that's worse than not being able to follow Tree. The streak trumps Tree.

I gear up and head out the door, a good thing because for some strange reason ideas come to me while I'm running. Without trying, by the time I get back I have the answer. It's a simple equation, basic Comedy 101: If you are not rich and famous enough for the crowd to shut up and listen to you just because you're rich and famous, the easiest and most sure-fire way to follow an outrageous character is with a character of equal or greater outrageousness. If Tree's going to costume up, I'm going to costume up. If Tree's going to tear a page from the Marquis de Sade, I'm going to tear a page from Shecky Guthrie's book: "Bound for Funny"!

O.T. PRICE'S

I get to O.T. Price's and the place is packed. Now I am having second thoughts. What if the shit doesn't fly? I'm always nervous when I am trying out something new, especially in front of a large crowd. Tonight is especially nerve-racking because I am following Tree. I'm pretty sure my new stuff is going to work, but there's no way of knowing absolutely positively until I'm up there and hear the audience response. The show starts and Tree gets up. It's last night squared. Tree leaves the stage: The building's shaking. Bottles are rattling behind the bar. Drinks are walking off tables. "TREE! TREE! TREE!"

A couple of encores later, Tree is on top of the world. The crowd is on its feet cheering as he stands there, hands on hips, surveying the damage he hath just wrought, like Caesar surveying Gaul after having destroyed it. He puts on his dark wrap-around sunglasses and exits triumphantly strutting past me. The crowd is cheering. I'm thinking, "Damn, this dude really does look like the Terminator!"

Tree is too much of a gentleman to say, "Top that, motherfucker!" But I know he's thinking it.

It's my turn. I hand the MC a napkin with my new introduction on it. He gets on the microphone.

"Ladies and Gentlemen…"

The room is alive with the energy of Tree. It's more intense even than last night, way more intense.

"Ladies and gentlemen, may I please have your attention…?"

They are not settling down.

"May I please have your attention? We have more show for you, we need to go on with the show…!"

Now they are down to a slow simmer.

"Tonight we have a special guest! Before I bring out our headliner, we are honored to have with us a very special guest, a legend in the Southwest, world champion beer drinker and chili eater from Waco Texas, please welcome: Butt Butane!

I am wearing a pair of faded wranglers, a hand tooled leather belt with a buckle about the size of a small dozer blade, a beat-up pair of Justin cowboy boots and a straw Resistol cowboy hat that looks like it's seen it's fair share of horse wrecks. In my hand I have a can of Lysol. I've got my best redneck face on. I walk on spraying Lysol everywhere Tree just was. I spray all around the stage. I get to the microphone careful not to touch it. There is total silence in the room. I now have their rapt attention. I look down at a lady in the front. "Mam, did you see? Was he a-spittin' when he was a-talkin' up here? Did you see if he was a-spittin' on the microphone?"

She says, "I don't know…"

I spray the microphone down good with Lysol hear titters in the crowd. I milk it for all it's worth and finally in pured redneck say: "Who-ee! Tree! Ain't he somethin'?"

The crowd lets out a huge cheer. When that dies down, I say, "Yeah, Tree, man…I never had to follow a guy before that talked about deviated rectums and dick smokin' and sack suckin'…Hell, that ol' boy didn't leave me nothin' to talk about!"

The crowd roars. I pause and look at Tree in the wings.

"Just don't let none of your damn branches start growin'

in my direction, boy!"

Another big laugh, I'm getting warmed up. "My name's Butt Butane and I am the world champion beer drinker and chili eater from Waco Texas. I just got back from the chili cook off in Terlinga and let me tell you, after a week of eatin' chili and drinking beer, you couldn't take away my gusto with a hot air balloon!"

More laughs.

"I'm mighty proud of myself! I just qualified for the World Cow Chip Throwin' Championships next month in Beaver, Oklahoma!"

Just the mention of "Beaver, Oklahoma" gets a laugh.

"Yeah, buddy, if it hadn't been for the dust devil that caught my chip and took it the extra 30 yards I'd a never qualified. I'm in training now. I'm on a strict diet: Mountain oysters and tequila..."

The tequila reference gets a big cheer!

"I knew it! Santa Cruz is full of hippie rednecks! We in KPIG country now!"

The KPIG reference gets an even bigger cheer.

"Speaking of tequila, why don't we all do shots?"

Now the bar is going crazy, within minutes there are 10 shots of tequila lined up on the stage in front of me. The management is ecstatic.

"Damn! It looks like we're fixin' to set some records at the bar.

Unlike the night before, this time after the show people are saying: "Great show, Butt!"

"Yeah, Butt, you're a real gas!"

Tree who?

BUTT

Ever since I read George Burns' books, I have been on the elusive quest to find a strong opening and a strong close for my act. Since I dropped the Ape Man ending, I really haven't had a strong close. I haven't had a strong opening since back when I used to come out as the Godfather. Most of the time I just get up and start talking, do my impersonations, finish with my football mime bit because it is a sure fire applause getter. Now, thanks to Butt, I have a strong original character to walk on as. I have an opening! Now all I need is a close. I ask myself. "What would George Burns do?" The answer is simple. "George would do a song of course!" I want to be like George, but I don't want to do anyone else's material, so my only choice is to write a song. I have never written an original song or even attempted to write one, but I have a pretty good idea of what needs to happen. When it comes to writing for my act, there are only two criteria. It needs to be original, and it needs to be funny.

As serendipity would have it, around this time I see the movie *Tender Mercies*. In it Robert Duvall plays a down and out country singer/songwriter. Duvall, one of my all-time favorite actors, wins the best actor Academy Award for his efforts. As impressive as winning the Academy Award is, for me the most impressive thing is when the final credits come up and I see Robert Duvall wrote his own songs for the movie. I'm thinking what the hell? If Robert Duvall can do it, so can I.

Hank Williams Junior is hot, and I'm a big Hank Jr. fan at the time, so I come up with the idea to write a satire of a Hank Junior song, not a parody, but an original satirical country song, signed, sealed and delivered by none other than Butt Butane his self. The first out the chute is a beauty if I say so myself, right up Butt's alley called: "You Can Keep the Baby, But Leave Me The Truck."

Jim as Buck

THE KEYSTONE

Tonight I have a gig at The Keystone in Palo Alto. I'm so jacked about doing the song on my way to the gig I get a ticket. Fuck it. I'll worry about traffic school later. Right now I just hope the song works. The most fun thing you can do if you're a comedian is to try out new material, but I'm saving it for my close, so I have to remember to be patient. I don't want to finish before my time is up. I know the song is going to work. I just need to relax and trust my instincts.

Now I'm on stage. There is great energy in the room. Everything is working. I'm excited about what I'm doing. The audience is on my side. I'm rolling right along. I have the tendency to race through my act, but I keep reminding myself of the words of the cop, "Slow down!"

Now the moment we've all been waiting for, the big close: "I'd like to dedicate this song to all you dee-vorced men out there. Do we have any dee-vorced men with us here tonight?"

Guys are yelling. "Yeah, I'm divorced! Yee-ha!"

This ain't exactly Hank Junior country, but then again, maybe it is. "Do we have any Hank Junior fans here tonight?"

There is a smattering of applause.

I have to cover for the fact I don't play guitar, so I say in my best Hank Junior voice. "I don't have no backup tonight because some squirrelly low life piss ant twinkle toe dip shit snot nose rat face motherfucker five finger discounted my guitar. I'd like to spit some beechnut in that dude's eye, I guarantee!"

I hear rebel yells. Oh, yeah, there are some Hank Junior fans here tonight.

"Since I ain't got no gui-tar I reckon I'm going to have to sing this one Acapelago..."

This gets a laugh.

"Here we go. You can keep the old hound dog..."

Now I'm singing, slapping my knee like I'm calling a square dance. The crowd is eating it up, stomping and clapping right along with me. I finish to huge applause. The crowd cheers as I walk off.

After the show a guy comes up to me and says, "You know, Butt, that song, I swear, you wrote my life! Everything you sang about happened to me, it's true no shit!"

Holy mackerel, Andy! I write satire and this dude thinks it's for real! Methinks I must be careful how I use my new-found super powers.

SONGWRITER

"Songwriting is Zen; Creating not knowing what will be. Do not birds sing their song not knowing what will be? As birds sing their song, so will you grasshopper."

"What does this mean, oh great master?"

"I don't know. I just pulled it out of my ass."

The songwriting bug done bit big time. Now I am writing songs around the clock. I think songwriting. I dream songwriting. In a month I write 100 songs. Of course, 99% of them are garbage so percentage-wise, I average one a month. Like the almond growers, "A song a month, that's all I ask…"

If I score a hit, I'll be on the map.

All I write is shit, mindless puerile crap.

I might become a star, may even write a book.

Anything is possible if I could find a hook.

KATIE ROSE

I am in full song writing fever when I meet Katie Rose, who is soon to become one of the more influential characters in my life. I first meet Katie at the Vallemar station in Pacifica, a place I frequent occasionally. I know it sounds like an oxymoron but it isn't. See, I perform there occasionally, but tonight I am not performing, I am frequenting. I'm not there to see Katie Rose per say. She just happens to be in there, doing her thing and I just happen to be in there and, boy do I see her! How can I miss her? Katie is bigger than life, way bigger! She's like a blonde-headed woman version of Pavarotti. The crazy thing, she can sing like Pavarotti! This chick is wild! So I walk in and Katie's onstage holding court and she really has the crowd going. She's banging out songs on a guitar, belting them out. Katie's a big voice woman, like Kate Smith or Ethel Merman or Sophie Tucker, louder than anyone in the room, louder than any heckler and rowdier.

A drunk is heckling her as I'm walking in. She actually plays with him for a while, like a cat would play with a mouse. She's up there capping on the guy and he's blathering away incoherently so she plays off that for a while and finally she decides she has had enough of the idiot, so she turns up the volume on her amplifier, and within seconds the guy's burnt toast. On stage, just her and her guitar, she is the master of her universe. As long as she is up there, the crowd is hers. And Katie is known for her ability to stay up there. She's halfway through a 3½ hour set right now, belting out requests, doing shots of tequila with the crowd. She hasn't stopped to take a piss and doesn't look like she's ready to anytime soon. The crowd is with her all the way. The place is packed and none of them look like they're getting ready to leave. I ask the bartender about it and he says the shots she is slamming are real. He says, "Katie is unbelievable. She doesn't even stop to take a piss."

Holy shit! This chick is heavy duty! Now I have to stay 'til the end. I wait until it's over and, as the crowd is thinning out and Katie is packing up her stuff, I come up to her and say, "Katie Rose, I'm Jim Giovanni. I'm a comedian I play here too..."

She goes, "Oh hi Jim Giovanni. I've heard of you. I hear you are really funny."

I say, "I am funny, Katie, but I can't believe you! You are unbelievable! You do what I wish I could do!"

She says, "Oh, really? What's that?"

I say, "I mean, I can do 45, sometimes an hour if I'm hot but I mean you're on stage for 3 1/2 hours! To hold their attention for 3 1/2 hours and not stop to take a pee, that's unbelievable!"

Katie says, "Well, I got to pee now, so would you mind watching my stuff for me. I hate to walk away and just leave it."

I say, "Yeah, sure, Katie. I'll watch it like it's the crown jewels."

"Watch it like it's your family jewels."

She walks away. She's not staggering. She's not slurring her words. Who is her father, Jackie Gleason? She comes back a few minutes later. I say, "Katie, I am a songwriter. I would like to write a song for you. What would you like me to write a song about?"

She says, "You know, I've always wanted a song about those guys that come up at the end of the night and they're always shitfaced drunk and they're slobbering all over the place and they come up to me and say, 'You know, hey baby, you know you look pretty good for a fat broad.' And they're always the guys with the 'No Fat Chicks' bumper sticker on their pickup truck. I'd like a song about those dumb ass peckerwoods."

I say, "You got it."

She gives me her phone number. The next day by mid-afternoon I have the song. I tweak it a little and call Katie around 4 PM. I wait till four because I figure that's probably about the time she gets up. Katie answers the phone. I say, "Katie, this is Jim Giovanni. I have the song!"

Katie says, "My, you do work fast!"

I say, "You want to hear it right now?"

She says, "I really am in a hurry to get out of here. Do me a favor. Do you have a tape recorder?"

"Yeah."

"Can you make me a tape of it and write out the words on a lyric sheet?"

I say, "I don't now know how to write music but I know someone who can..."

She says, "I don't need sheet music. All I need is a tape of the song so I can hear the melody and a lyric sheet with the words on it."

I say, "If I get one for you, do you read sheet music?'"

She says, "Not enough to hurt my pickin'. Don't worry about the sheet music. All I want is a tape with the melody and the words on a lyric sheet."

I say, "OK, how do I get it to you?"

She says, "I am at the Tar and Feathers tonight. Can you meet me there?"

I say, "What time do you start?"

She says, "Nine."

I say, "I'll see you there."

TAR AND FEATHERS

By the time I get to the Tar and Feathers, Katie is already on stage, singing, slamming shots, bullshitting with the crowd. I walk in and find a seat near the stage and just as I am sitting down, Katie spots me because I am waving at her and she says, "Oh, guess what everybody a friend of mine just walked in. Jim Giovanni, he's a comedian. He's really funny. Hey Jim, do you mind doing ten minutes while I take a leak?"

What am I going to say? "Gee, no Katie. I'd rather sit here and watch you suffer." I say, "Yes" of course. Twist my arm. I'm one of those guys the light bulb goes on in the refrigerator and I do 20 minutes. So I'm on stage in the Tar and Feathers and I am doing my sure-fire impersonations and the crowd's digging it, laughing at my stuff and about five minutes into it the front door flies open and in comes a rugby team en masse fresh from the playing field. They are grass stained and covered with mud and drunk as shit and they immediately start a scrum in the middle of the main bar and now they are knocking over tables and patrons are scattering out of the bar every which way. Talk about getting upstaged. There is no wall separating the bar from the showroom and you can see everything. The attention of everyone in the showroom is no longer on me, but rather on the scene going on out in the bar. The only thing I can think to do is to announce as loud as I can over the PA system, "Oh, look, the Aussies are here!"

This stops the scrum. Now they're all looking at me. One of them says, "Look at the faggot on stage, mate!"

So I say in my best Australian accent. "You Aussies are

the faggots, mate! Why do you think they call them from down under?"

This gets a big laugh. Now I am in uncharted territory. I've never pissed off an entire Australian rugby team before. I figure I am probably safe as long as I stay on the stage. Before I say another word, the heckler yells out, "You're the faggot mate!"

I say, "Gee, how clever! Where have I heard that before?"

"Faggot!"

"Is there an echo in here?

"A bloody pooftah, that's what you are!"

"I'm beginning to think you have an obsession with the subject, which indicates to me you may be a you a tailgunner yourself. You definitely look like a breechloader to me..."

"I'm no bloody poofter!"

"What is it then? Oh, I get it! You have a little itty-bitty cock, right? Am I right? You guys shower with him! Am I right?"

One of the other ruggers yells out. "You're right, mate! He's hung like a bloody field mouse!"

Now the rugby guys are laughing.

I say, "Gee, that's too bad. I bet the sheep are disappointed! Although when it comes to shagging gnats, I bet you're a real stud!"

This gets big laughs. Now I'm singing: "Tie me kangaroo down, sport. Tie me kangaroo down..."

Just as I'm beginning to think maybe I'm not so safe up here after all, the Cavalry arrives in the form of Katie Rose: I say, "Alright ladies and gentlemen let's hear it once again for the one and only, the Queen of the Kasbah,

Katie Rose…!"

The crowd cheers!

"Who I bet could drink this Aussie poof under the table any day."

Which immediately unleashes a torrent of hoots and catcalls. I walk off the stage and straight to where the Aussie's are. I figure I'm going to have to deal with the situation sooner or later and it might as will be sooner. They all have drinks. I can't believe the house is serving them, but they are. I guess the house figures it will be less trouble to serve them and have them destroy the place than not serve them and have them destroy the place anyway. The heckler draws an immediate bead on me. The minute we make eye contact I know it's on. This could get ugly quick. Within seconds he is in my face standing square in front of me blocking my path. We are toe to toe nose-to-nose, and he says, "What say we go outside and have a go, yank!"

I look him in the eye, smile and say: "She's right, mate!"

He gets a look on his face like he's thinking: "Maybe I don't want to do this, maybe this is not such a good idea after all." He hesitates, he looks at me eyeball to eyeball and says: "You know that bloody Jap shit, don't you?"

By now my smile is a shit-eating grin. I say, "She's right, mate!"

He hesitates. I can see the wheels turning in his pea brain. Finally he says, "Piss off!" and walks away.

Now the biggest guy on the team is staggering towards me. Just as I'm thinking, "Here we go!" he puts his hand on my shoulder and says, "I hate it when me mates can't handle their grog!"

I say, " It is a bummer, isn't it?"

"I like your style, mate! Buy you a beer?"

"Fair dinkum!"

He says, "I have a question, mate!"

I say, "What?"
He says, "How did you know we were Australian?"

I say, "Lucky guess, I reckon…"

So now I'm drinking beer with the Aussies waiting for Katie to come off. Around 1:30 AM, she finally does. I say, "You surprised me asking me to get up there. I thought you never had to piss."

She says, "I didn't. You just happened to show up right about the time the Aussies usually come in."

"Gee, thanks Katie."

I give Katie the tape and my hand-written lyric sheet and bid her adieu.

NO FAT CHICKS

About a month goes by. I've forgotten about it, the phone rings and it's Katie Rose. She says, "Man, I really owe you!"

I say, "For what?"

She says, "You know that song you wrote, 'No Fat Chicks'?"

"Yeah...?"

I'm kicking ass with that song, man. I'm making more money on tips. I had a guy come up the other night three times and throw a twenty-dollar bill down and say, 'Sing it again!' Three times he threw down a twenty! People love it, man. You wouldn't believe the tips I'm getting off that song! It's a hit! It's my most requested song!"

"Gee, that's great Katie..."

"I feel like I owe you, man."

"You don't owe me. If you record it I want the credit as the song writer..."

"Of course, but in the meantime I feel like I owe you, I've got to give you something..."

"You don't need to give me anything..."

"I know I don't "need" to but, you know how you were saying you wish you could play guitar?"

"Yeah...?"

"I've got a guitar I want to lay on you, man."

"But I can't..."

"It's a good guitar, man, it's a Takemini copy of a Martin D18 but it's a good guitar."

"Katie, it's not going to do any good. I don't know how to play..."

"You can learn. You're not trying to be Stevie Ray Vaughn. All you need to do is learn a few open chords, enough to accompany yourself on guitar. You're a singer/songwriter. You need to learn to be able to at least accompany yourself..."

"I'm not really a singer either..."

"Bullshit! I heard you! You gave me a tape. Remember? On it, you are singing. For the type of stuff you sing, your voice is perfect. I'm giving you the guitar. Get your ass over here right now before I change my mind. And I'm not giving it to you so you can leave it sitting in the case! Take some lessons learn your open chords you'll be playing in a week!"

There's nothing like a good swift kick in the ass to get one jump-started. Now I'm excited about getting the guitar. I'm going to do this. I get to Katie's, she pulls out a beat-up case with a KEEN Country sticker on it, opens it and pulls out the guitar, which like the case, looks it's seen its share of road.

"She's got a few dings in her and the fret board is a little worn but she still plays real good."

"You're going to have to find a guitar teacher, I got the name of a guy, you want to play country talk to Pete Charles. Pete is a country guy he has his own band. I'll get you Pete's number. Call Pete and take lessons from him. Pete teaches guitar. Call him and tell him what you want to do. All you need to do's start with your basic open chords, some basic strums. If want to do the Johnny Cash stuff, you have to learn the alternate base. Later on if you start getting good, you'll want to go to the bar chords like the big boys, but for now, for what you are doing, all you need is your basic open chords. That's all Johnny Cash plays. Look at him! I'd say he's done pretty well just playing open chords, don't you think? You say you want to learn to play like Johnny Cash? Call Pete."

"Gee thanks Katie! Thanks again for the guitar! Are you sure you don't want anything for it?"

"Are you kidding? Thanks for the song, man. I wish I could give you more but right now..."

"If you record it and it's a hit just remember I want the writing credit!"

"You got it man!"

I leave Katie's stoked, hyper focused on learning how to play. Katie's right. Within a few days, thanks to her and Pete, I've got sore fingers and just enough chords to get me into trouble. Less than a week after my first lesson I take the guitar on stage with me at Casa Caralita's. All I have is one song and three chords. I know the song works because I perform it a cappella and it always works, but accompanying myself on guitar is another story. This adds a whole other level of apprehension to the deal. I keep telling myself if I really suck, I'll make a joke about how bad I suck and get off. David Allen's advice about not burlesquing an instrument unless you can play the shit out of it is out the window. It's swim or sink time! There's a good crowd that night. They are rowdy but not too rowdy. They are with me all the way through my act. Now the moment of truth: I pull the guitar out and say, "I'd like to dedicate this song to all you dee-vorced men out there. Do we have any dee-vorced men with us here tonight?"

I get the usual response.

"Here we go. It's in the key of A. Alright 1,2,3,4..."

I start strumming the guitar. "'You can keep the old hound dog and...'"

Now I have my tongue stuck out looking cross-eyed at the fret board trying to find D and the audience is laughing. I'm fucking up and they are laughing. I finally find D: 'Brand new VC…' Oh fuck! Don't tell me, another chord change already? Only two strums of D and it's already back to A? Where the fuck is A? Here it is!"

They howl at this.

"'R! You can keep the stereo and (E is easy) you can keep the car. You…' A, where the fuck is A…?

"I found it! Fucking A!"

A big laugh and cheer!

"Where the fuck was I?"
"Who cares? Just keep going, Butt!"

"Oh, yeah, 'You can keep the ranch style house with the…' Where the fuck is D…?"

My tongue is all over the place trying to find D. The crowd roars. Women are screaming. "My, God! Look at his tongue!"

"I found it!"

The crowd cheers again!

"'…Neighbors who…' Oh shit here's that pesky A again! A! 'SUCK! You can keep the baby but (E is easy) leave me the (A) TRUCK!' Fucking A! I did it!"

I have to wait for the applause to die down. I say, "I've got another verse. Want to hear it?"

Another verse and two choruses, everything kills, afterwards people come up to me. "Hey, Butt! That shit's hysterical."

"Yeah, Butt, I remember when I first learned how to play guitar. That's some funny shit, dude!"

It's funny how that works. Sometimes the first time you do a bit it's the best. It's that good old white belt Zen, getting laughs without a clue how or why. Comedy comes so effortlessly and naturally, it's total spontaneity and it happens without trying. You can't duplicate it. It just happens. When it does, it's magic.

I call Jim Stafford the next day and tell him about it. Jim says, "That won't last long. Once you start getting good on the guitar you're going to lose that."

Jim's right. It doesn't take long. Right now I've only got three chords and three songs, but look out world! Here comes Butt!

GUITAR ACT

It's funny how after seventeen years of doing standup I am suddenly classified as a guitar act. Take a guitar on stage and I am immediately pigeonholed. I am in Tommy T's in San Leandro one night and a well-known headliner whose name I will not mention starts calling me out after I get a huge reaction with my guitar, saying, "That doesn't count!"

I say, "What 'doesn't count' the standing ovation I just got?"

"You'd never have got that if it wasn't for the guitar. You're not really a stand-up. You're a prop comic."

"Prop comic? What are you talking about? What props did I use? I didn't use any props."

He says, "The guitar. The guitar's a prop."

I say, "What? The guitar is a prop? I beg to differ. The guitar is not a prop. I actually accompanied myself with it so that makes it a musical instrument, not a prop. Besides, I did forty minutes before I ever pulled out the guitar. So what props did I use? I'm still waiting for you to tell me...!"

He says, "The cowboy hat and raincoat are props!"

I say, "No, the cowboy hat and raincoat are costume, which is a totally different department. You'd better not get Costume and Props mixed up if you go to Hollywood. The union guys will kick your ass. The musicians' union is strong too. You'd better not tell musicians their instruments are props."

He's dumbfounded. I can see the wheels turning. I say, "Oh, you know, I take that back, you're right, come to think of it, I did use props. Colombo's cigar and his notebook are props. Be sure to turn them into the prop department when you're finished with them or you'll be in deep shit."

He says, "What you do is not standup."

The wall in Tommy T's is adorned with giant black and white images of Laurel and Hardy, WC Fields, Charlie Chaplin, the Marx Brothers, Buster Keaton. I point to the wall and say, "Look at the wall."

He says, "Yeah...so?"

"All prop comics, every one of them, there is not a standup in the bunch, yet these are the most iconic comedians of the twentieth century. That's why their picture is on the wall of this and a lot of other comedy clubs. Unlike a lot of guys who call themselves standups, these guys are actually funny!"

The king of comebacks has no comeback. That's the last time he calls me a "prop comic" to my face.

I chalk it up to this: Comedians in general are a jealous bunch. Not all of them, I'm sure some are well adjusted, but to my experience, many are pretty insecure people. I know. I'm one of them. I have already documented my own insecurities here, especially in relationship to Robin Williams. But it's like getting snakebit. If you survive the initial bite, after a while, with each subsequent bite, you build up immunity. Pretty soon nothing bothers you.

Okay, so what's my next move? Join a Pentecostal group and handle actual snakes? Come to think of it, that would be a hell of a lot safer than some of the rooms I play. In some of these dives I'm less of a snake charmer and more of a lion tamer. The lion tamer analogy is good since every night I walk on stage is like sticking my head in a lion's mouth. Many of the rooms I play are notoriously rowdy. It's the eighties and it's the Wild West as far as the comedy scene goes. Many of the comics I have to follow aren't interested in getting on TV. If you are one of the ones who survive, if you are reading this, you know who you are. It's a safe assumption that when your whole act is talking about pussy and blow, chances are you are not looking to score a gig on the Tonight Show. Chances are you're looking to score pussy and blow. Since a healthy percentage of the eighties audience is looking to score pussy and blow, it makes your job easy. You are an evangelist at the Church of Pussy and Blow preaching to a flock of true believers.

I don't do cocaine. I never did. My reasoning is simple. I make a conscious effort not to complicate my life and nothing complicates like cocaine. In the eighties cocaine is ubiquitous. It is hard to avoid. There are times I am tempted, people say it won't hurt me, but I don't believe them. I always remember the words of a Dave Van Ronk song: "Cocaine: They say it's for horses and not for men they tell me it will kill me but they don't say when. Cocaine running all around my brain..."

It's a good thing I never get involved with coke. I probably would not be writing this book if I had. A lot of guys I know, some of them real good comics, go down the tubes fast behind it. It all starts with, "Just try it. It will make you funnier...!"

You have to admit it's a pretty good enticement if your whole goal in life is to be funny. The problem with coke is, pretty soon the initial funny wears off and all of you are left with is desperation in its purest form. Forget the funny. Now the only thing that matters is scoring more coke. I've seen it time and time again. You've heard the expression: "Don't knock it if you haven't tried it."

Here's my motto: DON'T TRY IT AND YOU'LL NEVER MISS

IT!

The only downside to not doing coke is it adds a degree of difficulty to the gig getting process. In many cases getting the gig depends on being part of the scene. Comics are turning on promoters and vice versa. If you're not part of the scene, forget about it. This locks me out of a lot of gigs. I tell myself this is a marathon, not a sprint. I want to be there at the finish line. Gigs come and go. Comics come and go. You want to be like George Burns, remember?

IT'S A SHITTY BUSINESS

I doubt George had to go through some of the shit I have. Promoters can be extremely petty people. If you work for this guy over here, you can't work for me and vice versa. I work for lots of people but I don't let anyone tell me who I can work for and who I can't work for. If I sign a contract to work for you exclusively, that's one thing, but petty turf wars between small-time promoters, I don't have patience. My act is a sure-fire crowd pleaser, I'm easy to work with, I promise to be on time and professional, but I am an owner operator and if you try to dick me around I will gladly tell you to fuck off. Most of these promoters know where I stand and don't pull the petty bullshit with me they pull on other comedians. They don't exactly put me at the top of their list for plum jobs either. Many times, they use me as a last-minute replacement for somebody who canceled. I'm the guy who comes out of the bullpen to save the game. Since many comedians during this time period are known for being notoriously unreliable, many of my gigs are under such circumstances.

I guarantee George Burns never had to play some of the dumps I play. I do comedy runs in the hinterlands drive hundreds of miles between gigs. I do one eight night hell run for $1200, average $150 a show and then the promoter makes me wait a month to pay me. When he finally does, he bounces a check on me for $1,200. As if that's not injury to insult, I'm doing a great job for the guy, kicking ass in famously tough rooms. A lot of comics wither in these rooms. But in these rooms Butt is in his element. It makes no bit of difference how rowdy the room, like Hank Jr. Butt will rowdy 'em up even more. "The rowdier the better!" is Butt's motto. Management in these places loves it. Butt sells beer! But that doesn't matter to the dickhead who bounces the check on me. All that matters to him is that he burns me for an extra $1,200 to shove up his nose. The really hard part is this happens at a time when the mortgage is due, bills are due. I'm counting on the money to make my nut, and this dirt bag screws me out of money that I busted my ass for and did a great job to boot. I figure when I do great it makes him look good. You think he would realize this, but this idiot not only doesn't realize or appreciate it, he doesn't care. And now that he's screwed me, not only does he not answer the phone or return my calls, he ceases to book me altogether in rooms that I did a great job in. I lose both the money I've already earned, and any future gigs working for the guy. It's a double hose job.

Make that a triple. He's fucked me, he's fucked the club owners and their audiences out of having me back, and he's fucked himself in terms of his own karma. Karma doesn't waste any time on this idiot. One day not long after bouncing the check on me, I hear the idiot got jacked up on drug deal gone bad and some not so nice guys left him in motel room, duct taped to a chair with duct tape over his mouth. They hung the "do not disturb" sign on the door and left him there for two days shitting in his pants. I have to admit I feel good old-fashioned schadenfreude when I hear that. Oh yeah, I believe in karma. If this isn't an example of karma biting a worthy recipient on the ass I don't know what is.

Another time a different douchebag promoter screws me out of $600, the irony being the gig is a fundraiser for the sheriff's department. I do the gig, it's in a theater, sold out, the place is packed, Butt kills, my act kills, the sheriffs love me. You can't go wrong playing Colombo to a room full of cops. I'm a hit and afterwards everybody's telling me how I should be arrested because I murdered!

So Douchebag the Promoter gets money from the sheriffs' department for me, probably a lot more than the six hundred he's paying me. He makes me wait a month for my money and finally he sends me a check for $600, and it bounces, which sets off a chain reaction causing me to bounce my mortgage check, etc. Now my wife's pissed off at me telling me to get a real job and it's back to the old drill of me calling him and him not answering my calls, and pretty soon I give up and write it off as another karmic rat fuck to come for Douchebag the Promoter.

Again, it comes sooner rather than later. I get to administer the karmic rat fuck personally myself which is especially delicious. I happen to be at a very talented musician friend of mine's house one day when Douchebag calls and tries to hustle my buddy for a gig. I can hear Douchebag on the speakerphone. I say to my buddy, "That's the douchebag who fucked me out of $600!"

My buddy tells Douchebag, "Don't call back here again until you pay Giovanni the money you owe him!"

Now I'm Groucho on the speakerphone: "If you don't want a karmic fucking, don't fuck the fucking comic."

CLICK!

Speaking of karmic fucking, how about those Cubs?

For a while there I work for another booking agent with an even more creative way of screwing the talent. He's so clever about it he hoses me good for a couple of years before I even figure out I am being hosed. Here's how it works. I am talent and I am hungry. I am doing a lot of shitty $150 headline gigs where I have to drive my ass off, eat crappy food, go without sleep and basically beat myself up on the road to eke out a meager living, such as it is.

So this guy calls me up and he says he's got a gig for me. I'm going to do six nights for $1,500. All I need to do is a half hour as opposed to my usual forty-five to an hour plus. And the best part is I don't have to go on the road to do it. The gig is a forty-five-minute drive from my house. Sounds like a great deal, doesn't it, $350 a show for six nights? To me it's manna from heaven.

So I agree to the thing, and he sends me a contract and I sign the contract. He tells me to dress up and keep my act clean. Unlike many of the comics working the circuit, he knows I am capable of squeaky. I can work PG, no problem. And I am consistent. I am sure-fire funny. He knows I am going to make him look good and the client happy. These are all pluses on the side of him taking care of me, right?

Wrong!

I get to the gig the first night and realize right away it's much bigger deal than I thought. It's in Palo Alto and it's a banquet dinner for 600 Hewlett Packard employees. I'm thinking $350 is a little light for this scene, but I agreed to it and I already signed the contract so I go ahead and do my act and I do great and the crowd loves it. I'm a star from Laugh-In and I do Columbo and Patton and the Godfather all these great impressions and I'm a hit.

Methinks he's billing me big with the folks at Hewlett Packard in more ways than one. I call him the day after the gig and I say, "Hey you know you're only paying me $350 to do thirty minutes of standup for 600 people. This is a corporate gig! I should be getting more than $350!"

And he says, "Oh, no, well, you know, I have all these expenses yada yada yada I have to pay the band yada yada and that's all I could get for you yada yada yada I'm not making any money on this myself yada yada yada and besides you signed a contract yada yada yada...!"

This doesn't pass the smell test, but yeah, you're right, I signed the contract.

I do five more of these shows, each a carbon copy of the one before, each a dinner for 600. Apparently, there are so many Hewlett Packard employees they can't do all of them at once, hence six dinners. My act kills at all of them. I'm not about to short the crowd just because I suspect this guy is shorting me. I have my pride. I do my best and my best kicks ass. At the end of the six nights I get a check for $1,500. His check clears, that's one good thing I can say about the guy.

FOOL ME ONCE

So here I am limping along living my life of quiet comic desperation wondering how I am going to pay the mortgage this month and the promoter calls again. This time it's a dinner for the plumbers' union in Oakland. He gives me the same song and dance how all he can afford to pay me is $350, there's nothing in it for him, he's doing a favor for a guy, it's for a small crowd yada yada yada...!"

For me the $350 is coming just in the nick of time. The crazy thing is that it always seems to work that way. Just as things look the bleakest, it looks like the swamp is about to swallow you whole, you get the gig that gets you to the next lily pad. I kind of have a hunch I'm getting screwed, but what can I do? Who knows? Maybe he is telling the truth. Don't argue with the guy. You need the money. Take the gig.

I say, "OK" and he gives me the usual spiel that I am going to be paid by him after the gig after he gets the money from the client he'll pay me and I am not supposed to discuss money with the client. So I agree and he sends me the usual bullshit contract, which I sign and send back to him.

I get to the gig and it's a big dinner, not as gala as the Hewlett-Packard affair, it's in a union hall, but it is a good size crowd, everybody's dressed up, it's a big event. It's a lot bigger than what is described to me on the phone. I get there during cocktails. There's a sleight of hand magician doing walk around showing everybody close-up magic tricks. Someone comes up to me and says, "Are you the comedian?"

I say, "Yes."

"Come on. I want you introduce you to the president."

It turns out the president of the plumbers union is a fan of standup comedy. He insists I sit next to him during dinner. He digs my jokes. We have a great time. After dinner it's the usual after dinner speeches, inducting new officers and stuff. Then I come on. I'm dessert, the icing on the cake entertainment portion of the show. I do my usual. My act kills. Everyone loves it. The president loves it. He thinks I am hilarious. I finish and get off and take my seat next to him and I'm sitting there and the magician comes over and asks for his check and the president hands it to him and I glance at the figure on the check and it's for $750. I don't say anything, but I kind of gulp and do an obvious double take and the president picks up on it and he looks at me and says, "What's wrong?"

I say, "I am somewhat taken aback...!"

He says, "Taken aback by what?"

I say, "By the size of the check you just handed the walk around guy."

He says, "What's the problem? You're getting fifteen hundred."

I say, "I am? He's getting fifteen hundred for me?"

"He's getting more than that. "

"How much is he getting?"

"I agreed not to discuss that with you."

Now my wheels are really turning. The $350 a show he paid me for Hewlett Packard, what was he charging them for me, $3,500 a show? This asshole has the whole agent/talent thing in reverse. He thinks it's 90% to the agent and 10% to the talent.

Q: What do comedians and hookers have in common?

A: When you've got "fuck you" money you don't need to be screwed by assholes.

It is a shitty business indeed.

TO SET THE RECORD STRAIGHT

On Saturday, December 23, 1972, at Candlestick Park in San Francisco, the Dallas Cowboys beat the San Francisco 49ers 30-28 in the divisional playoffs. With a few seconds left on the clock, driving and inches from being within field goal range, John Brody throws an interception to Charlie Waters and watches Waters run the opposite direction to end the 49ers season and advance Dallas to the Championships. I watch this "Oh, shit!" moment in real time on TV. The following Friday night I go on stage in the Holy City Zoo and perform it as Brody in a slow motion mime routine, complete with silent mouthing of the phrase, "What the fuck?" called time-out, sideline conference, more silent mime profanity, line up, silently mouthed calling of signals followed by interception and runback with Brody silently mouthing the words "Oh, shit!" as Waters runs by.

The bit kills and continues to kill to this day, forty-four plus years later. Of course it has evolved over the years as different quarterbacks have emerged as the goat, calling time out twice in a row as Marc Wilson, lining up behind the guard a la Bob Griese, but it's still variations on the original bit starring John Brody. It is arguably the best piece of original material I ever came up, the proof being that the bit has been ripped off by more comedians than any other of mine. So anyone who tells you it's his bit is full of shit. I first perform it on stage at the Holy City Zoo on December 29, 1972, so anybody who wants to argue with me about who's bit it is, there it is. If you can beat that date, power to you.

MERLE

Being typecast as a country comedian does have its upside. All of a sudden I get calls to do opening act gigs for big-time country artists. I've been a fan of many of these artists since I was a kid. Merle Haggard is the first big country name I open for. I open for Ray Charles at Keystone Palo Alto before that, but Ray is not known as country per se. When it comes to pure Country, Merle is the shit and when I get the gig I'm ecstatic. I decide to take some of the money I'm getting for the gig and hire a couple of sidemen to back me. Butt Butane and the Blue Flames are going to do it for real, opening for Merle Haggard no less.

I call Carl and his brother Paul, a duo of extremely talented musicians known as the Green Brothers. The idea is I'm going to do my comedy act, and at the very end I will bring the Blue Flames out to back me up on some original Butt Butane hits with Carl on pedal steel guitar, his brother Paul on base, and me on rhythm and vocals. The gig is at the Luther Burbank Center in Santa Rosa.

We get there the night of the show and are backstage and the stage manager comes up to me and says, "Are you the comic?"

I say, "Yeah."

He says, "How much time can you do?"

I say, "They told me do 30 minutes."

"That's not what I asked you. I said, 'How much time can you do?'"

Where have I heard this before? This has the distinct feeling of déjà vu written all over it. I say,

"I can do 45-50 clean, after that it's going to get a little raunchy..."

"Don't worry about it. Just get up there and do as much time as you can until I give you the sign to get off."

"What's going on? Why do you need me to do more time?"

The IRS just seized Merle's tour buses, they got 'em hooked up out in the parking lot and they're getting ready to tow all the band instruments, everything! Merle can't do the show until he negotiates a release for his shit..."

Suddenly I'm going through the mental Rolodex of every bit I know.

"The MC will introduce you just go out there and keep going until I give you the sign to get off."

"Aye Aye, sir!"

I am about to ship off into uncharted waters. The IRS. Lovely. So I'm waiting to go on, hanging out backstage with Merle's band guys, telling them how I have to come up with more material than I thought and I'm not sure how blue is too blue for this crowd and I ask if I can try something out on him. They say, "Sure. Go ahead!"

I sing a song I wrote about a donkey. The song is off-color, but very funny. Merle's guys think it's hilarious and tell me I should do it in my set. We are looking out through the curtains at the audience and it's a full house, packed, about twenty-five hundred people and I can feel the energy in the room. I'm standing there and I say, "I don't know. I'm still kind of nervous about this..."

One of the band guys says, "What are you nervous about?"

I say, "I'm nervous about being too dirty for this crowd.

Normally, I keep it clean out of respect for the headliner, out of respect for Merle…"

He says, "Are you kidding? You think Merle gives a shit? Look out there. Do you see any kids out there? I don't see kids. All I see is cowboy hats! They'll love that song! I'd do it if I were you!"

It's the story of my life. There is always someone there to egg me on, the bad angel on my shoulder.

The MC comes up and says, "Are you ready?"

I say, "Yeah."

The MC is a local DJ on the Country station in Santa Rosa. He goes out does his thing, makes announcements about upcoming events, etc. Then he introduces me. Unlike the time at The Great American Music Hall with Buddy Rich, this guy doesn't clue the audience in on the situation. I'm standing backstage, decked out in my best Butt Butane attire: Wranglers, cowboy belt buckle, Tony Lama boots, black T-shirt, Resistol straw hat. I look like a redneck trucker. The MC introduces me and I walk out and the audience is applauding and I get up to the microphone and say, "HOWDY!"

The crowd answers: "HOWDY!"

Ooh. Good crowd, I can tell already. I say, "My name is Butt Butane. A lot of you all may have heard of me. I got a band: 'Butt Butane and the Blue Flames' you may have heard of us…"

This gets applause.

"We have our fans, the Buttheads. Are there any Butt-heads here with us tonight?"

People start cheering. A guy yells out, "I'm a Butthead!"

"Looks like we got a whole bunch a Buttheads here to-night!"

Jim Giovanni

This gets a laugh.

"I love Santa Rosa! Santa Rosa is BIG BUTT Country!"

This gets a cheer followed by a delayed reaction laugh.

A guy yells out, "You got that right!"

He points at the woman sitting next to him. She starts hitting him.

"Whoa! Easy, mam, don't hurt the guy...!"

The crowd roars. This is almost too easy.

"Who-ee! We gonna have a time tonight!"
They cheer!

"Has anybody here ever been in jail?"

A lady yells out, "My husbands in jail!"

I say, "Your husband's in jail, mam? Why's your husband in jail?"

She says, "He got caught!"

This gets a laugh.

I say, "Why did he get caught?"

She says, "Because he's stupid."

This gets a big laugh. I haven't even told a joke yet and they're laughing. This crowd is into it. From then on I roll through my act like a freight train. About the time I'm around the 45-minute mark, I'm singing some song parody stuff solo on guitar and someone yells out, "Where's the band? You said you had a band!"

I say, "Are y'all ready for the band?"

This gets a smattering of applause.

"I said, 'ARE Y'ALL READY FOR THE BAND?'"

The crowd cheers!

"All right boys, come on out! I want to introduce you to, from Santa Rosa California, Butt Butane and The Blue Flames!"

Carl hits a few warm up notes on the pedal steel and the crowd cheers. This crowd is ready, oh yeah.

"Here we go, boys. One, two, three, four...!"

Carl hits the lead in on the pedal steel and the crowd goes crazy.

"'There's bullshit on my hat, bullshit in my hair'..."

The song is a great two-step. At least one couple gets up and starts dancing. We finish the song and a huge cheer goes up. I look to the wings and there is still no sign from management. I say, "Looks like we got time for another one, folks..."

The crowd cheers again.

"Not a problem for the Blue Flames. These guys can follow me anywhere in the key of A."

This gets a laugh.

No kiddin', folks. My goal in life is to write a thousand songs in the key of A. I have four to go!"

Another laugh.

"One, two, three, four...I ain't a comic genius. Robin ain't my name. Still I'm trying to make it in this business just the same. It ain't that I'm nasty and it ain't that I'm a slob, but if it weren't for dick jokes, I wouldn't have a job!"

The crowd roars on this one.

"Here comes one right now folks: A man one time found a donkey stuck in some quicksand. The human pulled the donkey out with his custom van. A year went by, the donkey found the man in the same fix. The donkey said, 'Don't worry, man, just grab onto my dick!' The donkey saved the human with his donkey dick. This story has a moral and the moral's this: I don't care if you're a donkey or if you're a man, if you got a big dick, you don't need a van!"

BOOM! The crowd goes ape shit!

I look over and now they're giving me the sign to get off, so I say "Goodnight!" and get off to big cheers. I'm backstage and everybody is slapping me five saying how funny I am and how great the Blue Flames sound. I'm a country star for a night! I'm anxious to meet the man and here he comes, the biggest star in the country galaxy with his entourage and he looks like he's been commiserating with his buddies Jim Beam and I.W. Harper. He doesn't look happy, so I figure it's probably best if I don't introduce myself at this very moment.

Merle blows by like a bad wind and now the roadies are setting up the instruments slapdash and next thing I know they are introducing Merle and he comes out and does thirty-five minutes and walks off and that's it, show's over. People are yelling for Merle to come back and he doesn't, that's all she wrote, "Badda beep badda beep a... 'That's all folks!'"

Now I'm out in the parking lot after the show and people are going, "Great show, Butt!"

"Yeah, Butt! Outstanding! You put on a better show then Merle!"

Two weeks go by and I get a call from the management of the theater. "Did you do some off-color material in your show when you were here opening for Merle Haggard?"

I think about it. "Off-color by whose standards? You mean the 'Bullshit Song'? I got the okay on that before the show."

312

"Not that song. The other song."

"You mean the donkey song? The crowd loved it!"

"Not everybody! People were offended. "

"Why? There weren't any kids there that I could see."

"There were ladies there that were offended you sung that song. This theater used to be a church!"

That explains it. Church ladies! I can hear them right now. "He sang about donkey dicks! This used to be a church! He sang about donkey dicks in a church! He's going to go to hell for that!"

Well, I may not go to hell but I sure as hell don't get booked back there, which once again proves the old show business truism: It ain't the ones that likes the show that writes the letters!

A DAY IN THE DIRT AT SAN QUENTIN

Bread and Roses is a group founded by Mimi Farina. Bread and Roses entertainers donate their services to perform at hospitals prisons, etc. It is pro bono work, a charitable contribution, if you will. I don't have much money but I can donate my time and services. One day I get a call from someone at Bread and Roses, and the Bread and Roses person asks me if I am interested in doing a show at San Quentin prison. I say, "Yes." I know Bread and Roses is an honorable organization. They do good work in the community and I am happy to help them if I can. It is also a chance to follow in the footsteps of one of my heroes, the legendary Johnny Cash. I can already picture the album cover: Me, dressed all in black with a guard tower in the background. "Butt Butane, live at San Quentin!"

This'll add to my country credentials: Nothing more country than prison.

Turns out I have no choice in the matter as far as clothing is concerned. They tell me that to do the show I cannot wear anything blue or anything denim. Even black Levi's are out. The deal is the prisoners wear blue and they wear denim and if there is a riot the guards on the catwalks with the M14s don't want to start shooting the wrong people. The best way for them to identify us performers is if we don't wear blue and we don't wear denim. "And oh, by the way, if there is a riot and you are taken hostage, they are not going to negotiate for your release."

"That's comforting to know. Anything else?"

"Yes. Do not under any circumstances bring contraband into the prison!"

"Smoke it before you get there, right? Willie's not the headliner by any chance, is he?"

"The headliner is Sheila E so keep it clean. It's a prison, but out of respect for Sheila E, we ask that you keep it clean."

"Roger that."

I get there the day of the show and I am all decked out in my best black dress slacks black pointy toe Tony Lama boots black dress shirt black Stetson hat black hand tooled leather belt with the silver Roy Rogers belt buckle. I am the man in black. I check in and they search me and now they are taking me through a bunch of metal doors that keep clanging shut behind us as we go. I have to admit, I have a somewhat romanticized image in my head of what this experience is going to be like. I picture them taking me to a mess hall where I will be up on the stage and there will be guards all around and the prisoners will be sitting in the mess hall looking up at me and they will all be white guys who look like John Dillinger with thirties style haircuts, Willie Sutton bank robber-types, and the whole scene will be right out of Jimmy Cagney in *White Heat*.

Wrong!

The next I know we're outside and they're taking me down a long ramp with a big cyclone fence running all the way down it. The fence separates the ramp from the main prison yard I presume to prevent the inmates from all getting out at once. We get to the bottom of the ramp into the main yard and I'm glad I brought a hat because it's about ninety degrees, and the sun is beating down, and there is no shade anywhere and now we are walking in the dirt because the ground is not asphalt. It's dirt.

So I'm walking in the dirt in my black shiny cowboy boots – which are now dusty black shiny cowboy boots – to the stage, which is set up to the right as you come off the ramp. It is a makeshift stage no bigger than a couple of large pallets on the ground in the dirt. The event is billed as: "A Day In The Dirt at San Quentin." This is ironic since they made me promise to keep it clean. I get to the stage and who is there but my old buddy Tree. Tree has no problem with the dress code. He's dressed in his usual black leather everything. Besides Tree, Norton Buffalo is there with his band and the Bread and Roses people as well.

I look out at the crowd and it's not *Escape From Alcatraz.* It's *Escape From New York.* John Dillinger, Jimmy Cagney, forget about it. Mad Max is more like it. These guys don't look like the "honor among thieves" crooks you see in the thirties gangster movies. It's the opposite of a rainbow coalition. White, black, Hispanic, Asian gangs segregated into sub-groups, buffed from pumping iron, shirts off tattoos in full display. The whole place is a tattoo convention of the jailhouse variety. Standing directly in front of the stage, surrounded by his crew, is a crazy looking white beard long hair biker dude with a swastika tattooed on his face.

Tree is first up, which kind of blows the whole concept of "keep it clean" right out the window. The Bread and Roses people tell me they want clean and they put Tree as the lead off act? When you want clean, lead off with the filthiest act you can think of, that's what I always say. Andrew Dice Clay is filthier but he isn't available. Tree is a good second choice. This crowd loves Tree. He gets to the part about slamming his dick in a Bible and the crowd cheers like it's the Roman Coliseum watching Christians get fed to the lions. I feel like a Christian waiting backstage to go on.

"Time to start praying, you're next!"

I am praying. I thank God I don't have to follow Tree. Norton Buffalo is going on between us. Tree wraps it up and gets off to his usual enthusiastic response, and the MC introduces Norton. Now Norton is on stage, and he's wailing away on the harmonica, and about halfway through his set Sheila E walks in. She is wearing a yellow dress and she is walking down the ramp with her entourage and it may as will be a fire truck coming down the ramp with the lights flashing and the sirens blasting because everybody in the place immediately forgets about Norton Buffalo and zeros in on Sheila E. Norton is on stage playing his ass off, and it's like no one even knows he's up there. And now I see why they have the fence because guys are jamming up against it like it's feeding time at the zoo.

"SHEILA E! SHEILA E!"
I get it. I'm the sacrificial lamb that gets to go on before Sheila E.

Norton wraps up and gets off and instead of applause it's "SHEILA E! SHEILA E!"

The MC introduces me. They are booing before I even walk out. "BOO! SHEILA E! SHEILA E! WE WANT SHEILA E! BOO!"

I am not deterred. My opening line is tailor made for these guys: "My name's Butt Butane and it's my first time here in San Quentin. I've never been here before, but I've been in jail. I was stupid. I shot up one of those deer crossing signs. Hell, they wouldn't have never caught me if I hadn't strapped the dang thing to the hood of my truck!"

"BOO! WE WANT SHEILA E! SHEILA E! WE WANT SHEILA E! SHEILA E! SHEILA E! SHEILA E! BOO…!"

I plow straight ahead for about eight minutes.

"BOO! WE WANT SHEILA E! SHEILA E! BOO! WE WANT SHEILA E! SHEILA E! SHEILA E! SHEILA E! BOO…!"

Finally realize, you know what? It's hopeless. I say, "All right guys, that's it. You win! I lose! Enjoy the rest of the show! I'm out of here!"

A HUGE CHEER goes up from the crowd. As I walk off I see my guitar and it's truly a last second play call at the line of scrimmage. I grab the guitar, turn around and walk back out to the microphone and say, "I wasn't going to do this, but fuck it! I got a song for you boys!"

I hit the first eight notes of Folsom Prison Blues, that famous eight note lead in everybody knows what's coming when they hear it. "BUM-BUM-BUM-BUM-BUM-BUM-BUM-BUM!"

A CHEER goes up!

"I hear the train a coming, it's coming after me. I'm stuck here in this hellhole I know I can't be free. Here in Folsom Prison let me tell you Bub, if you've got an asshole this ain't no country club!"

ROARS!

"I thought I'd be a big man and live a life of crime, but my lawyer sucked the big one and now I'm doing time...!

CHEERS!

"Here in Folsom Prison there's one thing I know. If you weren't born bowlegged, you will be when you go!"

ROARS!

"You think a life of crime, my friend, will make you feel big, but that ain't what you're feeling when your squealing like a pig..."

ROARS!

"Here in Folsom Prison there's one thing I know. You'd better not bend over if you drop the soap!"

"BUM-BUM-BUM-BUM-BUM-BUM-BUM-BUM!"

ROARS AND CHEERS!

I walk off and a guard says to me, "Boy, you hit 'em right where they live!"

Now I'm backstage which really isn't a backstage, you're just kind of there in the yard, and stage right there is a buffet set up for the performers and the crew. I'm standing there talking to a guy and it's like I'm looking at myself. We're about the same age I'm thirty-nine, I think he's thirty-eight, and we have the same salt and pepper hair. We start talking, I ask him where he's from, he tells me and I have cousins that live where he grew up. We start comparing notes and we have the same background Italian Portuguese Irish. He's wearing a brand new, out of the box black "San Quentin Day In The Dirt" t-shirt. I ask the guy, "Are you with Bread and Roses?"

He says, "No."

Just then I notice he's wearing blue jeans. I say, "Are you an inmate?"

He says, "No, I'm a convict." He points to the crowd. "Those guys are inmates. I'm a convict."

I say, "There's a difference?"
He says, "Yeah, there's a difference."

He nods.

I say, "Oh. How long are you in for?"

He says, "Life."

I don't know what he did, but I'm thinking, Damn this guy reminds me of me. Good thing I was never in a lineup with him. It might be me in here. I like the guy. He's polite. I bet he went to Catholic school too. Just then it dawns on me. He is our bodyguard. He is the guy separating us Christians from the lions. He must be okay, some kind of model prisoner. Prison officials must believe in him to give him this job. I tell him and I mean it sincerely when I say, "You seem like a good guy to me. I don't know what you did but you seem like a good guy to me, I'm just a nobody comedian but if it was up to me I'd take a chance on you..."

He says, "Thank you. I appreciate you saying that. That means a lot."

I see someone walk by with a bowl of ice cream. Wait a minute! I saw barbecue beef and chicken and beans and rice and corn bread and salad over at the buffet table they have set up for us, but I didn't see ice cream. I say: "Where is everybody getting the ice cream from?"

He says, "Do you want ice cream?"

I say, "Yeah...."

He says, "Come with me."

Next thing I know I'm walking across the yard with the guy and inmates are parting like it's the Red Sea. They all stand back as we walk through, and I don't know who this guy is but he must be heavy. I look up at the guards on the catwalks with M14s looking down at us. You know they're going, "Now what's this crazy fool doing? Is this guy nuts?"

We get into the prison commissary to where an inmate is behind the counter serving ice cream and the guy who I am counting on to keep me alive says, "What would you like? How about a sundae, do you like sundaes?"

I say, "I love sundaes."

"Okay, go ahead and give him a sundae. What kind ice cream do you like? Chocolate, vanilla, do you want both?"

"I'll have both, please."
"What else do you want on there? Do you like nuts?"

"Yes, I like nuts."

"Put nuts on there. How about hot fudge? Do you like hot fudge?"

"I love hot fudge!"

"Put lots of hot fudge on there. How about whipped cream? Do you like whipped cream?"

"Yes, please."

"Give him the works. Fix it up good. Put a cherry on top too."

He gets the thing and hands it to me and it is a mountain of ice cream and goop.

He says, "Is that good?"

I say, "It's great! Thank you!"

He says, "Let's go."

We turn around and head back the way we came, walk all the way back across the yard to where the stage is. Once again the Red Sea parts as the guards on the catwalks with the M14s look down. "Looks like the idiot likes ice cream!"

Pretty soon they are telling us it's time to go, and we are leaving and if you want to stay, fine, but we are leaving. I certainly don't want to miss the roundup getting out of there so I exit with the herd. As we are headed to the ramp inmates are asking for my autograph so I sign. I don't sign my real name, but I sign. Tree signs more autographs than me. He doesn't sign his real name either. He signs them "Tree." We are whisked out in a big group with doors clanging shut behind us as we go. We get out the last door and believe me, it may sound trite, but it's true, once you hear that last door clang shut behind you and you are outside those walls, I don't care who you are, if you have any connection whatsoever to Whomever or

Whatever you call God or the Great Spirit or your Higher Power, you breathe a sigh of relief and say, "There but by Your Grace go I."

SO YOU WANT TO HECKLE THE COMEDIAN?

A question I am frequently asked is: "How do you deal with hecklers?"

Every comedian handles this differently. There are no hard and fast rules on how to deal with hecklers. Although history does have a tendency to repeat itself, every situation and every heckler is different so the same approach doesn't always work the same way every time. There is no one size fits all method of dealing with hecklers. This is something that you have to learn by doing. There is no substitute for experience. However if I were to simplify down to three simple tools for dealing with hecklers it would be three Ps: Be Prepared. Be Patient. Be Positive.

BE PREPARED

When it comes to dealing with hecklers, it's better to have the material and not need it, than need it and not have it. By "material" I mean enough to cover whatever your allotted time is on stage. Once you start with a heckler there's no turning back. Once there is blood in the water, it's like sharks in a feeding frenzy. If you're the headliner and you're supposed to do an hour, and you get a heckler right out the chute, you have to be prepared to string him along or finish him quick. I don't know if it's like this for other comics but I suspect it is. At some point in your career as a stand-up, if you do it long enough, you actually start wanting hecklers to heckle. Of course, human nature being what it is, the minute you start wanting hecklers to heckle is the minute hecklers stop heckling. No one wants to pick a fight with someone who actually wants to fight, right?

Well, not necessarily.

There is always one shithead who decides it's his duty to give the comedians a hard time no matter what. In the case of one particular night at the Sunshine Saloon in Pleasanton, it happens to be a platoon of shitheads. It's a two-man show that night, me and another comic named Tyler Horn. Tyler Horn is used to a hard time. His day job is he's a porn actor.

Badda-Boom!

His movie name is Tyler Reynolds. I think Tyler Horn is a great porn name, but I guess it's against the rules to use your real name if you're a porn actor. If the goal is to remain anonymous, my guess is it is hard to remain anonymous when you are featured in what is arguably the most iconic porn film of time, *Behind the Green Door*. I say "arguably" because some would argue *Deep Throat*, and I haven't seen that one either. Don't get me wrong. I am not claiming to be goody two shoes here. I've seen porn. I just haven't seen either of those flicks.

Anyhow, Tyler's claim to fame is he's one of the five guys Marilyn Chambers is doing simultaneously in the big climax scene in *Behind the Green Door*. I miss my big chance to see Tyler's film debut. The day I meet with Artie Mitchell at The Mitchell Brothers Theater it's playing on the big screen and I miss the movie. What am I going to do? I have the meeting with Artie. Tyler is the guy that Artie uses to do John Wayne's voice in *Sodom and Gomorrah* when I turn the part down. I actually suggest Tyler to Artie. He's already on the payroll; his John Wayne is passable. People are going to fast-forward through the part where Tyler's talking anyway. Tyler is another want to be Jonathan Winters, but alas Tyler is endowed with different talents. Tyler is more Milton Berle than Jonathan Winters. Although I never see him in *Behind the Green Door*, another comic has a VHS tape of a porn feature where Tyler is the star. It actually has a plot, such as it is. Tyler has to "act" in it. Tyler is hilarious. Unfortunately for Tyler, he is funnier as a porn actor than he is as a comedian.

So Tyler and I are doing this gig at the Sunshine Saloon, a notoriously rowdy room. As big a star as he is in front of the camera, this crowd eats him alive. God knows I could never do what he does, and it doesn't look like he can do what I do either. As the wolves devour him I am loading the ammunition belts. There are three definite subgroups of hecklers I have to deal with. The two non-stop verbal manure spreaders directly in front of the stage are no doubt going to require immediate attention. The guy to the right of the stage who is really into it and who is getting more and more emboldened by the minute, the guy with the big mouth and the braces and the hair that looks like Khadafy, this guy is a sitting duck. He's next. I'm saving my heavy artillery for the back right corner of the room. There's a big table with about eight big frat boy looking guys sitting at it. They've been heckling the whole time and one guy in particular sitting at the head of the table is the loudest and most obnoxious and if I can help it, I'm saving him for last. It's all a matter of what order they go off in.

I feel sorry for Tyler. He has about as much chance as a cow trying to cross the Amazon in the middle of a piranha convention. I give him credit. He lasts longer than the cow. He must really need the money. He's probably worried about doing short time and not getting paid. Being a porn actor you must develop a thick foreskin. He hangs in there tough for a while, but sorry Tyler, no money shot tonight. Tyler mercifully wraps it up and tells the crowd he is leaving and the crowd jeers him off! This room is famously tough but tonight is ridiculous and I'm next up. It's a two-man show so Tyler's is supposed to introduce me. All of a sudden Tyler remembers this, so he turns around and walks back on to yet another barrage of catcalls. He quickly introduces me and walks off. I get up and I can't tell if the boos are for me or for Tyler. It reminds me of the old Jackie Mason joke: "The guy I had to follow was so bad that halfway through my act they started booing him!"

So now I'm up there and I don't even get a sentence out and the two douche bags directly in front of the stage go off. I don't remember what they say. It doesn't matter. It's in the right order.

I say, a la Redd Foxx: "Lookee here! Why you want to mess with me? I don't come around and mess with you when you working. I don't come on your job and slap the dick out your mouth!"

BOOM! The crowd explodes!

These guys are done, not a word out of them the rest of the night.

Khadafy is next, right on cue. I don't know what he says, but whatever it is, he is really proud of himself for saying it. He looks up at me with a big shit eating grin on his face, I mean, the reflection off this guy's braces are blinding people in his immediate vicinity. Now I'm Butt. I look down at him and say, "Who-ee! You havin' a big ol' time tonight ain't you boy?"

He looks up at me nodding still smiling really big.

"Boy, you look like Mommar Khadafy!"

He shakes his head no. His teeth are still showing but his smile is seriously starting to droop."

I say, "What you got in your mouth there, boy, one a them Black and Decker pecker wreckers?"

BOOM! That does it. He doesn't show his teeth or open his mouth for the rest of the night, and neither does anyone else at his table. Two down and I'm not even warmed up yet. Table number three, the Eddie Haskell looking dude is next and sure enough he goes off and his timing could not be better if he had been cued. Again I have no idea what he says. It doesn't matter. He says it in the right order.

I say, "I been waitin' on you, Bubba! I got a song for you!"

I grab the guitar: "One, two, three, four: There's one in every crowd it seems. At least that's what they say. There always is an asshole that wants to make your day. I may be an asshole too at least I get paid and I know why guys like you heckle because you can't get laid. Guys like you if they tried couldn't get a poke at a hooker's convention with ten grand and a pound of coke. I ain't bein' unkind and I ain't being snide, but the truth of the matter is, my friend, a girl's got to have some pride. You can heckle me all night still I won't be fazed. Call me anything you like (here's where the fight starts!) except what your mama raised. I ain't saying that you're nasty or that you are scum, but you must be talking through your ass because your mouth can't be that dumb. There's lots more things I could say to someone like you but it's apparent you're a jerk who doesn't have a clue. So sit on back, do your thing. Me, I'll do my part. But the next time I want to hear from an asshole if you don't mind I'll just fart. And I'd say that you have shit for brains but I know you ain't that smart...!"

The crowd roars at every putdown. The guy I'm in the process of trashing flips out, charges the stage. Now he's on stage screaming at me. "PUT THE GUITAR DOWN! PUT THE GUITAR DOWN!"

People in the crowd are yelling, "He's a cop! You better do what he says he's a cop!"

I stop and I look at the guy and I say, "Are you a PO-lice officer?"

He says, "DAMN STRAIGHT!"

"If you're a PO-lice officer, where are your badges?"

He says, "MY SHIT'S IN THE CAR!"

"Badges? We ain't got no badges! We don't need no badges! I don't got to show you no stinkin' badges!"

"I SAID PUT DOWN THE FUCKING GUITAR!"

Why should I? Why should I believe you're really a cop when you don't show me no stinkin' badges?"

"I TOLD YOU MY SHIT'S IN THE CAR!"

"Well, you'd better go get it, Bubba."

"DON'T TELL ME WHAT TO DO! AND DON'T CALL ME BUBBA!"

He doesn't like the fact I'm challenging his authority. He doesn't like it but he is in my domain now. As a cop he has to maintain control when he is on duty, but he is in my jurisdiction now. I am the comedian. This stage belongs to me. I'm the guy with the mike. These are my rules. It's easy to use reverse psychology on this guy. The more I tell him to go get his shit the less likely he is to do it. I tell him, "I don't believe you're a PO-lice officer. I bet it's all bullshit! Come to think of it I've got another song for you Bubba It's called "The Bullshit Song" and it goes like this right here: "There's bullshit in my hat, bullshit in my hair..."

"PUT DOWN THE FUCKING GUITAR!"

Every time I turn around bullshit everywhere...

"YOU'D BETTER STOP RIGHT NOW IF YOU KNOW WHAT'S GOOD FOR YOU!
"

The word "Stop!" triggers something in my head. I say, "Wait a minute! If you're a PO-lice officer, I got another song for you!"

"YOU'D BETTER NOT SING IT!"

There's a bar stool on stage and I say to the guy, "Look, you can take it sittin' down or standing up, either way you're gonna get it..."

"YOU'D BETTER NOT...!"

"He's a asshole cop, he's a bad ass asshole cop. If he says you better stop you better stop..."

The crowd goes crazy. The guy storms off the stage. "I'LL HAVE THIS PLACE RAIDED! I'M GOING TO HAVE EVERY-ONE HERE ARRESTED...!"

The crowd is yelling, jeering him, he turns around and points to me on stage and says: "AND YOU STILL HAVE TO DRIVE HOME, ASSHOLE!"

The Sunshine Saloon has big picture windows in front. A white limo is parked out there visible for all to see. I don't know who's it is but I point to the limo and say, "No I don't Bubba! That's my limo parked out there!"

The crowd CHEERS! He yells: "FUCK YOU!" And he and his buddies beat a hasty retreat out the back door to HOOTS and JEERS from the crowd. People are coming up to me afterwards going, "You got balls, man, those are all cops, all those guys are cops, man, you'd better watch it leaving here tonight!"

I am paranoid going home that night but nothing happens. Immediately I get booked back at the Sunshine Saloon for a show the following month and now I really have a reason to be paranoid because they put posters all over town in businesses and on telephone poles advertising the show. It's impossible to miss, like having a wanted poster with my picture on it plastered everywhere. "Butt Butane: Dead or Alive!"

I get there the night of the show and Bob asks what's wrong, and I say, "Well, I'm kind of paranoid, Bob."

"Why?"

"Because of what happened the last time I was in here…"

He says, "Oh, you mean the thing with the cop?"

I say, "Yeah."

He says, "Don't worry about him. I know his boss. He got his ass in such a sling over that, getting drunk in public and making an ass out of himself, disgracing his department. His boss says if he could ship him to Siberia that's where he'd be going. I wouldn't worry about him if I was you."

Nothing ever does happen but to this day I still can't help but look over my shoulder every time I go to Pleasanton.

The heckler song has come in handy on other occasions. One night I am doing a comedy show in a restaurant and the manager of another restaurant, which is part of a chain, brings his staff to the comedy show to celebrate a special occasion. It's obvious who these people are because they are broadcasting it to everyone in the room. I think they have the most sales in their district or something. So the manager is sitting there getting drunker by the minute along with about eight of his employees, and he decides it's a good idea to heckle the comedian who happens to be me. And these aren't good-natured heckles. These are drunken asshole heckles. Still I am patient with this guy. I really am. I really take my time with him. In a way I kind of feel sorry for him. I kind of hate to drop the hammer on him because I know how embarrassing this is going to be for him in the long run. Who knows? He may even end up having to transfer to another restaurant in Siberia or someplace.

So I give him the customary three complimentary unanswered heckles, and then I gently say to him: "I am giving you every opportunity to stop now on your own. If you choose to continue, you will leave me no choice. I will no longer be able to do my act. I will be forced to do an entirely different act! And guess what my act will be then? My act from now on will be trashing you! For the rest of the night every minute of precious time that I spend on this stage will be spent trashing your sorry ass. Oh, and by the way, my other act, Plan B, the act I have planned for assholes like you, is way funnier than Plan A that I originally was going to do for this nice crowd here, who if I'm not mistaken, is pretty sick of your sorry-ass bullshit too!"

The crowd cheers.

I say, "So now it's your choice. What's it going to be?"

He says, "Say something funny!"

"There's one in every crowd it seems, at least that's what they say. There always is an asshole that wants to make your day..."

By the time I'm halfway through the heckler song the guy has his wallet out and is waving cash at me offering to pay me to stop, but I tell him, "Too late now, Bubba, I have 22 minutes to go! What was the name of that restaurant you work for again? By the time I'm done with you, your ass will be in End of the World, Alaska, boy!"

Another Restaurant Manager bites the dust.

Moral of the story: Don't mess with the man with the mike.

Another time I'm at the grand opening of a club in Vallejo. I can't remember the name of the place because this is at a time when clubs open and close like I change my shorts. I do remember the comedians I'm working with. One is Henriette Mantell, who is just starting out at the time. Later on she gets a gig as the maid in the Brady Bunch movie. The other is another woman comic who I can see her face, but I can't remember her name. If she reads this she'll probably remember. This goes down as a hell night in anybody's comedy logbook. Anyhow it's the grand opening of a brand-new club owned by a bunch of Hispanic guys who are all related to each other and into martial arts. One of the co-owners is a Professional Karate Association full contact champion. The owners of this joint don't need to hire bouncers. They are bouncers.

So they get a pretty good crowd of their family and friends in there for the grand opening. Still, there are empty seats to the right of the stage. Henriette is first up, and immediately a heckler starts in on her, and this guy is brutal. Nobody does anything about it. I keep thinking with all these martial arts guys, somebody's going to deal with the heckler but nobody does, and I'm puzzled why they don't. As I recall Henriette leaves the stage in tears. I'm sure somebody is going to say something to the heckler but nobody does. The next comic gets up and the heckler starts in on her. At first I'm hoping she'll be able to turn the tables on him but she is quickly overwhelmed. Not by wit, because this guy has none. There is nothing clever about this guy. He is just an obnoxious drunk.

Finally, an owner comes over to me and asks if I think the guy needs to be ejected. By then it's already too late. I say, "No. Leave him for me."

I get up and the guy immediately says something, so I respond. I can't remember what he says or what I say. What is said is not important. What is important is his response. This guy can dish it out but he can't take it. He cannot handle the audience laughing at his expense. The fool comes flying at me and now he's on stage trying to kick me. I easily sidestep him, but he doesn't quit.

He comes at me again with a spinning back kick. It looks like he's been studying "Drunken Asshole" style. I never attempt to block or protect myself other than with footwork. My years of training pay off. I tear a page from Ted Gilchrist's book and, mike in hand, deliver one line counter strikes to each botched kicking attempt. Finally he winds up like a baseball pitcher before launching yet another misguided attempt at a spinning back kick. I side step him effortlessly, he flies off the stage and his momentum carries him head first into some empty tables and chairs stage right, I mean ass and elbows and tables and chairs flying everywhere.

Now I'm Redd Foxx. "Man, you pathetic! You couldn't whup a one-legged man in an ass-kicking contest!"

That does it! A couple of the owners grab the guy and boom! Out he goes! The problem is he doesn't stay out. Three more times he comes back. I don't mean "comes back" like calmly staggers through the door back. I mean three times he comes flying back through the door and three times he goes flying back out the door, and when I say "flying," I mean the guy is literally airborne. By back and forth number three, I'm starting to get paranoid. I'm starting to think, "What if this guy comes back with a gun?" Fortunately, three's the charm and it's the last I see of him, but try doing your act under these circumstances.

I find out afterwards the heckler is a friend of the family and a wannabe martial artist and he put all the flooring down for them for free, thousands of dollars worth in time and materials. That's why he gets to drink free and be an asshole in the club and no one says anything. But I guess there are limits to even that. This night is a case in point.

So when time comes to show Saint Peter my comedy logbook, I'll turn it over to him and say, "Check it out, Saint Peter. I paid my dues, no shit. I done spent my time in comedy hell!"

BE PATIENT

Don't be too quick on the trigger. Having the material and looking for an excuse to use it are two different things. It's like the guy who learns a few karate moves and then wants to go out and get in a fight. Unless you're Don Rickles, don't incite hecklers. If it's your schtick and you are mentally agile enough to make it work for you great! I have seen guys like Jimmie Brogan, Jay Leno, and Letterman as I have previously mentioned, and Will Shriner comes to mind as well. These guys are brilliant playing off the crowd. If you are in possession of that type of rapier wit, by all means, start shit all day long. If it's funny, do it! A problem occurs when the comic's act is insulting the crowd and it's not funny. I've worked with comics, male and female, who are themselves no more than glorified hecklers. Some of these folks it's like "get a heckler out of the crowd and give him/her the mike" time. That would never work for me. If I did that the audience would turn on me like a brown bear on a bag of Cheetos. But if the audience likes me and starts feeling sorry for me because I have a heckler who is picking on me and I am Mr. Nice Guy, the psychology is on my side.

Now when the time comes for No More Mr. Nice Guy, guess who gets to be the bear and who gets to be the bag of Cheetos? The key is, unless you are really certain of your ability to deal with the situation, don't be too quick to respond. Be patient. When you find the opening you will be able to exploit it for all it's worth. In rare instances where the heckling escalates to the point where the heckler becomes the act, maintain control by following this simple rule. Just like fishing, if you think a fish is on the line, don't jerk on the first or second tug. Wait until they swallow the hook. Then jerk on the line, set the hook, and reel slowly. Remember, if you're into it with the heck-ler on minute eight and you have another thirty-seven minutes of stage time to go, you'd better be prepared to reel real slow. I always like to start off with something nice and gentle like, "It must be a full moon! How did you escape from the asylum? Bed sheets out the window?"

More often than not the response will be drunken inco-herence.

"Just in case anyone thinks this guy is a plant, he's a plant all right, a potted plant."

If he is a truly belligerent, out of it drunk, be prepared to go all the way or until the gendarmes arrive. One of the ugly scenes in any live performance is when a heckler ac-tually has to be physically ejected from the show. Every-thing stops and people watch it go down like lookie-loos at a car wreck. It's hard getting back on track after that. The first time it happens to me, it's tough picking up where I left off even after the problem is removed. I'm thinking there has to be a way to incorporate this into my show so that the next time this happens and, oh yes, it will happen again, it's not such a downer. Fortunately for me, the incident serves as inspiration to write a song for just such an occasion, which is fortuitous because not long after that, sure enough in a different venue, it hap-pens again. This time I am prepared. I string the heckler along and milk the insults for as long as possible, sing "The Bullshit Song" and "The Heckler Song" to him. The crowd roars the whole time at his expense, but nothing fazes him. This guy is too out of it to be fazed.

Finally we reach the point where his presence is no longer viable, so I sing the song: "Mr. Bouncer, throw this asshole out. He ain't nothing but a god damn stupid drunken lout. Mr. Bouncer, please remove this hick. These nice folks here didn't pay to listen to this prick. Mr. Bouncer, please remove this fool. It's plain to see someone peed in his genetic pool. Mr. Bouncer, let there be no doubt. I believe the time has come to throw this asshole out!"

Now, instead of being bummed, the audience is laughing and clapping and singing along while the heckler is being ejected. Instead of a downer, it's a hootenanny! It leaves them wanting more!

"Encore! Encore!"

"Can we have the heckler come back out and take a bow?"

"Sorry the heckler has left the building."

Now the question is: How do I follow that? With a cover tune, of course: "Well it's 40 below and I don't give a fuck there's a heater in my truck and I'm off to the rodeo..."

Now they're square dancing. God, I love country people.

BE POSITIVE

If a heckler gets the better of you, go with the flow. Whatever happens, respect your audience. Never talk down to your crowd. A lot of comedians think highly of their own intelligence and a lot of them are highly intelligent people indeed, but just remember, no matter how smart you think you are, there's always someone out there who is smarter than you. He may be a Nobel Prize recipient or a member of Mensa or a Rhodes scholar. You don't want to get in a battle of wits with that person. Sometimes it is unavoidable. If they are the ones who start it, they leave you little choice. Just because they are really smart doesn't mean they can't get really stupid after a couple of cocktails.

One time I'm in the Flat Iron in San Rafael. I'm on stage, a guy starts heckling and he's not the standard drunken heckler. He's a smart drunken heckler, and he's wicked funny, and he's topping everything I say. I don't say anything to the guy to provoke him, I'm just trying to do my act, but it soon becomes obvious he's out to destroy me. Every time I try to do a bit he derails me with a funny line ridiculing me and/or my material. I can't just hit him with standard heckler comebacks because it will seem weak and contrived by comparison. Fortunately for me I have Colombo in my back pocket. So he says something at my expense and the audience roars. I don't say anything. I just calmly put on the Colombo coat and take the cigar and notepad and pen out of my pocket and now I am Colombo. I don't have to do or say anything. All I have to do is be Colombo. Everybody is mesmerized including the heckler. "Holy shit! It's fucking Colombo!"

I look at the guy with my eye askew and say, "Excuse me that was really funny, that was really terrific! How do you think of lines like that? I mean, how do you come up with them? I have to pay writers $100 a piece for lines like that and you're giving them to me for nothing. Do you mind repeating the last line just the way you said it? I mean I need to get it verbatim, just the way you said it otherwise it won't be funny. Do you mind repeating that? I mean, you're saving me a lot of money by giving me these lines for free, you know that gee where did you get dose shoes...?"

The heckler doesn't say a word after that. I guess he doesn't want to contribute to the betterment of my act, at least without getting paid.

"Ten bucks, would you take ten bucks a line? What happened? Did I go deaf? Where did the guy go? He was here a minute ago. I guess he must have passed out..."

ONE LAST THING

When all else fails, let discretion be the better part of valor. Sometimes it's best not to respond, especially if you suspect the heckler may be a mob associate or an escapee from the home for the criminally insane. Every now and then someone pops off, you look out and make eye contact with this individual and realize that either this person was actually raised by wolves or he is indeed a fugitive wanted in connection with a triple homicide. In this case it is best to just swallow your pride and pretend he doesn't exist. Only once does this actually happen to me. I look out and this guy's eyes come back at me like high beams on a bus that's out to run over me. Normally, I engage, but not this time. There are some people you know instinctively it's best not to mess with. This is where experience comes in. It is a judgment call. It is not easy to let a heckler destroy your act, but it is certainly preferable to taking a dirt nap in the trunk of your car or winding up chopped up in little pieces in a dumpster. On this particular occasion I weigh my options and do the prudent thing and punch this guy's transfer. If and when the time comes you will know it. If not, it's been nice knowing you.

I ALMOST FORGOT

No matter how drunk or obnoxious a woman heckler is you still have to remember that she is a woman. If the audience feels you are being too harsh or overly aggressive they will turn on you. Not can, will! So how do you deal with a woman heckler? Obviously, you cannot make fun of the size of her dick. Making fun of her ass can be tricky too, especially if there is a convention of big butt women in the place that night. Don't get me wrong. I like big butts. But talking about them on stage can be dangerous. And never use the C word. This is an absolute no-no, unless you're Irish. If you are Irish, especially if you are from the North, use it liberally in every sentence combined with the words "wee" and "fooking".

Ah, the Irish, such free-spirited fun loving people. I love the Irish. The thing I love most about them is they get my jokes! I can do stuff for Irish audiences that if I did it for an American audience, they would look at me like a lost pup. Impersonations like Sergeant Bilko, most American audiences nowadays wouldn't know about whom I am speaking, but the Irish get it totally. I do Bilko in an Irish pub and have the audience on the floor. There is a temptation to make a joke about how they were already under the table when I walked in. However, I will resist the temptation and tell you a true story. One night I am performing at an Irish pub in San Francisco for an all-Irish crowd. And when I say "Irish" I don't mean a crowd of hard drinking Irish from America with names like Conroy and O'Rourke. When I say "Irish" I mean a crowd of hard drinking Irish from Ireland with names like Conroy and O'Rourke. The term "hard drinking Irish" sounds redundant, doesn't it? Stereotypical or not, it works out great for me as the comedian because I'm funnier when they're drunk and this night I'm hysterical.

So I have a great set, finish, and I'm standing at the bar. The place is packed and a guy walks by and woman sitting at the bar says, "What? You went and got yourself a pint and you didn't bring me one, you wee fookin' coont!"

My ears do a double take. I can't believe what I just heard. This is a woman talking to a guy! I say, "Did you just call him a… 'coont'?"

She says, "Aye! He's a wee fookin' coont, that's what he is, he bought himself a pint and didn't bring me one the wee fookin' coont!"

I am a bit taken aback, so much so, she notices. She says, "What's wrong with that?"

I say, "There's nothing wrong with it, it is just that, well, Irish people from Ireland speak differently. To you the C word is no big deal, but if I as an American male was to use it in mixed company the women would want to cut my balls off."

She says, "That's because Americans are a bunch of uptight coonts, the wee fookin' coonts."

Note that in the English language the F word and the C word are normally four letter words to be used sparingly if ever. In Irish they become five letter words, suitable for use on even the most solemn of occasions. "I would like to say it's a great honor to be asked to deliver the eulogy here today for our dear departed brethren, Clancy, a man known and loved by all. What can I say, dear brother, other than, Clancy, you were a great fookin' bastard, you wee fookin' coont!"

The Irish get a pass. Anyone else, avoid the C word at all cost.

YOU HAVE THE RIGHT TO REMAIN SILENT

Here is my best example of how to deal with a drunken woman heckler. I say it's my best example because, in truth, I don't know how I'll ever be able to top this one. One night I'm at the Sands in Reno and a drunken woman heckler decides to take out whatever issues she has going at the time out on me, the comedian who happens to be on stage. This woman is not the standard pissed off "My boyfriend left me for my best friend and I'm going to take it out on the comedian" type drunken woman heckler either. No sir, this woman is a bone fide all-American pure-d homegrown corn fed hardcore red neck repeat offender type drunken woman heckler. Looking for a bull ride? Push her buttons and hang on. We're in Reno! Yee-haw!

So I'm onstage doing my act and she takes offense to something I say. To this day I don't know what it is, but I do know that whatever it is, it can't be that offensive because I always keep it squeaky clean in the Sands. The crowd there is Mr. and Mrs. Middle America from Nebraska or Arkansas or wherever and they appreciate the fact I work clean, so I always keep it clean in the Sands without exception, like it's a Branson audience. I wish I could say the same thing about some of the other comics but that's another story.

Anyhow I don't say anything offensive or direct any negativity towards her. I am just up there doing my act and she takes offense to something I say and she starts yelling at me. I guess because I play a redneck character on stage, she thinks I'm making fun of her or something. I don't know what her story is. Well, I know what her story is, but I don't want to give away the punch line. At the time I don't know what her story is. All I know is I'm on stage and she starts yelling at me something about she's mad because she thinks I'm from Texas, and all her exes are from Texas, and she hates them and all men in general. I give her the standard three heckles thinking this won't last long because the doorman is a Sicilian guy from Brooklyn who doesn't tolerate hecklers in his room and he is having a word with her. The last thing I hear him say to her is: "Look, lady, it's the last time I'm going to axe you. If you don't be quiet during the show I'm going to have to axe you to leave!"

Usually when this guy axes you; you stay axed. I'm thinking surely that's the last we'll hear from her for the rest of the night.

Wrong!

As soon as he walks away, she starts up again. What comes out of her mouth is pure obscenity laced incoherence. I look over to where the doorman usually is and I don't see him. He must have thought she was going to stay axed and he stepped outside for a cigarette. Now I have no choice but to respond. I go with a standard line always good for a woman heckler: A nice gentle middle of the road Norman Rockwell Americana kind of good-natured putdown meant to hurt nor offend anyone including the recipient of the insult. It's the kind of insult you could use on Lawrence Welk's show and not offend anybody. "Hey lady, nice outfit you got on there! Somewhere in Reno there's a jeep with no seat covers!"

Now she is yelling total babbling incoherent rage.

I say, "That's it, lady, have another 10 shots of tequila!"

She comes out of her seat like a Polaris missile, just in

time for the doorman to grab her arm. He says, "That's it! You're out a here!"

She turns and slugs the doorman. My mission is to keep the show going at all cost. As casino guards are hauling her out the door I'm singing: "Jose Cuervo, you are a friend of mine…!"

The crowd loves it. I get a standing ovation. I get back to the dressing room and am informed that Reno PD is now involved and they want to talk to me. I go back out into the showroom and there's a cop standing there. He has a pen and a notepad. He says, "Are you the comedian?"

I say, "I'm one of the comedians."

He says, "Are you the comedian that was on stage when she was arrested?"

I say, "Yes."

He says, "What's your name?"

Here at the Sands I'm billed as: 'Buck Butane.' My real name is Jim Giovanni, Giovannoni…"

"How do you spell it?"

"G-i-o-v-a-n-n-o-n-i. Officer, I didn't do anything wrong…"

"That's not what she says."

I say, "I don't care what she says, I am telling you the truth. I have a whole room full of witnesses…!

He says, "What did you say to her?"

I say, "I didn't say anything. I was very gentle to her. I used an old joke about her outfit looking like the seat covers of a jeep, it's a very innocuous old standard joke…"

"She says you said a lot more than that…"

"What does she say I said?"

"She says you called her names and used profanity."

"That's not true, I didn't call her any names and I didn't use any profanity. I never use profanity in the Sands. I told her to have another ten shots of tequila and she went bonkers…"

He is looking at his notebook. He says, "She says you called her "a fly on a pile of dog shit.
"

I'm confused. I stop and think about it and realize what has happened. I say, "I never called her that and neither did the comedian who told that joke either."

"Somebody else said that to her?"

"It was never directed at her. There was a comic on stage two guys before me named Geechy Guy who did a guest set who told a joke about two flies on a pile of dog shit, where one fly farts and the other fly says, 'Excuse me, I'm trying to eat here!'"

The look on the cop's face says it all. He closes his note pad and says, "That's all I need to hear. I have no further questions."

The cop leaves and the doorman says, "Even her own mother testified to the cops she should be arrested. It's bad when your own mother is saying it, know what I mean, Buck?"

I'm getting ready to leave and the bartender says, "Hey Buck, tell me something…!"

I say, "What?"

He says, "How did you know she was drinking tequila?"

I say, "I didn't. Just an educated guess, I guess."

NEVER SAY NEVER

I'm booked at a club in Chico. I can't remember the name of the place. I wish I could remember and no, it's not the Top Flight, subsequently named the Crazy Horse, the place with the mechanical bull and the upside down barber chairs kamikaze drunks do shooters in. It's not that place. Anyhow, the name is not important. What is important is, it is in Chico and at the time Chico is the number one ranked party school in America. So a few days before I'm supposed to do the gig I get a call from the owner of the club and he says he wants to cancel because it's Grad Night. Right away I'm thinking Grad Night, of course! Nobody's going to be in the club, they will all be off at private graduation parties and barbeques somewhere else. But I'm counting on the money from this gig to make my mortgage payment. I've already turned down other gigs because this one is booked. I tell the owner that.

He says, "Well, okay, you can do the gig but it's Grad Night and I don't think it's going to be a good night for comedy, but go ahead, show up and I'll pay you for the gig."

It's my first time playing this place. I get there and it is a medium size room with all the tables and chairs removed and a little stage that sits above the crowd. When the performer is up there his/her feet are at the head level of the crowd. It's like the Fillmore Auditorium in San Francisco on a smaller scale. You're on stage looking down at the audience, which in this case consists of a couple hundred drunken graduates and their friends, many with drinks in both hands. And to say they are packed in there like sardines would be an understatement. This place has got to be way over whatever limits the fire marshal allows. It's the opposite of a bust of a crowd. This place is busting at the seams. Booze is flowing. Bartenders are struggling to keep up with the demand. Judging by the amount of power drinking going down, there is no way the house loses money tonight. The cash registers are ringing like Johnny B Goode's guitar, but now I get what the owner means about Grad Night not being conducive to comedy.

Despite the challenge, I look at the crowd and believe this is doable, unlike the other comic, who takes one look at the inebriated masses and immediately starts freaking out. This particular comic who I'll call Ken because he looks like a Ken Doll starts in with: "This sucks. I'm never going to be able to do anything with this crowd. They're never going to listen, this sucks…!"

I keep telling the guy, "Negative waves, man, negative waves, you've got to think positive! You defeat yourself before you even get up there thinking that way, man. It's a self-fulfilling prophecy. Think positive. Never say, 'Never!'"

The power of positive thinking doesn't work with Ken. Nothing works with Ken. He has already convinced himself he'll never be able to pull it off, so he is right. He's never able to pull it off. He gets up there but even with a microphone and a PA you can't hear him above the din. It's like historical old Molloy's or the Abbey Tavern on St. Patrick's Day, shoulder-to-shoulder wall-to-wall, drunken revelries. He is supposed to do 30 minutes. He does less than five, throws his hands up and yells into the microphone. "YOU PEOPLE ARE NEVER GOING TO LISTEN!"

Even this the crowd ignores, so Ken bails and beats a hasty retreat back to the bar to the owner and now Ken is complaining, saying, "This sucks! They won't shut up, I told you they were never going to listen. I told you it would never work. I drove all this way for nothing. They are impossible! I'm never going to do this again!"

The owner looks at me and says, "What did I tell you? Forget it. You don't have to go up. I'll pay you anyway."

I say, "Can I at least try?"

He says, "Suit yourself. But you don't have to if you don't want to."

"I want to."

The MC, who is also the house DJ, introduces "Butt Butane." I walk on with my cowboy hat and boots and wranglers and guitar and big ass belt buckle and I get to the microphone and as loud as I can, I go: "WHO-EEEE!"

Everyone immediately stops and looks up. I say, "I FEEL LIKE I AM AT A WILLIE CONCERT! SHOW ME YOUR TITTIES!"

BOOM! Every woman I can see, which is half the humanity in the room, pulls up her top and out they come BOOM! I can't believe the timing of it, but there they are: Big tits, little tits, firm tits, floppy tits, pert tits, humongous tits, gorgeous tits, outrageous tits, you name it, all out on full display simultaneously, instantaneously, just like that! I had a hunch the move would get their attention but I had no idea it would work that well. From that point forward, I own the place. I do my time and Ken's and then some. The crowd won't let me off the stage. When I finally do get off, guys want to carry me out of there on their shoulders.

So my advice to young comics is: Never say, "Never!"

SINK THE
CONSTITUTION

In May of 1988, I write a song parody of Johnny Horton's "Sink the Bismarck," which is recorded by Commander Cody. Under Ronald Reagan's zero tolerance policy, yachts, boats, ships can be seized for finding so much as a marijuana seed aboard them. The Monkey Business yacht, the one that gains fame with the Gary Hart scandal gets seized for a couple of joints worth of pot, and it makes the front page of all the newspapers. I'm sitting there reading the newspaper drinking my coffee and inspired by the headline, right there at the kitchen table I knock this song out in about twenty minutes.

Right away I know the material is good. I'm anxious to perform it somewhere, anywhere. It just so happens I get a call later that day to appear on Marty Cohen's radio show the following morning. The next day I go on Marty's show and sing the song a cappella. I go home and there is a message from Bob Lacey that Commander Cody heard the show and wants to record the song. I make a rough demo of it and give it to Bob and he gives it to Commander Cody. Commander Cody records the song under the title of: "Sink the Constitution."

People ask me all the time. "Did you make any money on the song?"

The short answer: "No." When the song first appears in record stores it is on an album and they give me credit as writer of the words, but I never get any residuals from it. I talk to Commander Cody one time on the phone and ask him about it and he says the record isn't selling so therefore there is no money in it for me. I admit it's my fault for not pursuing it more aggressively, not that it would do any good. Recently I go on Google and find out it's on iTunes, and Johnny Horton is credited for writing the song. His publisher, Acuff Rose gets all the songwriter money. Hey assholes! It's one thing to take the money, but do the math. Johnny Horton died in 1960! I wrote the words in 1988! I have a copyright with the Library of Congress! I know going up against you guys is like David going up against Goliath, but I just want to set the record straight.

Thanks for helping me get that off my chest.

THE FEDS

One night in 1988 I'm doing my standup act headlining at the Dumphey Hotel in San Mateo. I do a long set that night, an hour and twenty or so. Everything kills; I close with Sink the Constitution. I walk off, people are cheering. Two guys walk up to me with big smiles on their faces and they pull out their badges and they're FBI guys. They say, "You're a real funny guy you know that?"

I say, "I know. Hey, do you guys still have that footage of me with Country Joe in 1969 at the peace rally in Berkeley? The one where I'm doing Nixon on the shitter? If you don't mind, I'd like to have that for my reel…"

"You are a real funny guy…"

Turns out they're just fucking with me. They can't get the movie either.

SEMPER PARATUS

Always ready, that's our Coast Guard. They're always ready to party every time they show up to see my show. One time I'm at the Eagle House Victorian in Eureka and four coast guards are sitting right in front. I dedicate "Sink the Constitution" to them. So I'm performing it for the same folks I am making fun of in the song, and they love it. They're going, "Holy shit! You're the guy that wrote the song about us!"

The head chief comes up afterwards and says, "We love your song. The words to your song are framed on the wall down where we work!"

Now I am the guy going, "Holy shit!"

The chief says, "I'm coming back tomorrow night and I'm bringing my whole crew."

He shows up the next night with about 20 more coast guards and they are all ready to party too. I walk out and there they are, all of them sitting right down in front. I look down and say, "Who-ee, bubba, you wasn't bullshittin' when you said you was comin' back tonight and was bringing folks with you. Well, Semper Paratus, Coast Guardians!" I sing the song and next thing I know there are drinks lined up across the stage from left to right or right to left, depending on which way you look at it. It's a big-ass stage, so if that ain't an example of reality reflecting art, I don't know what is. I sing the song three times that night, twice on stage and once more in the bar afterwards. You can't make this shit up.

RAT FUCK

Sometimes the best rat fucks are ones you don't plan. They just happen. A practical joke gets out of hand. The next thing you know, people are outraged. They don't get hurt. They just get outraged. Later on they laugh about it maybe but not at the time! No sir, at the time they are downright outright fucking outraged. And the most outrageous part about it is you never plan the outrage or rat fuck, as it were. It just happens.

One time I get a phone call from my old pal John Sanders, my football player buddy from the best of times. I had sent John a copy of Commander Cody's recording of Sink the Constitution. So one day I get a call from John and he says, "I love your song but I would also really love it if you could send me a copy of the real song by Johnny Horton. I love that song!"

I say, "I have a copy of Johnny Horton's greatest hits. That song is on there. All his greatest hits are on there."

He says, "Could you make a copy and send it to me?"
"Sure."

I have a dubbing deck. So now I'm bootlegging a copy of Johnny Horton's Greatest Hits on a TDK 60 cassette tape. Thirty minutes after I turn on the recorder a song finishes and three seconds later side A clicks off. Perfect! I flip the tape over and begin the next song. Everything works out great except side B ends up being twenty-two and a half minutes long. I've got to find another seven and a half minutes so as not to leave side "B" with a big gap like it's a Nixon tape or something.

I'm going through my records. Johnny Cash no, Merle Haggard no, he's probably got this already and then I come to an album that has a cut the exact perfect length. So I record the cut as the last seven and a half minutes of side B. The title of the cut is "You got To Wash Your Ass" by Redd Foxx. I label it Johnny Horton's greatest hits and send it off to my friend.

Now keep in mind I never ask him what he wants it for, and I fully expect him to at least listen to it before he plays it for other people. I figure he'll probably listen to it in his car and get a kick out of it and, if his family is there with him, there's a good ten or fifteen seconds were Redd doesn't say anything rude, so he'll have plenty of time to lean over and turn off the tape recorder before anyone is any the wiser. That's the theory anyway.

So I send off the tape via the US Postal Service and forget about it. About three days after Labor Day, which is a month and a half later, I get a phone call from John and he is major pissed off. I answer the phone and the voice on the other end of the line goes: "You son of a bitch! You asshole, I'm going to kick your ass!"

I say, "Who's this?"

He says, "John Sanders!"

I say, "Hey John what's up?"

He says, "You know that tape you sent me...?

Now I'm searching the mental Rolodex because I sent the tape about six weeks ago and I forgot about it. I say, "Yeah?"

He says, "I'm at the Mormon picnic on Labor Day and everybody is grooving to Johnny Horton: 'Way up north to Alaska, in 1814 we took a little trip along with Colonel Jackson down the mighty Mississip..., we got to sink the Bismarck because the world depends on us...I'm standing there talking to the bishop and I hear: "You got to wash your ass, not your whole ass, your asshole. I go: 'Holy shit! It's Redd Foxx!' Now I'm running across the campground trying to shut the thing off and the whole time I'm hearing: 'You might think no one knows, but the nose knows. You'd be surprised the amount of pollution you could find in a spot the size of a dime or quarter or a fifty cent piece. Hell, you may have a silver dollar! You know your own ass better than I do..."

See what I mean about the best rat fucks not being planned?

IRISH PAT

On my fortieth birthday I'm up and out the door at 4:00 A.M. I run a half mile to a high school near my house and then run another ten miles around the track. My plan is to spar three rounds with professional boxer Irish Pat Lawler at Newman's gym in San Francisco on my fortieth birthday. I think it would be a kick to get in the ring with a guy who defeated both Roberto Durand and Wilfred Benitez don't you? Pat's a pal of mine, so I know it's going to be a friendly sparring match. Besides, he's a middleweight and I'm a light heavy so how bad can he hurt me? Don't answer that.

So I get to Newman's at the agreed upon time, 8:00 A.M., and Lawler is there and he's there with his manager who's got a key to Newman's. He opens the door, and we get in there and I'm changing into my boxing shorts.

The phone rings, and Lawler answers it in Stewart's voice. "Yeah, this is Stewart, whatta ya want?"

I can't hear what the person on the other end of the line is saying, but by Lawler's response I know exactly what he's saying. Pat says, "It's Pat Lawler, Stewart…"

Pat listens for about thirty seconds and then hangs up the phone. He says, "Come on we gotta do this thing quick, Gio!"

I say, "Aren't we supposed to be in here?"

Pat says, "Never mind that, Gio. We're not supposed to be in here. Stewart is on his way down. We gotta do this thing quick!"

Now we're racing to change and get in the ring. Pat turns on the bell and for the next 11 minutes I regret running 10 miles before and not after. Now that I could use the gas my tank is empty. But it works out fine, a friendly little sparring match. I definitely would not want it to be anything otherwise, although Pat keeps encouraging me to try to land a shot. I do late in the third round a nice little overhand right that bounces off of Pat's head. Pat shakes his head and smiles and says, "Good one, Gio!"

The bell rings ending the third round. Pat says, "Don't bother to change, Gio. Grab your shit and get the fuck out of here!"

That's how I celebrate my fortieth birthday.

THE INDIAN

I had a sort of epiphany, I guess you could call it, right after the memorial for a friend. This was no ordinary friend. He was a two foot tall dwarf Cherokee Indian comic from Oklahoma. If that wasn't enough, he had a fatal bone disease that he never once mentioned, much less complained about. Everyone loved Ben Stewart, or "Stew" as we called him. Then his junkie roommate stole everything he had, and that terrible cruelty somehow resulted in Stew falling and breaking bones and dying in the hospital.

After the most loving tributes from all his comic friends and admirers at his memorial, I went for a ten-mile run that night on the high school track near my house. I was angry at the junkie and the world for allowing Stew to die that way. At the end of my long run, where I'd been throwing punches most of the way, I noticed what appeared to be eyes in the dark looking back at me. My mind told me it was light from the moon and stars, but my heart told me it was alive. It was a beautiful, perfectly composed and balanced painting in nature of a bear staring at me with a wolf and a mountain lion on either side. As I slowly walk away and the image faded, I didn't feel like kicking anybody's ass after that.

The Great Spirit had touched me. I felt at peace.

The next day I go to see a guy I often play music with. Like me, he's a country music guy. I love the twang of a telecaster and he plays a real good telecaster. I try to talk him into doing gigs but he's reclusive and doesn't like to play in public, a great player but a real private person. So

I'm over at his place the day after Stew's memorial, we're supposed to jam that day and I get over to his place and I tell him about Stew and what happened and how Stew was a Cherokee and about seeing the picture in nature. Now most people you tell them this story and they say, "What were you smoking?"

"Major endorphins dude it was crazy!"

I tell my telecaster playing friend the story and he says, "You had a vision. In Native American Culture this is a very profound spiritual event. You have been blessed."

"Cool."

"You say your friend is Cherokee. I am Cherokee."

I say, "From Oklahoma…?"

"My family is from Tennessee."

What a coincidence. Stew and this guy are both Cherokee.

My friend says, "I don't normally tell people this, but you had a vision so I am going to let you in on some thing that I don't share with most people."

I am intrigued. I say, "Go on…"

He says, "You have been given a gift. You are on a spiritual journey. I am a shaman. I can help you on your spiritual journey. I am going to give you some things to do but you have to do these things with an open mind and an open heart…"

"Mr. Open Mind Open Heart, that's me…".

"If you do as I tell you, many things will happen, strange wonderful things, you will venture down paths you never dreamed of. But you must do everything I tell you to do without question."

"You're not going to tell me to rob a bank are you?"

"I will never tell you to do anything that is illegal or immoral. Are you ready to do as I say?"

My friend is already aware of my frustrations with the show business career aspect of my life. I say, "Why not? I've tried everything else."

"This is not about show business or getting ahead in your career. This is about something much more important. Show business is an illusion. This is reality. To truly succeed in life you have to succeed as a Spiritual being. The rest is all illusion. You need to find your joy button."
"My what…?"

"Your joy button. You have lost your joy button. You need to find your joy button."

"What does that mean?"

"I don't know. It's up to you to figure it out."

I find all this difficult to mentally compute, but what have I got to lose? I say, "I'll do anything you tell me to do. Tell me what it is you want me to do?"

He says, "First you need to find a rock."

I say, "That shouldn't be too difficult. There are rocks everywhere. I can go out right now and find a rock in your yard."

He says, "Not any rock. This is a very special rock."

I say "Special? How so? What kind of rock am I supposed to find? I go to Hawaii a lot, a volcanic rock? A granite rock, a big rock, a little rock, a pebble, what kind of rock…?"

"You'll know it when you see it."

"I will? How will I know?"

"It is your rock. You will know."

The next day I'm on mile six of a ten-mile run. I'm running in the sand along the Pacific Ocean on the beach, my mind wandering not really thinking about anything. I look down and right there in my path is a well-worn – by rolling around for millions of years in the ocean – perfectly heart-shaped rock. I stop and pick it up. It's about as big as my palm, and it is a perfectly heart shaped smooth beautiful rock. As I hear the waves wash over the shore I feel a profound sense of peace wash over me. My friend is right. I see. Somehow I know. I bring the rock back to my friend, and I show it to him.

He says, "It is very old. It is a good rock. It is your rock. You have done well. You must go and find many more rocks and when you have found them bring them to me and I will tell you what to do."

Now I'm into it. Every day I run on the beach and I find more and more little smooth heart rocks from the ocean. Pretty soon I have a whole bunch of them and I go back to see my friend. I show him my rock collection, and he tells me very good and then he proceeds to give me a ceremony to perform, involving placing the rocks in a circle and performing a ritual. He says, "Go and perform this ceremony with an open mind and an open heart, and when you have finished come back and tell me what you have learned."

I go and do what he says to do. I finish and turn on the TV afterwards and see a piece on CNN about the Vietnam Memorial wall in Washington DC. I cry for the next two hours as I write this poem:

THE WALL

I used to think I was pretty tough. As a kid I never used to cry.

If I got hurt and had to go get stitched up, I'd grit my teeth and never bat an eye.

When I was born and the doctor slapped me, the story goes I never cried at all.

But I stood there crying like a baby when I saw his name up on The Wall.

When we were kids he was my best friend. In '68 he had to go away.

All those years I never knew what happened until I stood before the wall that day.

I know the type of person that he was. He proudly went and served when he was called.

Yeah, I stood there crying like a baby when I saw his name up on The Wall.

To this day I choke up every time I read that. On appropriate occasions I've performed it in public and had Navy Admirals and Marine Corps Generals come up to me with tears in their eyes afterwards and hug me and thank me for the poem. Don't thank me. Thank the Indian.

I go back to the Indian and tell him I performed the ceremony as instructed. He asks what "came up" for me. I read him the poem. He says, "You have a big cat in your totem. He runs with you. Listen for his footsteps. Someday you will see him."

I say, "What do you mean by a big cat? You mean like a bobcat. I see bobcats all the time. A couple of them I gave names: Red and Brownie. You mean Red and Brownie? I see them all the time. I talk to them…"

"I said 'a big cat'."

"Bigger than a bobcat, you mean like a mountain lion…?"

"You will know him when you see him."

"Oh great. This is just what I want to hear. I like running in the mountains. Some of the places I go trails are the only safe place to run. Run alongside the road with cars and trucks and no shoulder and you are taking your life in your hands. I have to run on trails. There's nowhere else to run! Now you tell me I'm going to be running with mountain lions!"

"Don't think of him as an adversary. Think of him as your spirit guide."

LOMA PRIETA

In 1989, an earthquake hits San Francisco. The quake occurs during the opening game of the World Series between the Giants and the A's. A friend of mine's life is actually saved because he picks up a load with his truck at the Oakland port and is off the Cypress Freeway seconds before it collapses. That night everyone who normally would be on the Cypress goes home early to watch the World Series. It is my friend's good fortune that the freeway is open and his life is spared.

I am booked that week at a new club in San Jose. Here's a tip: Never make your grand opening the day of the World Series opener, especially when it is between two local teams. Not only is the earthquake a crowd killer, the World Series is the coup de grace. Two people show up for the grand opening. The bottom line and it's another comic who's name I can't remember who I first hear say it is: "Dionne Warwick should sing another song titled: 'Do You Know Another Way To San Jose?'"

CRYSTAL GAYLE

One good thing about being on the West Coast and being typecast as country comedian is there ain't a lot of competition. All of a sudden it's: Loretta Lynn is in town and they want to have a comedian opener or it's Ronnie Milsap or the Oakridge Boys or Kenny Rogers and they want a solo act, preferably a comic.

"Call Giovanni."

"That doesn't sound like a country name."

"He also goes by 'Butt Butane'."

"Sounds like a fart joke."

"You've seen his act?"

Hey, don't laugh. Nothing country audiences love more than a good fart joke. Actually, I can think of a couple things they love more, but fart jokes are right up there, I guarantee. I love country people. Country artists are the best, and one of the greatest of all in my book is Crystal Gayle. One time I'm opening for Crystal Gayle at the Visalia Convention Center and I get there and check in and somebody says they're feeding the band up in the Sequoia Room. So I get to the Sequoia room and walk right in with no hesitation and, unbeknownst to me, it is Crystal Gayle's dressing room.

Crystal Gayle is standing there with a sister, I'm not sure which one but not Loretta Lynn, and I come walking in. All of a sudden it's like I'm in the presence of an angel or something. If you've ever seen that show "Touched By An

Angel," it's like that. I mean it's like she's glowing. Crystal Gayle is one of the most beautiful women I've ever seen and if it hadn't been for my experience with Frank Sinatra on *Laugh-In*, I probably would've been doing the Jackie Gleason "Hamana hamana hamana" routine. But I'm not because before I can say anything, Crystal Gayle says, "Hello, I'm Crystal."

I say, "Hello...hamana hamana hamana..."

"What's your name?"

I say, "I'm Jim, Jim Giovanni."

She says, "Are you with the Convention Center?"

I say, "No...I'm, I'm your opening act."

She says, "Oh, what do you do? Are you a singer/songwriter?"

"Well, yes I am, but mainly I am a comedian."

"A comedian, that's great. So you tell jokes...?"

"I do impersonations, some song stuff, impersonations of country artists. I can't impersonate you of course but I do other artists...'

"Oh, like who do you do?"

"The Highwaymen, Hank Williams, Merle Haggard..."

She says, "Gee, that's great. Well Jim, it's nice to meet you. If you'll please excuse me, I have to get ready. Oh, were you looking for someone?"

I say, "No I wasn't looking for anyone. They told me to come up here that they were going to feed the band up in the Sequoia Room. I thought this was where the dinner was going to be..."

She says, "No that's in the Redwood Room. Everyone is having dinner over there."

Now she tells me! I just barged in on Crystal Gayle and her sister and the whole time I've been in her dressing room without knowing my faux pas! I say, "I'm really sorry, I did not mean to come in here I really thought it was where they were feeding the band..."

She says, "Don't worry about it. Have a great show!"

I leave feeling half schmuck and half touched by an angel.

That night my act gets laughs in all the right places. Crystal Gayle comes out, and some women are even more beautiful in person than they are on television; Crystal Gayle is beautiful inside and out, and it's not an act. What you see is what you get and what you get is one hell of a dynamic stage performance. And it doesn't hurt every song she sings is a number one hit. The audience gets more than its money's worth at her show.

After the show I go out in the lobby and right away people are asking for my autograph. It's not often I get asked for my autograph, but with country folks, it's part of the deal. Most amazing is Crystal Gayle comes out in the lobby and signs autographs and takes pictures. I'm watching her, and she is hands on. She stays until every last person has got a picture with her or an autograph or souvenir and the only people left in the lobby are Crystal Gayle and her manager and me and my cousin who is a Kern County coroner.

There's a character for you. If you want stories talk to my cousin but don't talk to him while you're eating. You'll be sitting at the dinner table and he'll be saying stuff like: "We just pulled a guy out of a airplane that's been hanging upside down in a tree for three months. The plane went down in August. He's nothing but an oily blob, don't weigh nothing by the time we get to him..."

Not too many people go back for seconds when he's

around.

So Crystal Gayle and her manager and my cousin and I are the last ones in there and I learn another valuable lesson, which seems to come naturally to country folks. Your audience is number one, son. Don't ever forget it.

WILLIE

One day I get a call from my old pal Bob Lacey, whose house I stayed the night of the Old Waldorf show. "He says, "Hey, Jimmy, what are you up to these days?"

I say, "Not much Bob. What have you been up to? Have you had your couch fumigated yet?"

Bob says, "I got rid of that couch years ago. I live in the country now. My girlfriend has horses."

"So, what does that mean? If I come stay with you you're going to make me sleep in the barn?"

Bob says, "You're a country guy, I thought you'd be at home sleeping in a barn. Seriously, I know you're doing a country thing now so I recommended you to some people. I told them you'd be perfect. They're looking for someone just to do a solo opening, a comedian, I told him you were the perfect opening act for Willie."

"Willie...?"

"Willie Nelson. You'll be getting a call from a guy named Tom Lapinski. They want you to open for Willie at Paul Masson Winery."

"Willie Nelson! Great!"

"Tom will talk to you about money..."

"Yeah, sure, do I owe you an agent's commission or anything...?"

"Don't worry about it. I work with Tom. I help him book

other acts too."

"Gee, thanks Bob!"

"Kick ass, will you? Make me look good."

"You got it, Bob!"

I get there the night of the gig and I got on my big Resistol straw cowboy hat and my Wranglers and boots and I got my guitar case and gig bag in hand and I tell people I'm the opening act and they give me my backstage pass. I get backstage and the only guy back there is Grady Martin. I don't know who he is at the time, but Grady Martin is the guy that did all the fancy Spanish-style fingerpicking on the Marty Robbins song "El Paso." Grady is a big-time studio musician, a great guitar player, but not real friendly when you first meet him. So Grady is sitting there and he's got on a floppy old brown felt hat pulled down over his eyes and he's watching a baseball game on TV and I say, "Hi! What are you doing?"

Grady looks up at me with a look of utter contempt, like I am a dog that just came in and crapped in the living room. He says, "Watchin' baseball."

"Of course you are watching baseball. I should have known better than to ask a dumb question like that. Stupid me."

From the look on Grady's face the dog is now dragging his butt across the carpet. I can't get this guy to smile for nothing. I hear somebody behind me. I turn around and there is a guy standing there who can't stop smiling no matter what. He's about 6'2" with long white hair and beard. At first I think he's one of the ZZ Top guys. I come to find out he is one of Willie's spiritual advisers. He says, "Howdy! I'm Reverend Jim." Then proceeds to pull out a fatty and hand it to me.

Bush the First is President and he's declared a war on drugs even more severe than the one that's been going down for the last twenty years. I am paranoid. I don't want to get busted or even worse kicked off the job before I even get started.

I say, "You want me to light this here?"

He says, "No. Save it for later." He then proceeds to pull out a second fatty and fire it up on the spot.

I have a great set that night. The crowd is into it; I get a nice round of applause at the end, walk off and Poodie, Willie's stage manager, is right there. He says, "Willie wants to see you on the bus."

Now, even though Sinatra for the most part cured me from being nervous around famous people, Willie is a different story. Willie is not your normal everyday superstar. It's like meeting a legend of the Old West, like meeting Wild Bill Hickok or Sitting Bull or some iconic figure of that stature. Willie is short and wiry, so in that respect he's not big, but his aura sure is. Aura-wise, this guy has some serious wattage going on, some old soul heavy-duty karma or whatever you want to call it. Like Sinatra, it's palpable. I get into the inner sanctum and there are other people in there and someone introduces me to Willie. Willie is grinning like he just smoked something really good, which there's a high degree of probability he just did. He extends his hand and says, "Nice to meet you, Jim."

We shake. I say, "Nice to meet you too Willie."

"Meet Sister Bobbie, my wife Annie..."

"Nice to meet you."

"Pleasure to meet you too."

Willie takes a drag off what looks like a small torpedo and hands it to me. I'll just say this. Anybody that gets on Willie's bus who says they didn't inhale is full of shit. You can't help but inhale on Willie's bus. If you are breathing when you're on Willie's bus, you're inhaling. Willie's got a guy sitting at a kitchen table whose entire job as far as I can see, is to roll joints. This guy never stops rolling the whole time I'm there and as fast as he can roll them, Willie lights them. I don't know if it's an initiation because I'm a virgin on the bus or what but every torpedo Willie lights, he fires it up and hands it to me. I'm going with the flow as Willie lights one after the other. The whole scene is like it's not even real.

There is a beautiful blonde woman on the bus who is a local radio personality there to interview Willie. She says, "Why don't you have Willie sign your guitar?"

I look at my guitar, do a double take and I say, "I don't know if I want Willie to sign my guitar...!"

Willie gets a quizzical look on his face because people are always asking Willie to sign their guitars and I'm saying I don't want him to sign it?

I say, "It's my only guitar! I need this to gig with! Now everybody's going to want to steal it!"

Willie laughs. Willie understands because he is a musician and they guard his guitar like Fort Knox. I'm caught off guard because I'm not thinking about getting my guitar signed. I forget I even have the guitar in my hand and now Willie wants to sign it and I'm saying no? My reaction is honest and Willie sees the humor in it. I see my folly, hand Willie my guitar and I say, "Aw, hell, Willie, go ahead and sign it."

Willie laughs, picks up a Sharpie and signs my guitar. I realize I have something else that I forgot I had, so I pull out The Rev's fatty and proceed to fire it up. Willie gets a twinkle in his eye, well he always has a twinkle in his eye, but his eyes shine especially bright at the sight of the Rev's offering. He hands the guitar back; I hand the joint to Willie. Willie hits it and says, "I laughed my ass off at your shit."

Willie's wife Annie is sitting there and Annie says: "Willie's not kidding. I've never seen Willie laugh so hard. When you sung the song about toxic waste Willie almost fell over he laughed so hard."

Willie says, "I love it. You come out lookin' like George Strait and then the shit that comes out of your mouth…"

Poodie comes on board. "They're ready for you, Willie!"

Following Willie's lead, we all pile off the bus.

It takes several minutes to get to the stage. Willie signs autographs the whole way. He takes the stage and picks up Trigger, the guitar with the hole in it, and the place goes crazy. The band hits the lead in.

"Whiskey River, take my mind. Don't let her memory torture me…"

Two hours and change I'm down to cruising altitude.

"What's the difference between Willie Nelson and the Dallas Cowboys?"

"Willie can play on grass."

The engagement is three nights and Willie Nelson has three buses, so over the course of three nights I make the rounds of all the buses and pretty much meet the entire Family. It's kind of comical how the whole thing works. On the road the Willie Family is divided into three distinct groups. Each group has a different bus and each bus has a different personality. There's the Willie Bus for Willie and sister Bobbie and Willie's immediate family, which is I'll call the Green Bus for obvious reasons.

Then there's the Clean Bus, as in clean and sober Holy-Roller bus. That's Paul's bus. Paul English is the guy Willie sings about in the song, "Me and Paul." Paul is an old Fort Worth Character, always dressed in black with black hair and a black moustache and black chinstrap beard and black boots and black cowboy hat. Paul has been Willie's drummer and wingman since the beginning of time. It's ironic Paul looks so much like the devil because his bus is the one with all the reform drunks and religious folk on there, although if you stop and think about it, it does make sense the devil is a drummer.

Willie's bass player, Bee Spears, is on the Clean Bus. Bee is hilarious, one of the funniest people I've ever met next to Willie. I think that's why Willie keeps Bee around as well as the fact Bee's a damn good bass player, especially when it comes to playing Willie's shit. Bee is quick with a joke, most of which I haven't heard before, quite a feat in itself because it's hard to tell me one I haven't heard before. Every time I think I've heard them all, Bee comes up with a new one.

Billy English, Paul's brother, is on the Clean bus. Billy is a big Grizzly Adams kind of character, a teddy bear if he's your friend and a real honest gentle soul but you wouldn't want him mad at you. Billy himself admits he has a temper, cross him if you like being chased by a pissed-off bear with a claw hammer. Billy's a freight train of a percussionist and drummer and all-around great musician, who, like Bee, loves a good laugh.

Last but not sober is the Drunk Bus. I don't think anyone is in charge on the Drunk Bus. Maybe Jose Cuervo is. Poodie is on the Drunk Bus and Jody Payne and Grady Martin and a few others. They are on the Jose Cuervo Tour and Jose is on the bus, cases of him. The occupants of that bus are, according to Poodie, "a pile of Texas yahoos," whom every now and then need Paul's boot up their ass to keep them upright.

There are other distinctive individuals in the traveling road show known as Willie Nelson & Family. There's Ben the valet. They say Ben was valet for Hank Williams and John Wayne. He looks like he was valet for Methuselah. Ben looks like the character in the Tom T. Hall song where

Jim Giovanni

the guy is so skinny he has to drink a beer to keep his britches on his hip. Ben is a Willie look-alike. Sometimes I think Willie keeps Ben around as a head fake. Ben's got long hair and a beard like Willie and at a distance people think Ben is Willie. Ben walks out on stage and starts puttering around and people applaud because they think it is Willie. But it's not Willie. It's old Ben and people are going, "God, Willie really looks bad…"

When Willie does come out it's like a before and after picture. Willie looks like Charles Atlas next to Ben. People are relieved. "Gee, I'm glad to see Willie's all right. I thought for a minute there he looked like he was at death's door, but that wasn't Willie after all!"

"Nah, just old Ben."

There's also Gator and Tom and LG and Kenny and Tony the driver and Adeline, one of the ladies that sells the T-Shirts. I remember her because we talk and I find out she's Portuguese and I'm half Portuguese. There are also a whole bunch of other folks whose faces I see but whose names have faded in memory. Oh, and there's Mickey Raphael. How can I forget Mickey Raphael? Mickey is Willie's harmonica player. Mickey is normal. There is one in every crowd, right?

Over the next couple of years I open around twenty shows for Willie. I can't remember the exact number but it's somewhere around 20 or so. At first Willie is high on me. Willie is high period. He says, "We're going to take Nashville by storm and I'm going to be right there with you…!"

"You don't think Willie is going to remember this shit do you?"

Willie blew smoke up my ass, and boy is my asshole stoned.

CHEROKEE NUMBER THREE

When the Cherokee thing first starts I'm not thinking about stuff happening in "threes," but that's what happens: First Stew, then my shaman Indian friend, and Willie makes Cherokee number three: Willie Nelson, no less! How cool is that?

I'll tell you how cool. Willie Nelson, cool man, Willie Nelson cool. Early in this monologue I mention that in my experience, offstage, musicians are funnier than comedians. Not in every case but many times I find this observation to be especially true of jazz musicians. Willie is above all a jazz cat. Like most jazz cats, Willie doesn't generally exhibit funny on stage, but funny is a driving force and funny is what seems to keep him on an even keel no matter what obstacles life throws at him. I observe this at a time when Willie is going through a real rough patch. I watch him take it all in stride and wonder how anyone can be this cool. I have seen cool before but this cat is the coolest. And how can you be this cool and this funny at the same time? I mean Steve McQueen had the cool but not the funny. Willie is the whole package, super cool and razor sharp, quick witted funny. I think part of Willie's secret is no secret.

Willie is a people person. He is genuinely open and honest and he listens. He listens and has the ability to play off what other folks say with oft times hilarious results. One of the more outrageous examples of the funny of Willie: When called upon to reflect upon his advancing years,

Willie unflinchingly looks old age in the eye and says, "I think I outlived my pecker!"

One night we are on Willie's bus after the show and a guy gets onboard and it's obviously his first time on the bus. I know the awkward feeling of meeting Willie for the first time and not knowing what to say and now it's this guy's turn. His eyes are rolling around in his head; he's searching for an icebreaker. Finally he blurts out: "You know Willie, that old guitar of yours with a hole in it, I bet if that thing could talk it could sure tell some stories."

Willie says, "If that guitar could talk I'd have to shoot it."

ACCORDION SOLO

I'm opening for Willie at Konocti Resort at Clear Lake in Northern California. I just got a brand-new Acadian accordion and I'm walking through the parking lot with the accordion in an Anvil case. I can't see on the bus but Willie sees me from on there so the next thing I know is the door of the bus opens and Gator the driver says, "Willie wants to see you on the bus."

Now I don't know what Willie thinks is in the case, but I get on the bus and Willie says, "Hi Jim!" And immediately asks, "What's in the case?"

I say, "An accordion, Willie."

Willie says, "An accordion? Can I see it?"

I say, "Sure Willie." I open the case and inside there is a beautiful Acadian accordion, custom built, handmade for me by Marc Savoy in Louisiana. I pull the accordion out of the case.

Willie says, "Can you play it?"

I know one song. I say, "Sure Willie. Do you want to hear a song?"

Willie says, "Do you know what an accordion solo and a premature ejaculation has in common?"

I say, "What?"

Willie says, "You know it's comin' but you can't do nothin' to stop it."

WILLIE'S GOLF GAME

Willie knows I like to run. Willie does too but it's hard to find a place to run at Konocti because it's all narrow country roads with no shoulders. It takes some doing, but I manage to stake out a course off the beaten path. One day I'm coming back from a run. Willie spots me and says, "Where do you run up here?"

I try to explain it to him. Willie says, "Better than trying to explain it to me, do you mind if I run with you tomorrow?"

Do I mind? What an honor. Willie Nelson wants to run with me! I say, "Sure Willie I'd love to do a run with you."

Willie says, "OK. Meet me at the bus at eight A.M. tomorrow morning. I like to get it over early."

I say, "Sure, Willie. I'll be there."

Next morning I get there at 8 AM and Willie says, "Do you mind if we don't run today I just got invited to go play golf."

I say, "No problem Willie. I'll see you tonight."
That night after the show we're on the bus and I say, "How was your golf game, Willie?"

Willie says, "I lost 12 million."

I say, "12 million? How do you lose 12 million playing golf?"

Willie laughs. He says, "We start out at a thousand dollars a hole but it's progressive."

This is right in the middle of Willie's IRS woes.

He's obviously taking a light-hearted approach to the situation. I say, "Are you good at golf, Willie?"

Willie says, "Not really, but I have fun..."

"How'd you learn how to play?"

Willie says, "I'm self-taught just like my guitar. I do everything wrong but it works for me."

APOCALYPSE NOW?

Another time we're hanging out one on one and Willie says, "You know, if you read the Bible, it predicts a lot of the stuff that's happening today. A lot of what's going on in the world right now is predicted in the Bible, the end times in the Book of the Apocalypse and all…"

I say, "Willie, I don't spend no time worrying about it, not even a little bit. The way I look at it, I don't look for no trouble, and I don't start none but if it looks like it's going to land directly on me…"

Willie says, "You try to have fun with it!"

I say, "You got it, Willie!"

Willie says, "Me too!"

THE URANTIA BOOK

One time we're on the bus and The Rev is there. The Rev has two copies of *The Urantia Book*. He gives Willie and me each a copy. It's hard to explain *The Urantia Book* in a few sentences, but I will do my best.

First of all no one knows who actually wrote *The Urantia Book*. Some say it was Kellogg, the Kellogg's Cornflakes guy that wrote it but no-one knows for sure. One thing is for sure: whoever wrote it was out there, way, way out there. The first half I don't understand at all and the first half alone is over six hundred pages of small print. And this was written in the thirties, way before computers and word processors so whoever wrote it, wrote it by hand or with an old-fashioned typewriter, a monumental feat in itself. Just writing my book here, I realize how valuable the word processor on the computer is. I can't imagine getting it done without the aid of modern technology, yet whoever wrote *The Urantia Book* did just that and managed to produce an extremely well written work in the process. It is a monumental achievement. Whoever wrote this book created an alternate Bible with alternate Old and New Testaments except, no matter how you interpret the stories in the Bible – and different folks do have different interpretations – the Bible makes sense, maybe not to everybody but to most people. It makes sense to me. I get the Bible. I don't always agree with some people's interpretations of the stories in the Bible, but I get it. If a problem exists with *The Urantia Book*, it, for me, is that the entire first half of the book is over my head. I can't understand any of it, like whoever wrote it is a nuclear physicist or something.

Jim Giovanni

Come to think of it, I think The Rev is a nuclear physicist. Maybe that's why he understands the book and I don't. Sorry Rev, when it comes to the first half of the book I tried.

I finally gave up and went straight to the second half, which I read in its entirety. It is quite a read, over six hundred pages. Part Two I understand. It's about the life of Jesus, the missing years, how he worked miracles. The whole thing is like secrets of the magicians revealed only in this case the miracles are not magic tricks; they are real alterations of laws of the Universe. Like the New Testament in the Bible, according to *The Urantia Book*, Jesus really is Son of God and God really does work miracles. The difference is The Urantia Book explains how Jesus does it. For one thing God is not subject to time, so God can speed up the fermentation process to whatever he wants it to be. Voila! Water becomes wine! The second half of the book is filled with explanations like this of how miracles work. If you open your mind to the metaphysical, it all makes sense.

So I finish reading the second half of *The Urantia Book* about the same time I get booked back opening for Willie. Now I'm anxious to find out if Willie read the book and what he thinks of it. It's a short jump to metaphysical just getting on Willie's bus and, within a few minutes, we are metaphysical all the way. I figure now is as good a time as any to bring up the subject. I say, "Willie, did you get a chance to read *The Urantia Book*, the book The Rev gave us?"

Willie says, "I look at it from time to time."

I say, "What do you think? Isn't it an amazing book? I don't understand the first half, but the second half the part about the life of Jesus, where it explains how He did the miracles blows my mind. And it blows my mind it's so well written and nobody knows who wrote it!"

Willie says, "It is something, isn't it?"

I say, "Some people think the Kellogg's Cornflakes guy wrote it."

Willie says, "Whoever wrote it is a genius motherfucker."

I say, "Who do you think wrote it?"

Willie says, "Hank Williams."

CAJUN COUNTRY

One evening I'm at home, I get a phone call and it's a woman's voice and she is the slowest talking southern woman I ever heard. My wife is from the south and we have family members on her side that are slow southern talkers but next to the woman on the phone, my wife's family sound like auctioneers. This woman talks slower than a snail climbing a greased flagpole. She says, "Are you Jim Giovanni?"

I say, "Yes."

She says, "Are you the Jim Giovanni the comedian?"

"Yes I am."

She says, "My name's Jackie, I'm calling from Alexandria…"

I say, "Oh! My wife is from Alexandria. They were talking about getting me booked back there. Who told you about me? Was it one of the Hunts or Edwards…?"

She says, "I don't know none of them people."

I say, "How did you get my number then?"
She says, "I got your number from 'T Boy' Taylor."

I say, "Clark 'T Boy' Taylor the comedian?"
She says, "That's the one."

I say, "Clark Taylor's from Louisiana."

She says, "That's right."
I say, "Are you calling from Alexandria, Virginia?"

She says, "No. I'm callin' from Alexandria, Louisiana."

The snail is on his second lap.

It's like the joke about the stuttering Bible salesman. "I don't need you to read anymore here's the money, just give me the book."

By the time I hang up the phone I'm booked at the Cotton Gin in Alexandria, Louisiana on such and such date. They will send me an airline ticket. She leaves me no number to call back. Here I go again flying off half-cocked not knowing where I'm going or what I'm getting into until I get there. The trip starts out uneventful enough. I fly from SFO to Dallas. There is a two-hour layover in Dallas. I go into the bar and order a beer and now I'm sitting at the bar with an off duty air marshal and a Cajun guy who has been on and off planes for the last 26 hours coming back from working off the coast of Africa on an oil rig. I tell them I'm a comedian headed to Louisiana to play at the Cotton Gin and the Cajun guy says, "I know the Cotton Gin. My wife and I go there sometimes."

Turns out we are all headed in the same direction, to Alexandria, Louisiana. Finally, time comes to board the plane and it is a real puddle jumper, a twin-engine prop job. No sooner are we off the ground, the Cajun guy pulls out a silver flask and starts pouring whiskey. I guess we're cool because the air marshal does not object. The sun is way down as we fly into Alexandria. It is wintertime and it's dark, but I can still see enough to see we are flying over swamp in every direction and, if this thing goes down we are a smorgasbord for alligators.

By the time we land it's pitch black and I mean pitch black everywhere but the little tiny runway we are landing on. We exit onto the tarmac and into an itty-bitty terminal. I'm looking around, and the people that are supposed to pick me up aren't there to pick me up, and I'm starting to panic because I don't even know the name of the person I am working for. I have no contract, nothing is in writing. It is just someone's word over the phone that I am booked Friday and Saturday nights at the Cotton Gin in Alexandria, Louisiana.

And as if that's not playing it loose enough, the plane ticket they send me is for someone else's frequent flyer miles. My name isn't even on the ticket. Somebody else's name is on there. The instructions I am given are: "Don't say nothing to nobody about it."

I'm not thinking about that when I ask: "Are there any messages for Jim Giovanni?"

Some Sherlock Holmes airline employee puts two and two together and says, "That's not the name on your ticket!"

I'm thinking, "Oh, shit!"

Now I'm scrambling to explain. "I'm a comedian and I'm playing at the Cotton Gin tonight and someone is supposed to pick me up to take me to the to the Cotton Gin and they are not here and I don't even have a phone number of who to call…"

I have no idea what kind of illegalities I am involved in, but I've seen Cool Hand Luke. It's my first time down here and the last thing I want to do is end up on a chain gang in Louisiana. I look over at the air marshal and he looks at me with a raised eyebrow but by now I am in good enough with him he just looks the other way and doesn't say anything. Before anyone can say anything else the Cajun guy says, "I know where the Cotton Gin is. We drive right by there on the way home. You can ride over there with my wife and me. We drop you off over there."

My Cajun buddy's wife is sitting outside in the cab of an old Ford F150 pick-up with the engine running waiting on him. I figure I'd better git while the gittin's good, so I grab my bag and before anyone has a chance to say anything, I high tail it out of there with Mr. and Mrs. Cajun like it's an episode of *I Almost Got Away With It*. Now we're rolling along, and I'm glad Mrs. Cajun is the driver because her husband and I have been drinking buddies for the last three and a half hours, and he hasn't slept in two days. It is pitch black outside, and I can't see much of anything except what's in the headlights; what I can see tells me if we go off the road we are going to be in water. My Cajun friend explains my predicament to his wife and she doesn't say much but somehow I get the feeling she's mad 'cause he's drunk and, just as soon as I'm out of the truck, she's going to cut loose on him. She doesn't seem overjoyed by my presence either. So it's kind of a tense situation, we are in the middle of God knows where, no one's talking and all of a sudden she hits the brakes and the truck screeches to a halt. She says, "That's it."

I say, "That's what?"

She says, "The Cotton Gin."

I say, "That's the Cotton Gin?"

She says, "That's it."

I look at her husband. He nods his head. "That's the Cotton Gin."

"Are you sure?"
He says, "Yeah we sure we from here we know the Cotton Gin. That's it right there."

Up until then, I expected the Cotton Gin to be a comedy club located in a strip mall, "Cotton Gin" being a catchy name dreamed up by some local marketing genius. I figured that there would be lights and a sign that says "Cotton Gin" on it. I did not expect it to be an actual pre-Civil War era cotton gin, old wood and a tin roof in a field on the edge of God knows what, dark, with no signs, no lights, no nothing to indicate the presence of life. I've been to ghost towns after dark and that's what it looks like, a haunted structure where the only inhabitants are ghosts, except this time, instead of murdered gold miners, the ghosts are those of runaway slaves and Confederate soldiers. Who knows? Maybe Jean Laffitte himself is going to come walking up out of the Spanish moss any minute. My imagination is running wild as I get out of the truck. Are these going to be the last two human faces I see? My Cajun friend says, "Maybe we come back and catch you. It depends on the wife here." I know the drill. You won't be back.

I say, "That would be great. Thanks for the ride."
He says, "If I don't see you, pass a good time for me."

"I'll try."

They pull out, I watch their taillights fade into the distance. It is cold, spooky dark. Now is as good a time as any to start thinking about what I'm doing. I scare myself once I do. No one knows I'm here. My wife doesn't know I'm here. The airlines don't know I'm here. According to them, I don't exist. I was never here, but here I am, walking around what looks like an abandoned building in the dark, the only sound the sound of gravel crunching underneath my boots. I can't find an entrance, any lights or anything to signify that this is indeed the Cotton Gin. There is nothing, not even an old rusted out 7-Up sign from the 30's or anything else that would indicate we are even in the Twentieth Century. What am I in the Twilight Zone?

Panic is starting to set in. What is my next move? I have no phone number to call, no name of who to call even if I had a phone book to look it up in and phone to call from. Even if I do find a live human to tell my story, what am I going to tell them? "The woman I talked to, her name is Jackie."

"Jackie who?"

"Slow talking Jackie."

"Well, there's a lot of slow-talking Jackies around these parts, son."

Just as I'm thinking I should have thrown a flashlight in my bag, I sense a presence. I don't see him. I don't hear him. I sense him. I turn around and, like an apparition, he is just standing there, staring at me, grinning. In what little moonlight there is I know the long bill ball cap dirty flannel shirt bib overalls, gums and fang teeth ain't no apparition. His opening line is a real conversation starter. He says, "Hi!"

Whoa! Is this *Deliverance* or *Texas Chain Saw Massacre*?

I say, "Hi...uh, is this the Cotton Gin?"

He says, "Yes sir, yes sir..."

I say, "Uh, is there a comedy show here tonight?"

He says, "Yes sir, yes sir...you the comedian?"
I say, "Yes."

He says, "I like comedians!"

"How do you like them?"

He says, "Yes sir, yes sir..."

A couple more exchanges, I get the sense this guy is harmless. No matter what I ask him, his answer is: "Yes sir, yes sir..."

I decide to see if I can elicit a different response from him, so I say, "What's your name?"
He says, "Leroy."

I say, "Hi Leroy. My name is Jim. Glad to make your acquaintance, sir."

I extend my hand and Leroy shakes it. "Yes sir, yes sir..."

I'm standing there talking with Leroy and I see lights, looks like a pickup truck coming off the road, gravel crunching underneath the tires. I hear a truck engine being shut off a door slam. Crunch, crunch, crunch, someone's walking in our direction. A big ol' boy with a full beard on him appears out of the darkness, and he looks like one of the Cajuns who chase Keith Carradine and the other National Guards through the swamp in *Southern Comfort* and, when they get to the little Cajun village, these guys come up out of the swamp in a canoe. So this scary swamp running-looking dude comes crunching up out of the darkness and says, "You Jim?"

I say, "Yes."

He says, "Well, damn son, why didn't you wait at the airport like we told you to?"

I say, "Well I didn't know, I was there and there was nobody there, and I just decided it was a Cajun guy that gave me a ride over here, cause he said he knew where it was. I'm sorry, I guess I should've waited..."

He says, "Never mind that now. I see y'all met Leroy."

I say, "Yes..."

He says, "Don't worry about Leroy, son. Leroy's OK. He's OK. He just went to school on the little bus that's all."

I say, "I can tell Leroy's cool..."

"Leroy loves comedians, he just loves comedians, he really does..."

I'm flashing on maybe this is a horror film after all and Leroy is the Igor character.

"How does he love them?"

"Don't worry about a thing, son, we gonna take real good care of you. We gonna fix you up real good, don't worry about a thing..."

Don't worry about a thing? It looks like I just hit the trifecta of Southern Gothic horror film analogies. No one knows I'm here. I could disappear and no one would ever know. What's to worry?

"I'm Scott. Come on, son let's go inside. Y'all are thirsty? Let's go inside get you a beer…"

We get inside it is nothing like I expect. There are no medieval torture racks or chains with hooks hanging from the ceiling. It's a regular bar, Louisiana-style, funky, like something out of the Fifties but at least we're in the 20th century. Scott says, "Come on son, I got to open up, we going to have a big night tonight."

Scott starts flipping switches. Lights come on, neon beer signs. He sticks a long neck Bud in my hand, says, "Come with me."

As I soon find out, the Cotton Gin is not one, but two rooms with a partition down the middle. One side is the comedy club. Everything is neat and clean with tables and chairs and a mike on a mike stand and a barstool on stage like you'd find in any comedy club. The other side is all you can drink for five dollars draft beer and the legal drinking age in Louisiana is eighteen. Scott is a marketing genius. On one side drunken teenagers sucking up their five dollars worth and on the other, a comedy show for their parents. Something for everybody! Thank you Scott for the partition. It's better than chicken wire. So Scott's giving us a tour of the place and explaining that when it comes to the show, I'm it, so do as much time as I can because folks down here like to be entertained. I'm scrambling to remember every bit I ever did, except for stuff they might want to tar and feather me for and I sure do hope they like me because if not this could turn into *The Naked Prey* real quick.

Scarier still, it's getting late, and still it's just the three of us. All these crazy thoughts are going through my head. Where are the people? Maybe this whole comedy thing is a ruse and I am in a Southern Gothic horror film after all. My imagination is running wild and then it happens.

Everybody shows up at once, including the wait staff. One minute they're not there and the next minute they are there, a flash mob Louisiana style: Cajuns and town folk and military personnel, everyone out for a big Friday night. The place goes from nothing to jump started instantaneously, just add alcohol. "Aiii! Make us laugh, boy!"

My act kills that night. I have a crowd pleaser act and the crowd is pleased, so pleased people are arguing over me after the show. I say, "Why are they arguing?"

Scott says, "They fightin' over who's gonna feed you."

I say, "Feed me to what?"

Scott says, "You are funny, you real funny, son, you know that?"

Somebody says, "We want him Scott. He needs to go with us..."

"No, I got him tonight, son. Y'all can have him tomorrow night."

Leroy is grinning at me, nodding. "Yes sir, yes sir..."

"I told you Leroy would love you, son. Leroy just loves comedians, he really does. He thinks you're great..."

"I think Leroy's great too."

"I just want you to know, you done real good tonight, son, you done real good you really did."

"Thanks for saying so..."

"I mean it, I really do, son you done real good now come over next-door with me would you son we going real strong over there I got to take care of some business over there..."

We go over to the other side of the wall and it makes me gladder than ever there is a wall.

"Looks like we need to tap another keg, Scott!"

"Comin' right up, son, comin' right up…"

Finally the night's over, Scott says, "Wait right here y'all just stay with Leroy while I lock up, would you son?"

"Si."

"Now you talkin' like a Mexican you tickle me son you really do…"

Scott exits to go do his final lock-up. I look at Leroy and say, "So Leroy, did you have a good night?"

Leroy says, "Yes sir, yes sir…"

Scott comes back, says, "OK son, we gonna feed you now grab you a beer let's go…"

I grab a long neck Bud and head out to the parking lot, and the only two vehicles in the parking lot beside Scott's truck are two police cars from two different agencies. Standing beside their vehicles are two police officers. One looks like a County Mountie with the Smokey-Bear hat, and the other guy looks like Barney Fife. I come traipsing in their direction with a beer in my hand, see them, do an immediate about face and head back in the direction of the Cotton Gin just as Scott's coming out the door. Scott says, "What's the matter, son?"

I say, "Do you think I should be walking out there with an open container in my hand? There are two cops out there…"

Scott says, "Don't worry about them, son. They on the payroll, you in Louisiana now."

We head out in the parking lot and sure enough cops are going, "Hey Scott how you doin'?"

"Doin' fine, son how you all boys doin'?"

"We doin' fine, fine, fine…"

We get in the truck.

"See what I told you? Don't worry about a thing. You with me. 'Sides, it's legal to drink and drive down here. We got drive-through daiquiri…"

Coming from California where the drinking and driving laws are much stricter, this comes as somewhat of a culture shock. It turns out to be one of the stranger customs that I have encountered in my travels. The way it is explained to me is Louisiana has wet parishes and dry parishes, a parish being what most states would call a county. Most of the dry parishes are in North Louisiana and most of the wet parishes are in South Louisiana where the Cajuns are. It's the Protestant north versus the Catholic south, if you will. If you are in a dry parish, you can get busted for so much as a smashed empty beer can in the back of the bed of your pickup truck. If you are in a wet parish, you can drive through a drive-through daiquiri, which is like a Jack in the Box. You drive up, there's a drink menu there, and the voice comes over the intercom: "May I take your order please?" You give your order, pull forward and they give it to you in a small, medium, or large cup. You pay the person and drive right out the other side just like that. I'm thinking. Who wrote this law? The liquor industry and/or politicians who like to drink and drive? Hey! I've got a new slogan for your license plate!

LOUISIANA WE DO THINGS DIFFERENT DOWN HERE

When Scott says he is going to feed me after the comedy show, I imagine we will probably be going to a 24-hour diner, which usually is the case in the majority of locales I visit. But then again, so far on this trip, nothing has turned out like I expect, so why should this forthcoming culinary experience be any different? Turns out it's not. One thing, instead of going to a restaurant, we go to Scott's residence.

He immediately whips out a frying pan and starts cooking up grits and eggs and shredded meat that looks like pulled pork. At that point I am starving. I haven't really eaten since the plane meal and a couple bags of peanuts on the flight to Dallas and some pretzels in the bar at the airport. I tell Scott how I ran ten miles at midnight the night before, and I have been apprehensive about how I would go over down here, so haven't had much of a chance to think about eating, but now that the show's over, am famished. I am devouring it as fast as he can fry it up loads of everything including the shredded meat. Scott says, "Damn, son, you can really put it away. You know what it is you're eating?"

"Yeah, grits and eggs…what's the meat?"

"Squirrel."

"Squirrel?"

"That's right son you like it?"

I say, "Oh yeah it's great, this tastes great especially as hungry as I am…"

"You want more?"

"Yes, please…"

"Damn, son, I like you. Most of these comedians come down here and I try to feed them and when I tell them what they eatin' they say, 'Oh no, I can't eat that I'm watching my cholesterol I'm on a strict diet doctor's orders and you know that ain't it, son. You know that ain't it. But you ain't squeamish about it son you done run ten miles and come down here and say 'bring it all on me.' Damn, son, I like you!"

I must have eaten at least a Costco twelve pack worth of squirrel. Scott doesn't stop frying until I'm done eating. We finish and he says. "You sure you done son I want make sure you not going to starve at least 'til morning. I told you were going to take real good care of you. We going to put you up in a four star hotel and they got a real good breakfast in there real good they fix you up with everything bacon eggs biscuits gravy grits, got to have grits son, got to have grits don't worry about a thing son they got it all…"

I say, "I appreciate that, Scott, but to tell you the truth I'm not a real big breakfast eater. I like to have coffee and then run and eat afterwards. What time is it now?"

"It's about 2:30 in the morning so I don't expect you'll be getting up too early. I notice most of these comedians don't get up too early, son, but I would like to pick you up around noon, and I'll take you and feed you if that's OK with you. You think you can be ready to go by noon?"

"I'll be ready to go by noon. All I need is you to tell me where is a good place to run close to the hotel. I would like to get in ten miles if I can…"

Scott says, "Just go out the front door of the hotel and the levee's right there, son, you can run as far as you want on the dirt road along the levee there…"

"Great…!"

"Just be careful don't go over the side because you got a show tonight son and I don't want the gators to get you least not until after the show…"

"Oh. What about poisonous snakes?"

"Them too son, just stay on the road you'll be all right. Just be sure you back at the hotel and ready to go by noon straight up I'm going to pick you up in front of the hotel we going to fix you up real good, we gonna get you some crawfish. We gonna feed you real good, son. I'm going to show you how it's done, son."

I do just that. I run a little better than a ten-minute mile pace so I'm out the door at 10:00 A.M. that morning, and I make damn sure I stay on the road. I get back to the hotel in time to shower and get out in front before noon. At noon straight up I am standing in front waiting on Scott and he is right there in his white pickup truck with two giant what looks like oil drums tied down in the bed. He says, "Hop in son we going to feed you now!"

Once again I am picturing going to a restaurant. How silly of me. I soon find out we are not going to visit Chef Paul Prudhomme. We are going to eat crawfish with Cajuns off a steel table in a Quonset hut in the bayou. There are no place settings, no seating, not even chairs to sit on. There are no side dishes, not even rice. These guys are serious. The menu consists of just two items: crawfish and beer out of either a bottle or a can and the deal is you better get it while the getting is good because it's going fast. My first clue is we are driving along and we seem to be heading further and further away from civilization. I see a Quonset hut all by itself in the middle of the field on the edge of a bayou with several pickup trucks parked around. Scott pulls over the side and rolls up to where these guys are standing and kills the engine. He looks at me and says, "Come on son we gonna eat some crawfish now."

We get out and Scott says, "Hey boys, how are y'all doing?"

"We doin' good Scott we doin' real good…"

"Give me a hand would you boys?"

"Sure thing, Scott."

They unload the drums off the back of Scott's truck and carry them inside to a giant steel table with a rim around it I assume is normally used for butchering alligators and they lay newspaper on the table and turn the drums over and pour out two giant piles of crawfish onto the table. It's a very effective operation. Methinks these guys have done this before. They don't waste any time going to work on the crawfish either. It's not like somebody's going to say grace or wait for everybody to get to the table. As soon as the crawfish hit the newspaper these guys are on it. They are eating the little critters like popcorn, Scott is trying to show me how to open the first one up and I am not getting it. Meanwhile, the piles are disappearing like a sinkhole just opened up in the middle of the table. Scott says, "Damn son I better help you or you going to starve." Scott starts busting open crawdads and throwing them in a pile in front of me. He says, "There, that ought to do you for a while, son. Go ahead and eat up. Don't forget suck the heads, suck the heads!"

Not exactly what you'd call a leisurely lunch, it's over as quick as it starts. As the last crawfish head is being sucked, Scott looks at me and says, "Well damn son I notice you don't drink much while you eatin'."

"Are you kidding? How am I supposed to keep up with

you guys? You guys are professionals."

I hear Cajun music on the radio. I don't remember if it's coming out of a boom box or somebody's pickup truck but Cajun music is being played. I know it's a radio show because I can hear the announcer's voice and I can't understand much of what he's saying because of his accent and a lot of it is in French, but I know this much. We in Cajun country this is it, the real deal.

Word gets around I killed on Friday so Saturday is packed. I have a great show. Scott is happy. He's got a big smile on his face as he pays me. He says, "Son, you done real good you done real good son, we going to have you back I guarantee you done real good son yes indeed..."

Afterwards some of my newfound friends and I finish up at place called Red Beard's. Red Beard's is jumping. It's a Louisiana Saturday night. The next morning I fly back home. I am glad to be back, but that night I reflect back upon my adventure and feel strangely homesick for Louisiana.

True to his word, Scott books me back several more times after that.

MISSIVE FROM THE NINTH RING OF COMEDY HELL

It's summer of '91 and comedy hell has never been this hot! It's my last day of a weeklong comedy run which I have cobbled together piecemeal, a Butt Butane tour of Northern California if you will featuring such hot spot destinations as Red Bluff, Yuba City, Chico, and Redding. And when I say hot I mean hot. I mean hot temperature hot. Hot oppressive stifling hot! The only thing that's not hot is the crowd. Crowd? What crowd? There is no crowd. A lot of people think that California is full of surfers and Valley girls, but let me tell you, get up North and you are in redneck city. And when it's that hot rednecks don't go to comedy shows. They go to Shasta. They're out somewhere drinking beer and barbecuing, on a lake or up a river. They ain't at the comedy show, but I am, doing my act for 12 people at Buck's Crazy Horse Saloon in Chico on a Friday night. Usually in Buck's I'm used to playing for a crowd of at least a couple hundred people, but there's about twelve people in there that night. Why? I'll tell you why. Because it's hot! How hot is it? It's so hot even in the tongue on the mechanical bull is hanging out!

To make matters worse, I get back to the motel and the air-conditioner is on the fritz. I'm checking it out and the heater works, but not the air conditioner! It's still in the eighties at midnight, and that's outside. What little sleep I get, I dream I'm the Pillsbury doughboy and someone forgot to turn off the oven. The sun rises at around the same time I do. It's 6:00 A.M., and the thermometer is already inching into the higher eighties.

I figure I better get my run in while the getting's good. My streak is still alive, and my drill is, every morning before checkout time at whatever motel I am staying at, get up and run 12 miles. Saturday morning I wake up in Chico, and one good thing is that Bidwell Park is about half a mile from the motel. Bidwell Park is a great park with lots of shade and water fountains to hydrate. It's the place where they shot the original Robin Hood movie with Errol Flynn. Hey! What do you know? I'm in Sherwood Forest! So I run to Bidwell Park and do two laps around the park and then run back to the motel, which works out to around thirteen miles total, the extra mileage being a good thing because I'm extra frustrated after last night.

By the time I get back to the motel and shower and am on the road, the temperature is already pushing one hundred degrees. An hour and a half later I get to Redding, and get this. This is before cell phones, so to make a phone call I have to call from a payphone. I get to Redding, and I see a time and temperature clock and it says one hundred seventeen degrees. I'm not exaggerating. One hundred seventeen degrees! That's what it says! I get out of my car and go to an outside phone booth and I pick up the black plastic pay phone handle and I burn my hand. Now I have to go back to the car and get an old T-shirt I can use as an oven mitt just so I can pick up the phone. I ain't lying when I say comedy hell has never been this hot. I make my call being careful not to burn my ears with the phone and my wife answers. Before, I go any further let me tell you a little something about my wife. My wife routinely opens my mail thinking maybe there's a check in there or something. So my wife answers and before I can say anything she says, "Oh, a picture came in the mail for you today of you and Willie Nelson and it's really a great picture of you and Willie, it's really a cute picture!"

"There is a lot of ways I could think of to describe Willie, "cute" ain't one of them but go on...""Well I think it's a really cute picture and you are really going to like it!"

Jim with Willie Nelson

I tell my wife I'll see her around noon on Sunday, and I better get out of this phone booth pronto because the glass is acting like a magnifying glass, and I'm starting to feel like an ant who is about to spontaneously combust. I bid her a hasty adieu and get back in the car, and the steering wheel is too hot to touch. I look down and the plastic case for the Buck Owens cassette I've been playing is melted on the passenger seat. Now I'm searching around in the car for gloves I use when I have to run in the snow, and I only find one glove, but that will have to do for now. One hand is on the steering wheel, and one hand is on the shift, and I can't get to the motel too soon.

I get there before check-in, but the office is air-conditioned, so the desk person lets me sit in the office until my room is ready. I explain to her what a horrible night I had, and she assures me that the air conditioner in my room actually does work. She's not lying. When I finally get in the room it's already on, thank God! I don't know if it's possible to actually freeze hell over but I'm fixing to give it a try. When I leave that night to go do the show, I leave the air conditioner on full blast. Of course, stepping outside is like walking into a blast furnace.

I get back in the hot car, which is like getting into an oven on broil, I mean I actually have to roll the windows down and let it air back down to a reasonable one hundred seventeen degrees. That accomplished, it's off to the club, which at least has air conditioning. I get there and predictably there are two people in the audience, one lone couple by themselves. Time comes to do the show and nobody else shows up. I figure it's ridiculous for me to do my act from the stage, so I sit down at their table. The next thing I know, they are ordering rounds and I am doing my act at the table. I do about two hours. We have a great time. I do like Crystal Gayle and give them their money's worth. It isn't until afterwards I find out that the waitress and bartender are mad the whole time because they want us to get the hell out so they can shut the place down and go to Shasta.

I get back to the motel, and it's cold in there, just the way I like it. How cold is it? It is so cold stalagmites are hanging off the shower. Well, maybe not that cold. Cold enough for me to sleep and not sweat anyway.

Next morning I am out the door at 6:00 A.M. I figure I'll beat the heat as much as possible, get an early jump on the drive home, and do my run on the backend. I can't wait to get back to the cool California Coast. Homesick James is coming home. As I head down I-5, I get a feeling of overwhelming sadness, of lost opportunity, of defeat. As I see it, it's all but over. I'm forty-three years old. I don't know how many more runs like this I can take. I'm starting to think, as Kris Kristofferson says, "I have a brilliant future behind me." There's no one on the I-5 at that hour. I turn on the AM radio to the country music station. I don't know what it is about listening to someone sing about their fucked up life that makes you take your mind off your own fucked up life, but it works for me. Johnny Cash is on there singing "Sunday Morning Coming Down," a song guaranteed to make you feel melancholy if nothing else will. This is immediately followed by another Kris Kristofferson song, "Lord Help Me Jesus." I guess it's AM country radio's version of Sunday morning church services. Kris's lyrics hit home. "Lord help me Jesus I've wasted it so help me Jesus I know what I am. Now that I know that I've needed you so help me Jesus my soul's in your hand…"

When you are a songwriter, you never know when a good song is going to come. Many come when you least expect it. Some come when you are driving or when you are listening to another song or in the shower. In this case, it's two out of three. By Red Bluff I hear the song. It doesn't yet exist but I hear it. There's an old envelope on the seat of my car and I scribble on the back of the envelope as the lyrics hit me. It's in ¾ time, a waltz. By the time I'm passing through Vacaville two and a half hours later I have a finished song. I think it is Willie who once said: "You can't write the blues from the back of a Cadillac."

A PICTURE OF WILLIE AND ME

I thought that someday I'd make it. God knows I gave it a try.

Lord, it ain't easy, I nearly went crazy waiting for lightning to strike.

I have my share of good memories. I've had my share of success.

The Redheaded Stranger still is my hero. I've worked with some of the best.

But I'm getting older, the trail's getting colder and all I have left you can see

Is a seat in this bar a beat up guitar and a picture of Willie and me.

I once had the love of a lady. Lord knows I once had it all.

But she couldn't hide the tears in her eyes when I left to answer the call.

Now the lady I loved is a memory. Nothing's forever, it seems.

Just a roll of the dice, I guess it's the price you pay when you follow your dreams.

But I'm getting older, the trail's getting colder and all I have left you can see

Is a seat in this bar a beat up guitar and a picture of Willie and me.

An hour and fifteen minutes later, I am home. My wife shows me the picture. My wife is right. It is a great picture. Willie and I make a cute couple.

Christmas is fast approaching and I'm broke, a year older with nothing to show for it and no end in sight to the struggle. Old Man Desperation has set in and looks like he's fixing to stay a spell. Other people I know are making it or have it made, but for me it is a permanent recession with no end in sight. The crest of the 80's comedy wave has passed and I missed that one too. Most of the clubs I play are going or gone. The opening act gigs I'm getting aren't enough. Times are hard. At this point I am open to anything. I get a call from The Rev saying that Willie is doing a concert in Hawaii and do I want to be part of it? The Rev tells me it's not a paid gig, that it is a benefit for the Hawaiian people and I will be performing with Willie, but I have to pay my own way over there and pay my way while I'm there. I hear what The Rev has to say and I tell him give me twenty-four hours, and I'll get back to him. Now I have a dilemma. Do I go to Hawaii and put another thousand dollars on the credit card to work for nothing in the hopes that something may come of it, or do I skip the whole deal and save a grand and get a slightly less whopping credit card bill in January? If I don't go, I won't get the opportunity to open for Willie and maybe, just maybe get an inside track on copping the gig as Willie's opening act when he goes to Branson. If I can get into Branson as a regular my problems will be solved or so I think. Either way, I'm taking a chance. If I don't go, I may live to regret another missed opportunity. If I do go it's hope, but it's a crapshoot. I do what I usually do when confronted by a quandary such as this. I go see the Indian. I explain the situation. What he tells me is not what I want to hear. He says, "I see disaster."

I say, "Disaster? If I go it will be a disaster or disaster in general? Because my career can't be any more of a disaster than it already is...!"
He says, "It will be a disaster for others but you will be a shining ray of light. Your light will lead others out of darkness."

"What? Like the plane's going to crash and I'm going to be pulling people out of a smoldering fuselage?"

"Nothing like that."

"What then?"

"You'll know when it happens."

"Great! The last thing I want to do is have to play hero in some real life disaster scenario!"

"Don't think about it like that. Think about it as an adventure, as part of your journey."

I say, "What about Branson?"

He says, "It doesn't look good."

I say, "Branson doesn't look good for me?"

He says, "Branson doesn't look good for you or Willie."

"It doesn't look good for me and Willie...?"

"It doesn't look good for either of you."

"What's the point of me going then? At least if I have a chance to get into Branson, I may be able to breathe some life into my career! Why should I waste money I don't have if nothing's going to come of it...?

"Think of it as a learning experience."
"You think I should go?"

"Yes. It will be a positive experience for you. Good will come out of it, but you need to be open to it."

"And if I don't go..."

"Then you will never know, will you?"

Here we go again, betting on the come. I'll deal with January when it gets here. My wife is not happy about my decision, and we have an argument right before I leave. I'm bummed the whole way over on the flight, I mean really bummed. Every possible bad outcome is going through my head on a loop. Normally going to Hawaii is a good time, but this is not a pleasant flight for me.

We land on Oahu, a brief layover at the Honolulu airport and transfer to a smaller plane to Kauai which is scary because we land on Kauai in the middle of a monsoon which, looking back on it, I don't even know how they land the plane. But they do, and now we are on the ground, and you have to get off the plane onto a runway and, by the time I get from the runway into the terminal, I am soaked to the skin. I mean I am literally soaked through as if I had jumped into a swimming pool fully clothed. Everything I have is soaked through including my wallet and all the contents in it. Thank God I don't have a cell phone or that would be a goner.

I'm glad I'm traveling light. I just brought one bag and the only article of clothing I have pertaining to my act is my Colombo coat. I leave the guitar at home figuring I'll scrounge one when I get there and I am really glad I didn't bring my guitar now, being one less thing to worry about. I catch a shuttle to the car rental place and put that on the credit card. By the time I walk from the car rental place out into the lot to get the car, I am once again soaked through to the skin. At this point I am resolved to not give a shit.

I get in the car, and who cares if now the interior of the car is waterlogged? It's a rental car. It's a short drive to the hotel, and I know my way a little bit around Kauai, which is good because the water is coming down so fast I can't see anything. The wipers won't go fast enough for the amount of water that is coming down. There is one main road around the island, and I know if I just stay on that road, I'll hit hotel row, not literally I hope.

It's not far but under these conditions it's plenty scary getting from point A to point B. I'm driving along and pretty soon I see palm trees and hotels and there's the Islander and I pull in the parking lot and I don't bother to unload my bag from the car. I figure I'll retrieve it when and if it stops raining. By now I totally don't give a shit how wet I get, it's a warm wet anyway, so I casually stroll in the downpour from the car through the parking lot in the front entrance through the lobby all the way to the front desk, leaving a small river in my wake. I tell the front desk person I have a reservation.

She says, "Name please?"

I say, "Jim Giovanni."

As she pulls up my reservation a pond forms around me. All we're missing is the frogs and lily pads. I figure someone with a mop and bucket will come along. In fact, I'll be surprised if an army of mop and bucket guys don't come along.

"The desk lady says, "Oh, yes, here you are..."

Now comes the part I hate most. I pull out my thoroughly drenched wallet and before I can ask her for a towel to dry off my credit card, she says, "Here you go Mr. Giovanni, here is your room key. I just need you to fill this out and sign..."

I hold up my wet credit card. "Do you need this?"

She says, "Your room has already been taken care of."

Whoa! Things just got a whole lot better. Maybe Santa is not going to leave a lump of coal in my stocking this Christmas after all! She hands me my room key and now I am thinking about whether or not to go back out to the car and get my bag. I look out the main entrance to see if the rain has let up even a little bit. The timing could not be more perfect. The rain is still hammering down but I see a white stretch limousine pulling up out in front and say to myself: "I bet that's Willie!"

It is Willie. The first familiar face I see is The Rev, which means Willie can't be far behind. Next I see a guy I don't know and there's a couple guys I do know and there's Willie and a famous face I haven't met and here they come sweeping through the front entrance with Willie leading the charge. He spots me and says, "Jim. Have you met Kris? Jim, Kris, Kris, Jim. Come on, we're headed to the suite."

I shake Kris's hand on the fly. He eyeballs me hard or so I think, and we literally speed walk through the pathways of the hotel all the way to the suite and pile inside and the door closes and one of the guys pulls out a hermetically sealed bag and cuts it open and starts immediately rolling joints. Just like the bus, Willie's got a guy in Hawaii who's job is rolling joints.

And this dude is efficient, let me tell you. Within a minute of the door closing he has about three fatties rolled and he hands the first one to Willie, Willie fires it up, takes a drag and hands it to me. I follow suit and hand it to Kris. Kris doesn't say anything but the way he looks at me makes me think I don't belong here. This guy has a stare that can pierce through ~~ease~~ hardened steel and right now the stare is piercing through me. He never takes his eyes off me as he takes a hit and passes the joint to The Rev. Kris then turns and walks all the way through the suite out the sliding glass doors onto the outside balcony where he stands under an overhang staring at the ocean with the rain falling in absolute monsoon. The whole time nobody says a word.

The rolling guy is hard at it cutting open hermetically sealed bags and now joints are all over the place. So I'm sitting there with a joint in each hand, Kris is out on the balcony staring at the ocean, Willie is sitting on the bed puffing away and I'm starting to feel a little paranoid. I don't know if it's the weed or because nobody is talking, but the silence is making me uncomfortable. I'm thinking maybe I don't belong here, like any minute I'm going to get kicked out and it's going to be Kris's doing because the way the guy looks at me I don't think he likes me very much. I'm still standing pretty much on the same spot right where I came in, having not advanced much into the room. Kris is at the furthest point away from me that you could be in the suite. I am close to the front door and he's all the way out on the back balcony.

I stand there, wishing someone would say something, anything, for what seems like forever, and finally Kris turns around and walks back inside. Now he's walking straight towards me, and his eyes are like a wolf's eyes – intensity squared – and he's walking straight towards me. He gets about as close as you can get – nose to nose, eyeball to eyeball – right in my face. I expect him to say something like: "What the hell are you doing here?" or "Take a hike." Instead, in a long slow drawl with his voice that sounds like he gargles with rusty nails, Kris says, "This is some good shit!"

Willie says, "What did he say? What did he say…?"

I repeat in Kris's voice: "He said, 'This is some good shit!'"

We literally don't stop laughing for three days after that.

I don't know until I get there, but I find out the concert is supposed to be held in a football stadium. A whole bunch more Hawaiian guys show up, and everybody's freaking out. Already it's a disaster for artists whose work is on display at the stadium. Most of it is already gone, washed away by the monsoon. The entire Island is under deluge. Houses are being swept out to sea, people are dying and the rain does not look to be anywhere near letting up. At about 11:00 P.M. there is a powwow with the Hawaiian guys in another room. Willie and Kris stay in the suite. I go with The Rev to meet with the Hawaiians. I need to find out when my call time is for the next day. No one has told me anything, and I'm concerned about how and when I'm going to get my run in.

We get there and the Hawaiian guys are major uptight. They are trying to figure out what Plan B is. The rain is still torrential with no end in sight. What starts out as a benefit for the Hawaiian people starring Willie Nelson has turned into a disaster epic starring: Mother Nature. Everyone knows the rain is going to let up eventually. It's just a question of when. Whenever it does, all the people who have bought tickets to the concert who are now huddled in shelters all over the island are going to want to either see a concert or get their money back. And even if the rain does let up by say noon tomorrow, setting up electrical equipment in what is sure to be a flood zone is hazardous to say the least. In the midst of all this, there is a lull in the conversation. I sense an opening. I say, "What's the call time for tomorrow?"

The Hawaiians have an expression: "stink eye." Looking back on it, I suppose it is a dumb question. Not only that, here I am, a stranger, a haole and I dare to speak and ask a dumb question no less?

The leader of the group tells me 8:00 A.M., which is the original call time. With the rain coming down in buckets at 11:30 P.M., I don't think so but that's what he tells me. And I believe him because I am gullible. But hold on, there's more to the story. I'm not done stepping in it yet. Usually one "stink eye" from these guys is enough but not for this haole. I double down and commit the cardinal sin. I ask a follow-up question. I say, "Where's a good place to run around here?"

Looking back on it, I see the absurdity in this although at the time it seems perfectly logical to me. The Hawaiian's response is less than friendly. He says, "No place is a good place for you to run around here, haole!"
I sense animosity. My natural instinct is, of course, to triple down. I say, "Why? Is it dangerous around here?"

He says, "For you, haole!"

I perceive his response to be just short of a direct threat, which, of course, is my cue to go all in. The next question is my coup de grace, delivered in my best Louisiana backwoods accent: "Why? Y'all got poisonous snakes and gators around these parts?"

By the time The Rev and I leave, the Hawaiians think I'm crazy which is okay by me. Just in case this guy is right and call time really is 8:00 A.M., I do the math. To be at the football stadium by 8:00 A.M., assuming that the rain stops by then, I have to get up and run at 4:00 A.M. to get my ten miles in. So that's exactly what I do, proving to everyone once and for all that I am indeed crazy.

At precisely 4:00 A.M., I drag my ass out into the deluge and begin slogging through water, which at some points is up to my knees along hotel row just a few yards from the ocean. Unbeknownst to me at the time people are actually dying in this shit, but here I am at 4:00 A.M. running in it. By the time I get back to the hotel room and out of the rain and into the shower I feel great. Not that I need a shower but I take one anyway. I've done my run, the day has begun, and I'm ready for fun, son. It doesn't take long. The Rev is an early riser and he is out and about. He advises me that the stadium is not happening and they are looking for another venue to have the concert in. "Hang tight, Willie and a bunch of us are fixing to go have breakfast at the coffee shop by the hotel."

We get to the coffee shop and I am more than a little ready to see what is on the menu. Only four of us make it to the breakfast: Willie and The Rev and Brian, the guy that sells Willie's hemp shirts, and me, a nice cozy little group. The problem is, going anywhere in public with Willie, or anyone famous for that matter but especially Willie, no matter where you go, it doesn't stay a cozy little group for long. The rain has let up briefly, but more rain is expected. We walk over to the coffee shop and we get there and the waitress seats us and now we're sitting there, and Brian the hemp t-shirt guy says, "You know, this morning I get up at 4:00 A.M. to smoke a cigarette, and I'm out there on the balcony, and it's pouring rain, and some fool is out there running in that shit."

I say, "That was me!"

Willie says, "That was you?"

I say, "Yeah."

Willie says, "How far did you run?"

I say, "Ten miles."

Willie says, "Ten miles! That's great!"

About then the waitress shows up to take our order. I say, "You know, I know I really should go for the pancakes but that cheese omelet looks really good."

Willie says, "Hell, order two you already paid for your day!"

All of a sudden, everybody in the coffee shop knows that Willie Nelson is in there. People start approaching asking for autographs. Any attempt at conversation from that point forward is an exercise in futility. I can't help but notice how gracious Willie is. He's like Crystal Gayle, a people person. People love him, and Willie loves people and it shows. He's even nice to one jerk off that comes over and tries to pull his chain. This guy is the perennial ugly American, the ultimate bad tourist. He's probably pissed off the monsoon dared to fuck up his vacation. Now he is going to take it out on Willie. From the get-go he makes it clear he does not approve of Willie's appearance or his lifestyle or for that matter, the company he keeps. It's unspoken but the attitude is unmistakable as he looks at us all with utter disdain. He says, "My wife asked me to come over and get your autograph. I'm not a fan of yours, but my wife is. I don't care for your music, but she does. I like that one song you do: 'I left my heart in San Francisco.'"

I'm thinking, "What a dick!" I look at Willie and in my best Gomer Pyle voice, I say, "Willie, he thinks you're Tony Bennett!"

Everybody at our table erupts in laughter. The guy does not look happy that the laugh's at his expense. When will they learn? Don't heckle the comedians.

We leave the restaurant and it is raining again. It's sporadic, but when it comes it comes down hard, not the insane crazy rain that was yesterday, but still a good day to stay indoors. When we get back to the suite Kris is up and Kimo, the Hawaiian guy who saved Willie's life the time Willie's lung collapsed, and he was drowning, is there. Rolling guy is there as well and he is already hard at work. Word is until we hear the verdict about the new venue, it's "hurry up and wait" time. Sounds like a plan to me. If you're going to have to hole up during a monsoon what better guys to hole up with than Willie Nelson and Kris Kristofferson?

We laugh our ass off the whole time we're there. Willie is funny and Kris is funny, both of them quick-witted smart funny. Willie is obviously of high intelligence and Kris the Rhodes scholar is right there alongside Willie and I'm on a roll that day myself. Other people say stuff but mainly it's the three of us who are going at it. I can't remember every joke told, every ad-lib and funny line. I do remember this: It's non-stop.

At the time Willie is in the middle of his IRS tribulations, so lots of jokes are made at Willie and/or the IRS's expense. I figure, if I were the one on the hot seat, I wouldn't be laughing, but I'm not Willie. Willie's seen troubles that make the IRS look like a minor speed bump, so he takes the whole brouhaha pretty much in stride like he does everything else. At least it appears that way to a casual observer like me. It's like watching a Zen master. I don't know if Willie's ever met the Dalai Lama, but the two have to be on the same wavelength for sure. There's an old Buddhist saying: "All paths lead to the top of the mountain." Willie and the Dalai Lama are perfect examples of guys who take different paths and end up in the same place.

"Why am I holding two joints?"

Here are a few of the highlights I do remember:

Rolling Guy says, "Hey, Willie, I saw where in the National Enquirer it says you're homeless and destitute. It has a picture of you on the cover looking homeless and destitute. Are you homeless and destitute, Willie?"

Kris says, "Hell, Willie always looks homeless and destitute, but he's got two grand in his pocket right now I know of."

Kris picks up a guitar and starts strumming and singing a song he wrote. Kris finishes and hands the guitar to Willie. Willie sings a song he just wrote called "Valentine" and asks what we think. I say, "I think a lot of guys are going to get laid off that song, Willie."

Willie hands me the guitar and says, "You play one."

I hit a chord and sing: "Other night I watched a preacher preaching on TV. With these ol' boys what you get ain't always what you see. Jesus needs your tax-free dollars, so their message goes. But what they do with your money, God only knows. If Jesus hadn't risen, He'd be rolling in his grave. He came to save us sinners and so his life he gave. But these boys think that Salvation's theirs for them to sell. If this is what the good Lord wants Heaven's gone to Hell."

Kris loves it. He says, "-goddamn I love it that's great!"

Willie says, "I want you to do Farm Aid this year."

I'm thinking, "This is my big break! These guys are treating me like an equal. Willie asked me to do Farm Aid!"

There is talk about Branson. I am glad I came. I hope the Indian is wrong about Branson not working out for Willie and me. Now I'm more determined than ever to write a hit song of my own. I ask Kris how he writes songs. He says, "Write from the heart. Try it. I did and it worked for me."

I ask Willie: "How do you write songs, Willie?"

Willie says, "I always find it helps if you start with a sentence."

SHOWTIME

People are coming in and out of the suite all day long. Finally, someone comes in and says, "They found an auditorium, but now they're going to turn the house and we have two shows..."

The Rev says it's time to go to the venue, so I go to my room, which is just two doors down, and grab my Colombo coat. We ride over in the limo and, as I recall, the limo is not a smoke free zone. By the time we get to the venue, it is early evening, the sun is out, and it is no longer raining. There are overnight showers in the forecast, but the monsoon is over.

Inside the auditorium is a madhouse. The place is packed. The Hawaiian promoters are going nuts. People are running around trying to set up. Someone takes us to the appropriately named green room backstage, where the smell of burning pakalolo permeates everything. A steady stream of Hawaiian guys approach Willie with their offerings. It never lets up the whole time we're there. After a while it gets to be too much. After all, how much can you smoke?

I leave the green room and go to the backstage area to see what is going on, and I see Andy Bumatai, a Hawaiian comic I know from the Punchline in San Francisco. Bumatai has a following called the "Bumaheads" that follow him around wherever he goes and show up at all of his shows. He is one of the headliner comics not happy when I go on before him and kill. Last time we play the Punchline he tries to pull rank on me and tell me to not close with the guitar. Screw that. I close with the guitar, and the Bumaheads love it! I get them all singing along, "I'm fuckin' off! I'm fuckin' off!" which endears me even less to Andy Bumatai. Now here I am in Hawaii, his home turf. I say "Hi, Andy!"

I get the "stink eye" and a cold shoulder to boot. Oh, well. At this point, what do I give a fuck what Andy Bumatai thinks? Now I see Bumatai talking to the Hawaiian guy in charge who doesn't seem to like me much either, the same guy I was talking to about gators and snakes from the night before. I come to find out he too is a comedian, leader of a sketch comedy group called Booga Booga which Bumatai is also a part of. They are looking in my direction and I don't know if I am just being paranoid but it looks like they are talking about me. A few minutes later the Booga Booga guy comes over. I say, "When am I going on?"

He says, "You not going on, haole!"

Normally I would be bummed, but at this point I truly and unequivocally do not give a shit. Even if I don't perform, the trip has been worth it. Just the experience of hanging out with Willie and Kris is worth the price of admission. Screw what Andy Bumatai and the rest of these assholes think. Now that I know for sure I am not getting on, I have an ever increasing capacity for not giving a shit. I head back to the green room, where not giving a shit appears to be the direct order of the day.

The show goes on without me. Several Hawaiian musicians perform and individuals, and groups do okay, but the show comes off disorganized to say the least. Andy Bumatai and Booga Booga do comedy sets in between the music. I don't know if the crowd is bummed because their houses just washed away or what, but I notice the comedians don't get many laughs. It's got to be tough. Think about it. The comics are trying to be funny in a show that they themselves are promoting which has turned into a disaster of epic proportions. It's a tall order under such circumstances. They are bummed and, believe me I know how hard it is to be funny when you're bummed.

Another thing: Every comic who's been around the block more than a few times knows how tough it is to play for the same audience over and over without coming up with new material. I get the definite sense Booga Booga and Bumatai's stuff is the same old spam refried to this crowd. How can you laugh again at the same shit you've already seen a million times, especially after you just watched everything you own float out to sea? Willie and Kris close the show with what seems like half the population of Kauai joining them on stage for what starts out as a jam and quickly devolves into a major clusterfuck. When the show ends, I don't get the sense there are many happy people. The people leaving the auditorium don't look happy, the promoters don't look happy and Willie sure as hell doesn't look happy.

I'm happy. I'm happy because I hung out in the green room most of the time. Kris looks happy. Kris hung out in the green room most of the time too. Like me, he's just along for the ride. The key to happiness is not giving a shit, and I get the definite sense Kris doesn't much give a shit either. He comes off after the first set grinning like a tick at a dog show. He doesn't say anything. He just grins.

Willie tells management the second set is just going to be him and Kris, no other musicians on stage while they're up there. Willie also is not happy with the guitar they gave him. Willie didn't bring Trigger and they need to find him something he feels comfortable playing pronto. It doesn't take long before a steady procession of Hawaiians cues up to offer Willie their guitars. I watch as he sits and painstakingly checks each one out. If my recollection is correct, Willie finally settles on a Chet Atkins hollow body jazz guitar.

I'm backstage, and the next thing I know Willie comes up

to me and says, "How did you do?"

I say, "I didn't get on, Willie."

He says, "What do you mean you 'didn't get on'?"

"The Hawaiian guys said 'no.' They're not letting me on and, to be honest with you Willie, I don't really care. At this point, I'm just happy hanging out with you and The Rev and Kris and the rest of the guys. If those guys don't want to let me on, I really don't give a shit."

Willie looks irritated. He says, "Wait right here."

Willie makes a beeline straight to the Hawaiian guy in charge. Boom! Willie tells him what's what. Willie turns around, walks straight back to me and says, "You go on next show before me and Kris."

Willie walks away and less than a minute later the Hawaiian guy comes over and tells me the same thing. "You go on next show before Willie and Kris."

I say, "How much time do I get?"

"You get fifteen minutes."

Gee, that was fast! So that's what it looks like when thunderbolts come down from on high. Come to think of it, Willie is a little Zeus looking motherfucker. I'm going on next set prime time! Holy shit! Now what the fuck do I do? I start thinking about what the fuck I'm going to do, that's what the fuck I do! I look at the crowd and I say this will work, and I know this will work, and John Wayne will work and Colombo will work for sure with this crowd and the Godfather's sure fire, and everybody loves the football mime bit, and I'll close with the guitar, but I don't have a guitar, so I need to get a guitar quick.

I go back into the green room and say, "Anybody got a guitar?" It doesn't take long before someone hands me an acoustic Gibson guitar but I still need a pick so I say, "Does anybody have a pick?"

Kris says, "I've got one. Here, have one of mine. It's got my name on it: Fender Medium."

Kris hands me the pick. He is grinning bigger than a weasel in a henhouse. Methinks Kris is having a magnificent time. The second show starts, the sound guys and technical guys have got it much better together this time around, performers are settled down and more sure about what they are doing, the audience is in a slightly better mood. It's like the first show was a bad dress rehearsal. This show goes much more smoothly. From time to time I go out to see what's happening on stage, but more often than not. Since I know I am not going on 'til right before Willie and Kris, I figure I might as will just hang with these two for as long as I can. The opportunity ain't always going to be there, know what I mean? So we're hanging out, and a Hawaiian artist comes in, and he's got a beautiful portrait he did of Willie. He shows it to Willie and Kris says, "All it needs is a big green leaf growing out of the top of his head."

Finally someone comes in and says I'm on next. Willie looks at me and pinched between his forefinger and thumb he has a big fat resin dripping roach. He holds it up and takes a hit off it and then looks me directly in the eyes with those dark Cherokee eyes of his, and puts it in my fingers and it's one of those delicate handoffs, where you have to be careful lest you fumble. I look Willie in the eye and take a hit. I don't know if this is a test or what, but if it is, I'm fixing to pass it with flying colors. Willie says, "Have a good show."

I say, "Thanks, Willie."

I go out, they introduce me, and for the next fifteen minutes everything kills. About six minutes into it, I put the raincoat on to do Columbo and, before I say a word, the crowd is roaring. I milk Columbo for awhile not saying a word. This crowd is red hottest hot! Every bit I do is out of the park. Now it's time for my big finale. I pick up the guitar and start singing a parody of a Dave Dudley "Six Days On the Road," singing: "I'm higher than a kite and I'm hauling toxic waste." The crowd goes sideways! I look over at Willie and Kris standing in the wings, and both of them are sideways. I'm rocking, the crowd's rolling, someone yells out: "Do Willie!"

What happens next I swear is an audible at the line of scrimmage. I didn't plan it this way but all day long it's been non-stop jokes about Willie's situation with the IRS and the primary joke maker is Willie himself, so it's not like he's sensitive about it or anything. Earlier that day, I thought of a parody of a Willie song, but I never really had a chance to share it with anyone. Now I'm up on stage in front of a full house and a hot crowd who's laughing at everything and there's Willie and Kris standing right there in the wings watching me, and I figure if I don't go for this I don't have any balls at all. So I look at Willie standing there and say, "Please don't hate me for this, Willie!" And in Willie's voice I sing: "Maybe I didn't pay them quite as often as I should have. Now they're always on my ass..."

The crowd goes hysterical. I look over, and Kris is laughing his ass off. Willie is going: "What did he say? What did he say?"

I close with a parody of Jambalaya about a guy who eats a bowl of bad gumbo and is now bemoaning the consequences. It's one of those songs you can dance to: all the way to the loo. The crowd goes wild. Everybody's stomping and clapping. Hawaiians are yelling like Cajuns. It's one of my over the top kick ass best sets ever. I come off and the place goes crazy. Kris is right there, grinning like Cheetah in a banana plantation. He bear hugs me and says, "God damn you are a funny motherfucker!"

Willie and Kris go out and I'm backstage watching from the wings and the head Hawaiian comes up to me and says, "Bra I can't believe it you save da day, bra, you save da day…"

I say, "What do you mean 'I save da day'?"

He says, "Everybody is bummed, bra, everybody is bummed. Nothing is going right, bra, all day long nothing going right. I try to make them laugh, but no can do, bra. Andy Bumatai they don't laugh at his shit neither. Nothing is funny nobody wants to laugh. Then you get up and make everybody laugh, laugh hard bra, you make me laugh so hard I think I hurt my side. I look around me, everybody around me is laughing. Now everybody is happy. You make everybody happy. You save da day!"

Holy shit! That's what the Indian meant! Me being a shining light in a disaster leading others out of darkness, it makes sense! The Indian predicted it! I bask in the revelation, in awe of everything that is happening, watching Willie and Kris live just a few feet away from me, feeling really good like I'm actually worthy of being in the company that I'm in, basking in the afterglow, watching Willie and Kris center stage unplugged, the audience rapt, spotlight on Willie, a quiet moment, Willie sings: "Maybe I didn't love you quite as often as I should have…"

The audience laughs, and it is a big laugh. I say to myself, "Oh, fuck!"

Willie does not look happy. He finishes the song, and he and Kris sing a few more songs and come off. Willie has dark Indian eyes that pierce right through you, and as he walks by, they pierce right through me. He doesn't say anything, but I know. My Indian shaman friend is right again. Kiss Branson goodbye. Good going, champ. There's another fuck-up to add to your resumé. Kris comes off looking more ebullient than ever. He says, "God damn, you're a funnier motherfucker than I thought!"

Which once again proves the old adage: The best rat fucks are ones you don't plan.

After the show, I figure I better make myself scarce around the suite, so I head down to the bar and a bunch of people are in there hanging around to see if they can catch sight of Willie and maybe get him to sign a program or their guitars, some of them locals, the rest tourists who were at the show earlier. Many of them saw my act. All of a sudden I'm a celebrity and everybody wants to buy me a drink and/or tell me a joke. I am in a state of happy exhaustion, still marveling at the accuracy of The Indian's prediction, sure glad I made the trip after all.

I go to sleep that night dreaming of dancing doobies in hula skirts. There's Willie in a hula skirt. Willie is a dancing doobie. It's one of those endless loop dreams that drive you crazy. I wake up and I am glad I'm awake. The Sun is bright! It's not raining! Now I actually will be able to see where I ran yesterday. I drink free hotel room coffee and pull on my still soggy running shoes. It's always hard getting started but I better get this over with because I don't know what adventure lies just around the corner; whatever it is, I don't want to miss it.

I take off down the stairs and onto the hotel pathway into the muggy Hawaiian humidity, even more intense than usual because of all the moisture in the air. Folks who have been to Houston or South Louisiana in the summertime know what I'm talking about. It's that kind of humid. The ground is saturated and I am slogging through areas, not normally marshy but are now, slipping and sliding my legs splattered with mud, exhilarated happy with the satisfied thrill feeling of victory, of knowing I pulled the motherfucker off. I do the distance, and now I'm jogging down the hotel pathway back to my room, a hot sticky gooey happy muddy mess and who do I see walking down the pathway in my direction but ol' Willie himself, and he's got The Rev with him. Willie says, "Went for a run, did you?"

I say, "Yeah, Willie."

"How far did you go?"

"Ten miles."

"How was it?"

"I'm sweating hash oil!"

This gets a big laugh out of Willie and the Rev.

I say, "No shit, the stuff's oozing out my pores like tree sap. I can smell it!"

The Rev says, "Far out!"

Willie says, "Come on by the suite later."

That's cool. Maybe I'm not in as much trouble as I thought. I don't know if it can be attributed to Willie's forgiving nature or short-term memory loss, but either way, he seems to have forgotten about last night. I go back to my room and shower and change into clean clothes and now I'm back on the walkway thinking about getting some food. I run into Brian, the hemp-shirt guy, and he's thinking the same thing, so the two of us go over to the restaurant. We're sitting there and Brian says, "You know, Kris hasn't smoked weed in eight years, or so I'm told, and the first joint he took a hit off in eight years, you handed it to him."

I say, "No shit. That's hard to believe. I'm a bad influence on Kris Kristofferson? He hangs out with Willie all the time, and I'm the guy that knocked him off the weed wagon? It does explain why he's so happy..."

A couple of cheese omelets and pot of coffee later, Brian's story and my breakfast are barely digested, and we head back to the suite. As we are walking I absentmindedly start doing a bad impression of pidgen English. I'm not thinking about it, I'm just doing it because I hear so many people around these parts talking pidgen, and I'm grooving with it, not thinking it ain't cool to be talking that way with locals around, especially when they hear you. I am blissfully unaware of the large Hawaiian man accompanying an older Hawaiian woman with gray hair pulled back in a bun wearing a muumuu walking on the pathway a few yards ahead of us and I say something to Brian in faux pidgen.

The large Hawaiian man turns around, and it's "stink eye to da max, bra, I mean total out!" He says, "Hey! You make fun of us or what?"

Now I am trying to explain how I'm not making fun of Hawaii or the Hawaiians. I am a comedian and I was in the show last night, which was actually a benefit for the Hawaiians and sometimes I start doing voices and accents before I realize I'm doing them and I love listening to Hawaiians talk and pigeon is such a colorful language. The whole time I try to explain myself, he's looking at me like shark bait and nodding the nod I'm sure he always nods right before he kicks haole ass. I finish my explanation and he says: "No laugh me, haole!"

Well, that settles that. The big guy turns back around, and he and the lady continue walking. My day is already off to a good start. He's not going to kill me. Ah oh, looks like they're headed where we're headed, the suite. Turns out, she is the Hawaiian Queen, and she's headed to a meeting with Willie. The big guy is a Hawaiian named Frank who I assume is there to make sure no one messes with the Queen. We get inside, and Willie and The Queen and Frank and The Rev and a few other Hawaiians who are there go off to the side and have their powwow.

I'm sitting on a couch in the living room, not paying much attention to what is going on, waiting for the meeting to get over with, so we can get down to the business of the day, and the next thing I know The Queen gets up and walks right over to where I'm sitting, sits down next to me and introduces herself. We start talking, and right away I get the sense the Queen is cool. So now we are talking and laughing and having a great old time, and all of a sudden the Queen stops and looks at me and says, "You Pot-a-gee!"

I say, "That's right! My mother is full-blooded Portuguese!"

The Queen says, "I knew it! You Pot-a-gee! You remind me of my first husband! You have da gift of gab!"

HONOLULU
COMEDY CLUB

For several years I have a two-week Hawaiian Islands run a couple times a year, courtesy of the Honolulu Comedy Club. Headliner pay is $1,000 a week. The money isn't great but as a working vacation, it's a pretty cool deal if the trade winds are blowing. If it's Kona weather it's like Houston in July. You're sweating at midnight, but that's another story. Fortunately, most of the time, the trade winds blow, and I don't.

However, on one occasion it gets pretty hot and not because of the weather. Most of the comics I work with are cool. Anita Wise is hot, but good hot and pretty dang cool at the same time. Our first night on the big Island she says to the audience. "It's my first time here and I'm looking at your street signs and wondering what happened? Did the Muppet ship wreck and all you were left were the letters K and H and a bunch of vowels?" My favorite line of Anita's, she says, "A lot of people think that big-breasted women are stupid. I think it's the opposite. I think when there's a big-breasted woman around it's the men who get stupid."

Anyhow, if you're reading this Anita, you're one of my favorites. When I say on one particular occasion it gets hot, I mean ugly hot, angry hot.

It starts the first night of the run. I get there and the other comedian is a self-styled cross between Sam Kinison and Andrew Dice Clay. He has a giggly little evil laugh like Kinison, but he wears a black leather jacket like Clay. It's like this guy has a personality conflict. He doesn't know whose act to steal. I honestly don't remember the guy's name, having downloaded it out of my brain long ago. I do remember him, however, because the whole two weeks we're there, he pushes relentlessly. He establishes opening night he is pissed off he's not the headliner. He even tells this to the audience. He is determined to prove to them, the management, me, Mr. and Mrs. America and all the ships at sea that he is the rightful headliner and not I. Suffice it to say, it is not a friendly rivalry.

So here's how the whole thing works. I fly from the mainland to Honolulu. From there I change planes and catch a smaller plane to the big Island. There I hook up with the other comic. We do two nights on Kona, one show each night. On the third day we fly back to Honolulu and then catch a flight to Kauai. The third fourth and fifth day we do one show a night on Kauai. The sixth day we fly back to Honolulu and then catch a flight to Maui. We do the sixth and seventh day on Maui in on the eighth day we catch a flight to Honolulu. The remainder of the tour is in the Honolulu Comedy Club at the Ilikai on Waikiki Beach, one show a night and two on weekends.

It almost sounds like work doesn't it? It is, especially when you're working with someone who is as big a pain in the ass as this guy. Not only do I have to work with him, I have to fly with him and ride in the rental car with him. The whole time he's bitching he's not the headliner.

One thing should be made clear. In our contract it states explicitly that we are expected to work clean and that all profanity should be excluded from our act. It also states that use of the word "fuck" is cause for immediate dismissal. Any comedian who utters the word "fuck" on stage will have their employment immediately terminated and they will be sent home without pay without exception. Of course, this guy figures that he's the exception. His act is a virtual cornucopia of pornographic word imagery, but when it comes to actual use of the word "fuck" I must admit, he never actually uses it. He does however describe in vivid detail his first sexual encounter at the age of fifteen with a fifty-year-old woman who has a foot fetish and how he has to disinfect his foot afterwards with bleach. Following this for fourteen shows is yet another ring of comedy hell. He has no compunction about making it clear that is what he is trying to make it for me.

Most of the time I can follow the guy, and it's not all that difficult. It's not easy, but I am able to do it relatively painlessly thanks to Buck. I am able to keep it clean but still maintain control as the headliner. This is true for all but one show. It's our last night on Maui. I don't know what it is but there are a bunch of Canadian tourists in there that night. Looking back on it I think they must be a swingers group or some kind of sex tourists or whatever, but these folks eat this guy's act up, especially the part where he has to disinfect his foot with bleach. He gets a standing fucking ovation! I have to follow this. It's like it's the climax scene in a porno flick and someone splices in Mr. Rogers. Hey sorry gang, I have a clean act. What are you gonna do? It's one of my roughest nights ever. I am what might best be described as the perennial punch in the turd bowl. Get the fucking punch out of here we want more turd! Fortunately, this is the only night of the run that this happens. Our next performance is in Honolulu where the owner of the club resides. After the conclusion of the run, he indicates to me that he is happy with my performance and, to show his appreciation for my efforts, he books me back immediately

My counterpart is not so fortunate, at least in relation to his association with the Honolulu Comedy Club. Immediately after the show on the last night the audience has pretty much cleared out, and I hear a heated argument ensuing in the lobby between the club owner and my nemesis. I hear them going back and forth and kind of have a hunch what it's about. I walk into the lobby and Mr. Not So Clean points to me. "He is my witness! You're my witness! I never said 'fuck' all week!"

I hate to corroborate the guy's story, but I don't have to. Before I can say a word the owner renders it moot. With utter disdain he says to the guy, "You reek of the word fuck!"

THE ENERGIZER BUNNY

At this point, my running streak is in the fifteenth year. I am up to 14 miles a day and have been for several years now. Where I live people call me "The Running Man." I wear a ball cap when I run and, when the movie comes out, people start calling me "Forrest Gump." Indeed, one might say there is a certain Forrest Gump-ish quality to my running style. Straight ahead, eyes on the ball. So one day, it's a Saturday, I'm Forrest Gumping along, I pass by this guy's house, which I pass most days for years now. If I'm out of town I run somewhere else, but I've run by this guy's house at least a few thousand times by now. It's on a direct route to the ocean from my house. From his house it's about a mile to where the debris meets the sea. The crazy thing is: He sees me all the time, but I never see him.

So what happens is one day I'm running past this guy's house, and he's getting ready to go get married. He's getting his tuxedo on, and he is looking out the window; "there goes Forrest Gump," and the guy doesn't think anything about it. He proceeds to get married, and now him and his new bride are on their honeymoon on the beach at Waikiki two days later where I am performing the Honolulu Comedy Club at the Ilikai. Him and his new bride are sitting on the beach taking in a view of the surf at Waikiki, and who should come running by?

I hear: "It's the Energizer Bunny!"

THE WHITE BRONCO

Some gigs I am able to remember, not so much for the gig itself as for some major event it coincides with. For example, the night I'm scheduled to headline the one-year anniversary of The Planet in San Carlos is the night OJ decides to make a run for it. I expect you probably remember where you were at the time too. It starts, I'm at home getting ready for the gig. I turn on the TV and there's OJ in the white Bronco leading a slow motion chase down the LA freeway with a parade of cop cars on his tail. I'm mesmerized watching it on TV like everybody else. But I have a gig, which starts at eight. A year earlier I headline The Planet's grand opening, perform to a sold out house. The planet is a 350-seat room. I've been told tonight's show is sold out. Then OJ decides to make a run for it in the Bronco. I keep waiting for it to be over with, but it just keeps going on and on, with no end in sight! Now I know how every team in the NFL but the Bills must have felt in 1972. Somebody stop this guy! But the motherfucker ain't stopping. I wait until the last second to bail and drive to the gig. About 20 people show up at The Planet that night. Everybody stays home to see what's going to happen to OJ.

Reality TV is born.

DADDY GOT A SQUEEZEBOX

If you had told me in 1989 that I would mortgage my house to buy an accordion, I would've said no way you're crazy it will never happen. But stranger things happen every day and this is one of them. No sooner do I get to Louisiana, the Cajun music bug bites me along with several mosquitos and a large horse fly. It starts that first day I'm eating crawfish with the Cajuns. I hear a radio station playing Cajun music and I'd heard it before as background music in movies, but I never really sat and listened to it. Now that I think about it, few people sit and listen to Cajun music because it's hard to sit when Cajun music is being played. You have to dance unless you are Johnny, and you can't dance. That's an inside joke for any of my Cajun friends who may be reading this.

For you non-Cajun music aficionados, "Johnny Can't Dance" is the song that gives Schultze the blues, another obscure reference I feel a need to explain the meaning of. See, Schultze is the protagonist in an award-winning German film in which a retired German salt miner hears "Johnny Can't Dance" on the radio and is immediately bitten by the same bug that bites me. Like me, Schutze hears the sound, and it is a clarion call. The difference between Schultze and me, Schultze plays a large piano accordion, an instrument I have no interest in playing. "Lady of Spain" ain't my demitasse of espresso.

That's why I would've said no way I would walk across the street if you were going to give me an accordion, let alone mortgage my house to buy one. But as they say, you don't pick the instrument, the instrument picks you. Thankfully, the accordion that picks me is not a Lady of Spain accordion. It is a Cajun button accordion, otherwise known as a melodeon otherwise known as a squeezebox. It is a diatonic instrument that operates on the same principle as a harmonica. It produces different notes depending on which way air passes over the reeds. This creates a unique sound, unlike any other, a sound, which can only be produced on a squeezebox. The other thing about a squeezebox is, although small in size, they put out much more volume than a regular accordion. They are loud, almost like a bagpipe! The original instruments come from Germany. It is historical fact that every German U-boat had one. Known as the "shit fuck love you" or "sailors' piano," it was standard issue on all U-boats.

A lesser-known historical fact is that any sailor with the temerity to actually pull one out and play it in the confines of a U-boat was summarily shot. My personal favorite name for the instrument, one which I coin myself, is the "Cajun enigma machine." This is because since obtaining one I've discovered that, like the enigma machine, which was also an item found on every U-boat, the Cajun accordion is designed to confound. I'm hanging out with my buddy Jim Boggio, a world-class jazz musician and zydeco accordion player, and I tell him I want to play Cajun music. He thinks I mean Zydeco, so he lays a small piano accordion on me and shows me some Clifton Chenier Zydeco riffs. I like what I hear, but I can't figure out how to play it. Even though I can play the melody on the piano keys, I'm not getting the rhythmic thing, and the bellows confound me because either way you push the bellows you get the same notes, and somehow it doesn't feel right to me. It doesn't sound right either. I try to describe the sound I'm looking for and finally Boggio gets it. He says, "Sounds like you're talking about a button box, man."

I say, "A button box? Is that different from a regular accordion?"

"Yeah, man. It's a different box. The sound you're describing you need a button box for."

I say, "Can you play one?"

He says, "No. I tried. No way I could figure that fuckin' thing out. I think you got to be dyslexic to play that motherfucker."

Boggio's another one of those funny jazz musicians I've been telling you about.

The first time I see Beausoleil live it's a Cajun music festival, and I hear it and it's the sound. I look to see what is making that sound, and I see this accordion this weird little accordion with the four stop sticking up out the top of it, and it is being played by Jimmy Breaux, and it mesmerizes me. I am watching him play this thing, and I say to myself this is it. This is the instrument. Forget the five-string banjo or bagpipes. This is it! This is the axe! Unfortunately there is the little problem of not having cash to buy one. I'm always jumping from one lily pad to the next, and I never have enough month at the end of the money to buy one outright, what with that pesky mortgage payment due all the time. So even after seeing one live in action, I go for four years thinking if I ever get a little bit ahead I'm going to buy a Cajun accordion, but I never get a little bit ahead so I never do. All the while, I am buying records and listening to the music.

Then one night I dream I am playing a Cajun accordion. Although I've never touched one before, I can feel it in my hands. I am not playing Cajun music on it, I am playing an Irish jig, but I am playing it. I wake up knowing I can play the thing if I can get my hands on one. I go to the Indian and tell him about my dream. I ask, "If I get a Cajun accordion, will I be able to get good playing it?"

He says, "Of course, if you learn how and practice your ass off, dummy."

THE PLUNGE

That does it. I need to do this before I change my mind. I call my old friend Scott at the Cotton Gin. "Hey Scott, "This is Jim Giovanni."

"Hey Jim. How are you doing son?"

"Great Scott. How are you doing?"

"Everything's goin' real good, son, goin' real good."

"Scott I got a favor I want to ask you..."

"Sure thing, son, what can I do for you son, how can I help you?"

"Scott you know those little accordions like Jimmy Breaux plays in the Beausoleil band?"

"Yes I sure do, son, I know the guy that builds 'em."

"Scott, how do I get me one of those?"

"You need to talk to Mark Savoy son, he's the guy that builds 'em. I'll get you his number. Mark's the guy you need to talk to, son."

Scott gives me the number. I thank Scott, hang up the phone, and immediately pick up again and dial the number. The phone rings twice and then I hear: "Hello, Savoy Music Center."

I say, "Hello, my name is Jim Giovanni. I'm calling for Marc Savoy."

"This is Marc Savoy."

I say, "Mark, Scott from the Cotton Gin over in Alexandria gave me your number and he says you build Cajun accordions."

"Acadian accordions, that's correct."

I say, "Mark, I would like to buy an accordion. How much are they?"

Mark says, "Well, Jim that depends on what you want, if you want a customized instrument, what kind of wood is available..."

Marc is the exact opposite of the stereotypical Cajun portrayed by Justin Wilson. Talking to Marc is like talking to a college professor. He is the expert and pre-eminent master builder and player. He is also a pretty darn good salesman too, although in my case it doesn't take much selling on his part. I immediately decide to go all in and buy a customized Acadian accordion with my name on it, burnt-orange curly maple with tiger stripes that jump out at you. I go for the anvil case, a strap an instruction video the whole deal. No half steps here, no cheap used or mass-produced instrument for me and no shortcutting it. I am either going to do this thing right, or I'm not going to do it at all. I'm going all in, therefore, I want my instrument to be one I can't wait to practice on; a box I am going to look forward to playing every possible waking moment. To me it is an investment, not as a short-term material possession that will certainly increase in value, but as a long-term investment in my future coolness as an old dude. When I am old, sitting, playing, and people are dancing, I want pretty young women to come over and rub my head and say, "Isn't he cute?"

That's what I call growing old gracefully.

"Hey, Mr. Bank Man, can I use the equity in my home as collateral?"

THE JOY BUTTON

I order the accordion in June. It takes four months to build and ship to California from Louisiana. It arrives late in late October. That day there is a huge storm with hurricane force winds that knocks out power for 10 days. My neighbors are bummed there is no power. I'm the opposite of bummed. The power outage is a gift. I've found my joy button(s). Now there is no distraction from doing what I really want to do, which is figure out how to play my little Cajun enigma machine. For ten days I sit in the dark pushing buttons. As I said, these things are loud, especially when you first are figuring out how to manipulate the bellows.

We live in a townhouse. My neighbors are none too thrilled about it, but I am. For them it's a nightmare but for me no electricity is a godsend. The worm has turned. For once I don't have to listen to rap music thumping through my walls at all hours, but they have to listen to a badly played Cajun accordion. More than once I hear someone scream out the window, "God damn accordion!"

Those neighbors move shortly after that. Our new neighbors are much quieter, and so am I. I've learned how to manipulate the bellows. Ever since then most days for a couple of hours a day, you can find me hammering away on my melodeon. Twenty years later, just as the mortgage is finally paid off and I am officially entering senior citizen-hood, I'm starting to get the hang of it. Everything is working out according to schedule.

I learn a lot along the way. For instance, I learn one... well, maybe five things.

Number one: The Indian is right! Once again, the Indian has demonstrated his amazing prescience! When he tells me I need to find my joy button, I have no idea what he is talking about and neither does he, but he says when I find it I will know, and he is absolutely right. I do know when I find it or should I say them, all twelve of them, not counting the air button. Believe me, pushing the buttons is great, better than Prozac!

Another thing I learn: a squeezebox is a great way to get people's attention, especially if you're dealing with a rowdy crowd. And women love it when you sing in French. I know this for a fact because every time I do, the bass player gets laid. The bass player will do the gig for nothing as long as at some point in the evening, I sing in French.

Another thing is making people dance is almost as much fun as making them laugh and sometimes even more fun. To tell you the truth, if I knew getting old would be this much fun I'd have done it a long time ago.

The last thing I learn and most important is this: You know a woman really loves you when she'll listen to a badly played squeezebox all those years. You know you found the right one. Thank God we don't live on a U- on a U-boat, 'cause Daddy got a squeezebox and boy, are mama's ears tired.

Jim Giovanni

Jim with his joy button | Photograph by Stephen Somerstein

MY SPIRIT GUIDE

I'm staying with friends in rural Sonoma County. It's too dangerous to run on the narrow little shoulder-less roads up there, so I decide to go run up on the mountain trails. I set out to do a ten-mile run, and about an hour and a half into it I realize I am lost. This is before cell phones or at least before I ever have one. And even if I did, it wouldn't work anyway where I'm at, which is only God knows where and what's this? It looks like skunk-hair confetti everywhere and strong smell of skunk but no bones or blood or anything, just skunk-hair confetti everywhere on the trail.

This is weird! I'm barreling down the mountain because I know the main road is down there somewhere and, if I don't figure out soon where I am, I'll be late getting where I am supposed to be. So I'm running fast, feeling good running strong at a quick pace down the trail with the mountainside on my left and to my right; if you go off the trail, you're down the side of the mountain.

So I'm hauling ass down the mountain, and I get to where the trail curves and I hear footsteps. Boom! I stop, do a one-eighty, and off my left shoulder running down the side of the mountain behind me is a mountain lion. Of course, this makes perfect sense. You wouldn't expect to find a mountain lion in the ocean. You would expect to find a mountain lion a on a mountain. So I'm running down the mountain, and there he is right where one would expect him to be, although, to be honest with you, at the moment, it's the last thing I'm expecting. But he's there now, so I stop and he stops just like that, out in the open in broad daylight. Even though he has a natural camouflage, I know he's there because I saw him move, and I see him now plain as day. He's not moving, but there he is, bigger than life, crouched down like he's stalking prey, like cats do. The words of my Indian shaman friend immediately snap into my head: "You have a big cat in your totem. He runs with you. Listen for his footsteps. Someday you will see him."

I say to myself: " Damn! The Indian was right again."

Don't ask me why I do what I do. I don't plan it. I just do it, my impression of Alphoso Bedoya from "The Treasure of the Sierra Madre": "Hey! Que paso, amigo? Bueno senior! Are you who I think you are? The Indian told me about you! I have been expecting you! Ha! Ha! Ha!"

I slowly advance towards the mountain lion to the edge of the trail to get a better look. The mountain lion doesn't move. I stop and stand facing him. " Are you what I think you are? O, si senior, you have beeg tail!"

So I'm talking to the mountain lion, and the whole time this cat is absolutely motionless staring at me like a statue with teeth, so now I start doing Robert De Niro. "OK. You're supposed to be my guide, tell me something I don't know, like for instance, where, the fuck, are we? Do you think you could tell me that?"

Absolutely nothing from the mountain lion but staring.

"You don't think I see you, but I see you, you, you! Huh, you think I don't see you is that what you think? I see you, you, you, you talking to me? Huh, huh? You talking to me?"

The mountain lion has got to be thinking, "I don't know what this is but this is not prey." Thousands of years of evolutionary DNA is going, "This is one of those ape things and these things are historically bad news."

I don't know. Maybe he really is my guide, and he's saying, "This way asshole!"

Anyhow, I keep talking until I finally run out of mountain lion material. I say, "Well you've been a terrific audience thank you very much, but I have to get going... bye now, see you later, hasta la vista..."

I start backing down the mountain watching the cat the whole time and still the mountain lion is not moving but I do not want to take my eyes off of him lest he decide to follow me home. Finally I get around a bend in the trail where I can't see him, and he can't see me. I can't see him but I hear him take a couple of steps. I hear leaves crunching, so I pick up a rock about the size of a grapefruit that happens to be handy and a tree branch that's lying there, about the length of a samurai sword, and I throw the rock against the tree at the corner of the trail, and the rock crashes down the mountain.

I start whacking the tree branch against a tree doing my impression of Torishiro Mifune in *Yojimbo*, I stop and listen. I hear nothing, no sound at all, so I back down the trail very slowly. It turns out I'm about a half a mile from civilization, after all. I get to the bottom of the trail and there are vehicles parked there and a guy standing there with an English accent. He says, "What happened to you? You're bloody white as a sheet!"

I tell him the story and he stands there listening intently. I finish what I am saying and he says, "That's bloody fantastic!"

I say, "I can't believe it happened..."

He says, "Do you think he was really trying to eat you?"

I say, "I don't know. If he's hungry enough to eat a skunk!"

I go back and tell the Indian the story and he says, "You have a way with animals. Someday it will save your life."

I say, "It already did."

He says, "I said, 'will save'!"

I say, "What's next, a bear?"

He says, "You'll know when it happens."

Note: When I refer to my friend as "The Indian," this is his preference. He does not want his name revealed. He does not want people showing up at his door wanting their fortunes told. He does not tell fortunes. He would never call himself a soothsayer or a prophet. He himself explains it this way. "I do not see what will be. I see what is."

NOW FOR THE REAL SPOOKY SHIT

On September 11, 2001, I get up at 3:00 A.M. and begin writing. It's my first attempt at writing a book, and I've been following this protocol for several months now. The book is a series of philosophical musings by none other than Butt Butane his self. The title is: *Eat Dessert First*, subtitled *The Wit and Wisdom of Butt Butane*. I've been at it about three hours, and at about six something A.M. West Coast time my wife walks in and says her alarm clock went off and told her that a plane just hit the World Trade Center. It's time to refill the coffee cup and take a break anyhow, so I say, "I'll go downstairs and turn on CNN. They'll have it on there for sure."

I go down, get my coffee. I'm in no hurry. I figure I'll turn on CNN and see the tail of a Piper Cub sticking out of the side of the World Trade Center. He probably got off course coming up the Hudson, oops! So I leisurely fill my cup, turn on CNN; the first thing I see is a huge hole and flames coming out the side of the World Trade Center! I say, "Holy shit! I didn't think a Piper Cub could do that!"

Still I'm thinking this is nothing more than a major fuck-up on someone's part. By now my wife has joined me, and we are watching this thing unfold, and in comes the second plane and holy fuck, le flame passé all le way through le building! I turn to my wife and say, "Welcome to the first day of World War Three!"

I go back upstairs, pick up a copy of an Amplified Bible

and open randomly, stick my finger on a page and here it lands. Jeremiah, Chapter 50 Verse 9: "For behold, I will raise and cause to come up against Babylon an assembly of great nations from the north country. They will equip and set themselves against her; from there she will be taken. Their arrows will be like (both) an expert, mighty warrior and like his arrows, none (of them) will return in vain."

I immediately call the Indian and he tells me at the exact same moment as me he randomly opens the Bible and gets the exact same chapter and verse in Jeremiah. I say, "We are going to invade Iraq!"

He says, "I know."

What are the odds?

CRYIN' TIME

The Friday after 9-11 I have a gig in Reno. It's a convention of Moose Lodges at John Ascuaga's Nugget. Driving up, American flags are hanging off every overpass. Every other car has an American flag on it. My guess is the cars that don't have American flags are probably headed right now to buy one.

I get to the Nugget, and everyone is walking around in a state of shock. I'm thinking how am I going to make this work? Who is in a mood to laugh? I've risen to the occasion in the past and I'm getting paid well for this one, but this might well be beyond my pay grade. I am supposed to perform for about fifteen hundred conventioneers and about six hundred show up in a room that seats more than fifteen hundred. The Head Moose gets up to address the assembled Meese and breaks down in the middle of it and starts crying. Then he introduces me. I get up. I'm up there over an hour and during my entire set, I alternately laugh and cry and the audience alternately laughs and cries along with me. I don't think it's possible, but that night it all works. There's great relief and real satisfaction in pulling it off under the circumstance.

The audience is greatly relieved as well, greatly relieved to let it all hang out, laugh/cry let it all go. And let it all go they do. I get more standing O's that night than ever before or since – four, which is a personal record. That being said, it's a record I sure as hell hope I never have to break.

Do I get an "amen" on that?

HERE COME DA JUDGE

One of my more unusual gigs is performing after-dinner entertainment for a circuit court full of federal judges. The dinner is not in the court obviously it's in a fancy restaurant, and wives and significant others are there as well. I won't tell you which circuit court because I don't want to cause the head judge any embarrassment.

I did great that night, that isn't it. It's that usually judges don't want the publicity so unless I hear from the judge it's OK for me to use his name in the book I'm not going to use it. The last thing I want to do is piss off a federal judge. So here we go.

It starts when the judge sees my act and thinks it will be hilarious if he introduces me to his fellow judges as a character he dredged up at the Tasty Freeze in San Antonio. The whole thing is designed to be a practical joke on the other judges. The judge doesn't want them to see me before the show so he has me eat dinner in a separate room with federal marshals who are there to escort the judges. So I'm sitting there at dinner cracking jokes with the federal marshals and now they all know who I am but the judges don't. Pretty soon someone comes in and says they are serving dessert so get ready, the head judge is about to introduce me. So now I'm dressed for the dance standing in the shadows in my big ol' Resistol straw cowboy hat, shirt, big ass silver overlay rodeo buckle with the rider gettin' throwed, wrangler cowboy cut blue jeans stacked on Tony Lama pointy toed cowboy boots, D18 guitar strapped on me, shit howdy boys it ain't none other than ol' Butt Butane his self! I hear the judge say, "I would like to introduce to you a clever fellow I met at the Tasty Freeze into San Antonio. Please give a warm welcome to Buck Butane!"

I go out. "Well thank you, Your Honor, for cleaning my name up for me. Don't worry I ain't wanted, not for nothin' federal anyhow. There is a warrant well it was stupid. I shot up one of those deer crossing signs. Hell, they'd have never caught me if I hadn't strapped the dang thing to the hood of my truck...!"

The judges howl at every word out of my mouth. They think it's hilarious the head judge would bring an outrageous redneck character like me to perform after dinner entertainment for an august body such as themselves. For the next ten minutes the judges roll with everything. Then suddenly I drop character as Buck, put on the raincoat and start doing Colombo and the looks on these judges face is worth it even if I don't get paid. Jaws drop collectively. I look over to the side of the room and the head judge and the federal marshals are laughing their asses off! Now I'm Colombo going: "What's so funny?"

There is an adjustment to be made. Slowly but surely the judges get back up to speed, but it's a gradual build.

"Gee, those are nice shoes you got there. Do you know where I could get a pair like dat? If you don't mind my asking, how much did you pay for those shoes? I bet you must have paid at least thirty dollars for a pair of shoes like dat!"

From then on the judges all look at me with one raised collective eyebrow, laughing, but they realize they've been had and one thing about federal judges, federal judges don't like being had. Afterwards they are all very gracious and tell me how funny and what a rascal I am. In the end, the judges are cool. Will Rogers said it best when he said: "I never met a man I didn't like." It's true. I like these judges, men and women.

MR. SATURDAY NIGHT

It starts when a comedian friend of mine, Mickey Joseph, recommends me to Hostel Elder. The audience at Hostel Elder consists mainly of elderly Jewish people. Mickey tells me I'm perfect for the gig because for this group you have to work clean, and I can work squeaky. So Mickey tells the management of the Hostel Elder about me; they hire me, and now it's the Twilight Zone again, only this time the movie is Mr. Saturday Night and I'm Billy Crystal.

Before I go any further, let me explain how Hostel Elder works. Wherever they live, Hostel Elders receive a brochure in the mail (or I'm sure nowadays they can look it up online) that has programs, mostly educational, they can participate in. They pick whatever program, then fly, drive, take a boat or whatever to wherever the Hostel Elder is being held, and over the course of a few days, a week or whatever, they experience Hostel Elder. Hotel accommodations and meals are included in the package. Throughout the day, Hostel Elders have classes, some with actual professors. In the evening there is an after dinner session. The title listed in the schedule for my performance is: "An Evening of Jewish Humor." I'm not Jewish, but for me it's not a problem because I work clean and most of my jokes are not only clean, they are funny and many are older than I am, a pre-requisite for any self-respecting Borsht Belt comic. "So what if this is not the Borsht Belt and I'm not Jewish, what do you expect in my price range? Henny Youngman?"

The session is in a meeting room in the hotel where the Hostel Elders are staying. It's supposed to last an hour and fifteen minutes. At exactly 7:30, or whenever the Hostel Elders straggle in from dinner, the host, the person in charge of the group, is going to introduce me.

I get there and the host is already in the room. He says, "You must be the comedian."

I say, "Yes, I'm Jim Giovanni."

He says, "You look older than your picture."

I say, "Yeah I'm a little older, but it still looks like me, doesn't it?"

He says, "You understand that you are going to do thirty minutes of comedy followed by thirty minutes of question and answer because the group likes to talk and they like to participate so when there's about fifteen or so minutes left after the question and answer portion you will lead the joke off and you'll get them up there, whoever wants to tell a joke, they want to tell jokes, don't forget the joke off, they're really looking forward to this and if it's going good you could do 20 minutes, don't worry about the time if it's going good, we don't have anything after this and at the end by applause let them pick the best joke…"

Sounds straightforward. I give the host my introduction which I've written in advance, consisting of three major credits: "He was *on Laugh-In*, the *Merv Griffin Show*, he plays a police sergeant in the movie *Tucker: The Man and His Dream*, please welcome Jim Giovanni."

He says, "Is this it?"

I say, "That's it! 'Keep it short and sweet' is my motto."

So now the Hostel Elders are coming in and they are all wearing name tags, and pretty soon the room fills up and there are about thirty in the group. So the host does a quick head count, and then he makes announcements about what is going to happen the next day, and now time to introduce me. So instead of reading the introduction I gave him, the guy gets up and starts reading my entire resumé verbatim plus some stuff that's not even on there. I hate it when they say you've been on the *Tonight Show* and you haven't. As of the writing of this book I have never been on the *Tonight Show*. Who knows? Maybe this book will change things, but I mean this guy is telling the group of thirty or so Hostel Elders I've been on the *Tonight Show*, and then he starts reading credits, I don't know where he gets them from, the Internet or something.

He's going on and on and his delivery is like the guy that does the Clear Eyes commercial that plays the professor in Ferris Bueller, he's droning on and on, "And he's headlined Caesar's...Steak and Salad, and he's headlined the Sands...Road Kill Café, and he's headlined Aladdin's... Crab Factory..."

I'm standing there waiting for the guy to finish, and I don't usually get embarrassed but I am. Everyone's looking at me, and he's not stopping.

"He's headlined Bally's...Barbeque and he's headlined the Hacienda...Taqueria and he's headlined Bellagio's...Pizzeria..."

What deep recesses of his colon is he pulling these credits from? Finally he finishes and introduces me. I say, "Wow! What an introduction! You remind me of the famous Chinese comedian: On Too Long!"

Somebody yells. "We can't hear you!"

"What?"

"Turn on the mike! The mike is off!"

What the...!" It was working a minute ago when the host was introducing me! I'm hitting the on off switch, and that's not doing anything. It's a crappy hotel sound system anyway, so screw it. I'm better off without the mike. I put it back on the stand and I can project. So now I'm projecting but there's one guy that can't hear even with the mike, so now after every punch line the guy is yelling out, "What did he say? What did he say?"

Other Hostel Elders are repeating my punch lines to the guy. "He said, 'That's tomorrow,' Morty!"

"What's tomorrow?"

"'That's tomorrow' is the punch line!"

"What's the punch line?"

"'THAT'S TOMORROW!'"

"What is? What are we doing tomorrow?"

"'THAT'S TOMORROW' IS THE PUNCH LINE!"

"'That's tomorrow' is the punch line?"

"THAT'S RIGHT! THAT'S TOMORROW' IS THE PUNCH LINE!"

"I don't get it."

Now people are explaining the joke to him. Talk about a momentum killer. Meanwhile the host is off to the side clomping around trying to fix the microphone. Trying to do my act is trying to start a car on a cold day. You're having a hard time getting the car started, and you finally get it to crank over, and you drive ten feet and it dies again. (Make car cranking engine sounds.) For the next half hour it's: (Make car cranking engine sounds.)

The guy is still trying to fix the mike as I'm closing with the football mime bit, which is great because it requires no sound. I'm doing the quarterback calling signals in pantomime and Morty's still going, "What did he say? What did he say?"

"He didn't say anything, Morty! He's doing mime!"

"Mine? What's mine?"

"IT'S A PANTOMIME, MORTY, HE'S DOING A PANTO-MIME!"

"IT'S QUESTION AND ANSWER TIME?"

It's hopeless to continue with the mime piece, so I say, "You know what? Actually Morty's right! It is question and answer time. Does anybody have a question…?"

A lady raises her hand. "I have a question!"

I look at her name tag. "Yes, Hannah, you have a question?"

Hannah says, "This was billed as an evening of Jewish comedy. Why are you here? You're not Jewish!"

I say, "No, Hannah, I'm not Jewish, but my jokes are. Some of my jokes date back to the time of Christ. He's Jewish, isn't he? What is: 'I, II, III, IV, V?' The Roman army counting off! Ba-da bing!"

So now Morty says, "Oh I get it! He's a stutterer!"

"He's not a stutterer Morty!"

"He keeps repeating himself…!

I'm determined to plow straight ahead. "So there's this Roman Galley, see, and the drummer guy is up there leading the rowers and he says, 'I've got good news and bad news. The good news, you all get double rations of food tonight!' And all rowers cheer! Now for the bad news: The Emperor wants to water ski!'"

Morty says, "The umpire is in Mississippi?"

"No Morty, 'The Emperor wants to water ski!'"
"Who does?"

"The Emperor!"

"Why does he want to do that?"

"It's the punchline, Morty!"

"I don't get it, "Why does the umpire want to go to Mississippi? Why are we talking about baseball?"

"THE EMPEROR WANTS TO WATER SKI, MORTY!"

"The Emperor wants to waterski?"

"YES!"

"I don't get it."

"IT'S A ROW BOAT MORTY!"
"What is?"

"THE JOKE IS THE EMPEROR WANTS TO WATER SKI IN A ROW BOAT!"

"What's so funny about that?"

(Make car cranking engine sound effects.) I must keep going at all costs. "Does anyone else have a question? Yes, Maxine...?"

"I have a question: Why are all these young comedians so filthy? I mean, what's with the 'F' word, why do they have to use the 'F' word all the time? Why do all these young comedians think they have to be filthy to be funny?"

I say, "You know, I agree with you Maxine, a lot of comedians overdo it with the profanity but there is a time and place for it, especially if the word is absolutely necessary for the joke or if the character that you are portraying uses profanity, for instance, it would be hard to do an impersonation of General Patton without using profanity, but you have to know your crowd and obviously I'm not going to do Patton and have him swear or use profanity in front of a bunch of Catholic nuns or the Widows of the Masonic Lodge..."

Now Goldie jumps into the fray. "I agree with Maxine! I think it's terrible the comedians today, the filth, I don't get why they all have to talk that way, don't you think it's terrible, Al?"

"Yeah, it's terrible."

This is definitely the ninth ring of Comedy Hell. We get through another twenty minutes or so of how terrible comedians are nowadays and how much better Jack Benny was than any of these young comedians. This works for me because I do a pretty decent Jack Benny. So now I'm doing Benny, and the crowd is into it and, the best part is, doing Jack Benny I can be silent for long periods of time without Mort asking what I just said.

By the time I exhaust the Benny repertoire, there's hope for a strong finish yet. The host gives me a sign.

I say, "OK everybody now for the part of the program we've all been waiting for, the joke-off! Okay, I'm going to kick it off with a good clean joke and, believe me, it will be absolutely clean. I'm not going to say anything profane or off color. I am going to be absolutely one hundred percent squeaky clean tonight, and the best way to get any joke-off jumpstarted is with a good clean joke. So I'd like to kick it off with my favorite clean joke, here it is my favorite clean joke: So a guy goes into a bar, and he's got a dog with him, and the bartender says, 'Hey, buddy, dogs aren't allowed in here.' And the guy says, 'He is not just any dog. This dog is special.' The bartender says, "What's so special about him?' The guy says, 'This dog can talk!' The bartender says, 'Get out of here. Dogs can't talk!' The guy says, 'This dog can! I'll bet you fifty bucks I can get him to say something.'

"The bartender grabs fifty out of the cash register and slaps it on the bar and says, 'You're on!'

"The guy looks at the dog and says, 'What do you call

the top of this building?' And the dog says, 'ROOF!' The guy goes to grab the fifty and the bartender says, 'Wait a minute, buddy, not so fast! What do you think you are trying to pull here? You think I'm stupid? Any dog can say roof! My dog can say roof! That doesn't prove anything! The dog doesn't talk! You owe me fifty!'

"The guy says, 'He talks and I'll prove it! What say we go double or nothing I get him to say something else?' The bartender says, 'Double or nothing?' He thinks about it and says, 'OK. But this time he'd better really say something.'

"The guy looks at the dog and says, 'Name the greatest Yankee slugger of all time? The dog goes 'RUTH!' The bartender says, 'That's it, you're out of here!'

"He grabs the guy and the dog and throws them both out the door. They land in the street side by side sitting there and the dog looks up at the guy and says, 'Was it DiMaggio?'"

For the first time, Morty doesn't ask to have the joke explained. He is absorbed deep in thought, no doubt trying to remember the joke he wants to tell.

I say, "OK, now it's time for the joke-off everybody! Anybody that wants to get up and tell a joke, now's your chance! Anybody? Who wants to go first?"

"Morty, you have a joke, Morty has a joke! Get up and tell your joke, Morty!"

With impeccable timing the host says, "I fixed it!"

Suddenly the microphone works again, just in time for Morty. "Okay, Morty, come on up and tell us your joke!"

Morty says, "What did he say?"

"He says it's time to tell your joke, Morty!"

Morty says, "Oh!"

Morty gets up and walks to the microphone. I give Morty the big Ed McMahon introduction: "OK everybody, here's Morty!"

Morty gets on the mike and says, "So Jesse James and his gang are robbing this train..."

Someone yells out: "We can't hear!"

"So Jesse's robbing this train, see..."

"We can't hear! Turn up the microphone!"

The host cranks the volume on the mike as loud as it will go.

Morty says, "Jesse James and his men are robbing a train, and Jesse says, 'OK everybody this is a stick-up, see. I'm Jesse James, and I am going to rob all the men and fuck all the women!'"

I hear groans. Irv yells out: "You got it backwards Morty! It's 'Rob all the women and fuck all the men!'"

"That's what I said! Rob all the men and fuck all the women!"

"It's the other way around. It has to be 'Rob all the women and fuck all the men!' Otherwise the joke doesn't work!"

"I said, 'Rob all the men and fuck all the women!' That's what I said!"

Now Sadie, who has a voice like Ethel Merman, chimes in: "IRV'S RIGHT MORTY! IT'S FUCK ALL THE MEN AND ROB ALL THE WOMEN! OTHERWISE THE JOKE DOESN'T MAKE SENSE."

Now Mort is yelling in the microphone: "THAT'S WHAT I SAID! ROB ALL THE WOMEN AND FUCK ALL THE MEN! ROB ALL THE WOMEN AND FUCK ALL THE MEN!"

Did I mention a Pentecostal church group is in the meeting room next to us? I walk out in the lobby afterwards and people are looking at me like I'm the antichrist. Another week goes by I get my reviews from the Hostel Elders. I won't be back. I'm too dirty.

DESERT STORM

A side effect of wearing a cowboy hat on stage is from time to time I get gigs entertaining cowboys and want to be cowboys on trail rides. These are unusual gigs in that most of them even Google doesn't map. I mean Google maps up to a certain point. After that, directions on how to get there usually include instructions such as: "Take the side road a hundred yards off where the main road forks to the right and you take that fourteen miles until you get to the gate with the padlock on it and then you punch in 92136 and then go through and put the gate back the way you found it and then you got to drive 5 miles till you get to the next gate and then you open that gate and drive-through and then be sure you close that gate too so the cows don't get out then drive another 10 miles or so over some real rough road. It's steep and it's best to have four wheel drive if you got it and when you get to the last gate be sure you close that one too and when you get up there, you'll see a bunch of trucks and horse trailers parked around. Park anywhere you can find that's out of the way and walk a couple a hundred feet or so and you can't miss us, we'll be right there where we're at."

So now I'm on my way to the gig. I've already gone 146 miles according to Google map and this last stretch of road is so desolate I haven't seen another car in over an hour. I get to the point where the road forks and there's nothing about a side road off a right fork on Google map and was that it I just passed? Cop a U and sure enough that's it or at least I hope that's it so turn off on that road and go fourteen more miles and there's the gate with the padlock on it. I get out and punch in the numbers and the padlock doesn't open. I double and triple check and I'm punching and punching and the padlock is not opening and I'm hoping this is the right gate and the right padlock but I'm not sure about anything except I am going to be late for this gig if I don't get this padlock open quick. It's dusk and it's October and it's getting cold and I still have a ways to go in the dark through a bunch of fences of not letting cows out. I'd like to appraise the guy who hired me of the situation, but we're so far out in the boonies nobody's cellphone works anyway so there's no way I could call him even if I could. Good thing there's no one else around because at the moment I'm hopping up and down like Yosemite Sam cussing up a storm calling the padlock every name in the book and lo and behold here comes a truck with a couple guys in it pulling a horse trailer and it pulls up to the gate! Hallelujah! I explain to the driver my situation and he says he is going to the same place. I say they must've given me the wrong combination and he gets out and he pushes in on the lock and it pops open! I had the right combination all along. I didn't know you had to push in on the lock to open it. Duh! Well at least we're through the gate, but now I'm afraid to make a wrong move so I tell the guy, "I'll follow you. You know where you're going." Which is stupid move number two because I fail to take into consideration the fact I'm going to be following a pickup truck dragging a horse trailer for fifteen-plus miles on a dirt road. Good news is at least someone else gets to open the gates. By the time we get to where the camp is I have a pretty good idea of what folks went through during the dust bowl. The worst part is, it's my wife's car. Oh, well, at least we're here and cowboys are where they say they are going to be: at the bar. Hey, just because this is a camping situation doesn't mean they don't have a full bar with all kinds of hard liquor, ice chests full of cold beer, a Mexican crew cooking full on Mexican food on site, a dinner table consisting of large pieces of ply board set up on sawhorses complete with white table cloth and place settings with bottles of fine wine and centerpieces consisting of candles sticking out of large fresh cow pies. The good news is cowboys are relatively well behaved during dinner. The bad news is once dinner's over and the toasting starts the inevitable drunken cowboy gets up and runs down the center of the makeshift table, scattering plywood and sawhorses and tortillas and carnitas and bottles of fine wine and cow pie everywhere, which is, of course, a sure sign dinner is over and it's time to start the show before these guys get in any more of a festive mood than they already are. Fortunately for me, being the bona fide party ringer I am, my act is tailor-made for this crowd. They love Buck Butane and they can't get enough of Redd Foxx. I do over an hour and even after the show's over, the show's not over. It's joke off time and everyone's got at least one and one leads to the other and I've got one for everyone they got and the jokes go on into the wee hours. By then the campfire is dying out, everyone is headed off to whatever makeshift sleeping arrangement they've got set up for themselves. I'm watching them fade, going, "Now what do I do?" And someone says to me, "What's the matter? Didn't you bring a sleeping bag?"

"Now you tell me."

Sleeping on hay and dirt on hard freezing uneven ground covered by nothing but a filthy old horse blanket isn't my first choice of accommodations, but since day light is just a couple of hours away and I have little choice otherwise, I make do and even manage to get in about fifteen minutes sleep before a dang rooster starts crowing. Pretty soon the mess crew's clanging, banging around putting out our breakfast, the usual fare of bacon and eggs, beans, sausage, biscuits, coffee and whatever leftovers anyone wants to make a burrito out of. The table and seating arrangement is back to the way it was sans tablecloth and cow pie centerpieces.

Chow down and coffee up, boys, because next thing we saddle up the horses. Cowboys are in the chow line, sitting at the makeshift plywood table. Everyone is stuffing their face, next thing I know somebody says something that gets a laugh, which triggers me to come up with a line, and in nothing flat we're back to full bore with the jokes but I need to get going and so do they. I look at the time and say, "Well, gents, I hate to leave, it's been fun but I have to get going. I promised my wife I'd be home by 2 PM and it's a long ways..."

"You can't leave now, funny man!"

"Sorry, but I got to go..."

"You can't leave now funny man you got to stay with us!"

I say, "You guys are going riding, I have to get on the road..."

"You got to come with us. We got a horse for you."

"I promised my wife I'd be home..."

"Call her and tell her you ain't comin' home."

"I can't. Cell phones don't work here."

"Paul, take him to the ranch house, will you? They got a landline over there. Paul will take you and you can call from the ranch house."

"Where's the ranch house?"

"It's about a half mile from the main gate where you come in. Paul will take you over there. You can call from there."

"I was only supposed to do one night..."

"Aw, hell, stay with us. We got a horse for you!"

So now we're in Paul's truck driving fifteen miles down dirt road opening and closing gates so we don't let cows out until we reach the gate with the lock on it. We unlock that and lock it back up again and get back on the road headed east, at least I think it is east, and about a half mile down the road off to the left is a ranch house. We pull in there and I call my wife and explain the situation to her and promise I will be home the following afternoon and yes I will wash her car before bringing it back. So now it's schlep all the way back up the mountain opening and closing gates until we get to the camp. We get there and guys are already on their horses, stragglers are saddling up. I hear, "There's the funny man! Hey funny man! You come back after all!"

"I don't have to go back now until tomorrow."

"Real good real good funny man. Well, come on let's get you saddled up. We got a horse for you we got a real gentle horse for you..."

"A gentle horse...?"

"Oh, yeah, he's real gentle."

"What's the gentle horse's name?"

"Desert Storm."

Climbing into the saddle isn't as easy as I remember. I'm sixty. I used to be able to spring up there, but looks like my spring's done sprung. I put my left foot in the stirrup grab a hold of the saddle horn: "I can make it I can make it, get your hand off my ass, cowboy, I don't need your help! I can make it I can make it up goes the hernia! Oh well shit howdy I'm here now!"

At this point I'm feeling mighty proud of myself for still having enough left in me to make it up on Desert Storm's back by myself, a sentiment apparently not appreciated by Desert Storm who from the get-go gives the distinct impression he is not exactly overjoyed by my presence. I try talking to him and making friends with him being the horse whisperer that I believe I am, but all it seems to do is piss him off even more. The more I talk the more it pisses him off, and I'm half Portuguese, so I have a difficult time shutting up to start with.

The "Why the long face?" horse jokes don't endear me to him either. I can tell by the time we're about a quarter mile up the trail, Desert Storm is ready to kill me. I try to explain the situation to him that since we're stuck with each other, let's make the most of it, shan't we? I try reasoning with him, using time-honored principles of logic I learned from Jesuits, but that doesn't work because he's a horse.

The only thing he understands is first chance he gets, he's going to dump me unceremoniously on my head or my ass, whichever hits the dirt first. So we are operating under different motivational principles, namely, I want me on, he wants me off, and he thinks if he can get going fast enough it will be easy to get rid of me. So now all he wants to do is run. He keeps trying to take off, and I keep yanking back on the reins, which pisses him off even more. Every now and then I'll give him a little bit of his head and as soon as I do, he immediately starts to run and now I got the trail boss yelling at me to stay with the group, which consists of about twenty guys on horseback and one guy pulling a loaded up pack mule.

So now I'm back with the group, and I don't know if I'm better off just letting Desert Storm take me for a ride because these guys are passing a bottle of tequila around and the pack mule's not the only one that's loaded up. Oh well. When in cowboy land do like the cowboys, the theory being at least if you crash, it won't hurt as bad. That's the theory at least.

It's about three hours from that point up the mountain. By the time we get to the top, the Mexican crew is already up there and they have got a full spread set up with tortillas and carnitas and rice and beans and cold beer on ice. It is a hot late Indian-summer day, but they find a nice shade spot to set up, so we tie up the horses.

I still have plenty of gas in the tank in terms of comedy

material, so I do about a half hour impromptu show at lunch. The Mexican crew especially likes the San Joaquin Valley farmer jokes. "How do you clear out a fiesta in Gustine? 'Manuel, Tony, your cows are out!' Did you hear John Deere has a new tractor with no seat and no steering wheel? It's for the farmer who's lost his ass and doesn't know which way to turn! How can you sell those axe handles for fifty cents when you paid a dollar for them? Beats farming!"

The material is a hit. You got to know your crowd.

We finish lunch, and the boss makes an announcement: "Every man for himself going down the mountain."

I say, "Does that mean we don't have to stick with the group?"

"That's what it means. Just be sure you make it back before dark."

Desert Storm and I have no problem following that instruction. As soon as I'm back in the saddle, he wants to go, and I figure he knows where he's going so I let him. I hold on to the reins and saddle horn tight with my left hand, and with my right I'm doing my best to keep my brand new straw Resistol cowboy hat, which I just paid $80 for and don't want to lose, on my head.

We barrel down the mountain full speed all the way. We're at a full gallop on a steep straightaway, and all of a sudden Desert Storm decides to take a shortcut. No warning, he makes a forty-five degree right off the trail over the side down the mountain, down an incline I wouldn't go in a jeep. Survival instinct kicks in, I let go of the hat and grab the saddle horn with both hands, simultaneously throwing all my weight back on his left haunch to keep from being thrown head first over his right shoulder or, even worse, him going down with me on top of him and rolling over me.

As it is, it's close. He stumbles, it feels like he's going down, but somehow he stays upright with me on him all way to the bottom. It takes about three and a half hours to get up the mountain and less than ten minutes to get back down and Desert Storm still ain't stopped. This horse ain't stoppin' 'til he gets to where he's going. We finally get where he wants, and Desert Storm screeches to a halt and stands breathing furiously. I get off and tie him up. The look in his eyes is even more furious than his breathing. I offer him a lump of sugar, which he turns his nose up at. He snorts and looks at me with pure hate exuding from every pore. I know what he's thinking. "How dare you stay on, you green horn piece of shit!"

I look Desert Storm eyeball to eyeball. In my best Robert De Niro/Jake La Motta voice, I say, "You couldn't knock me down, Ray. You couldn't knock me down, Ray...!"

Jim Giovanni

Photograph by Stephen Somerstein

EPILOGUE

By Jim's Daughter, Jessica Giovannoni

My father did not make it to seventy; he died unexpectedly three weeks shy of his 67th birthday, of what his doctor believed was a heart attack. When Robin Williams had died, almost two years prior, my father was deeply affected by his passing. He was very saddened, and I watched him sit quietly, pensive and reflective. Several months before my dad died, he said to me... "You know, Jessica, all my life I was so focused on my career, on making it big. You know for the first time in my life I don't care at all about that anymore. I am perfectly content with the way my life turned out. I have you and your mother... And EMMA..." He trailed off. Emma is my daughter – his granddaughter, and the highlight of his life. He was ecstatic in anticipation of the day she was born and helped care for her until the day he died. He would play with her like a child, having butt races down the stairs, singing his own original children's songs for her with his array of unique instruments and building towers out of all the paper towel rolls they would bring home from Costco. She had been such a gift to him and was all he could talk about, as anyone who ran into him would confirm. Now that is not to say he had given up his love of being an entertainer. He had been over the moon when he landed two national television commercials in his final years and had performed in a live show just two nights before he died. Still, Emma had given him a new outlook on life and blessed him with the greatest role of his life: the role of being a grandfather. The conversation he and I had surprised me because in all my life I never thought I'd see the day my father didn't care anymore about the big break. But he went on to say that although he had always dreamed about having what Robin had, he realized now that he got the one thing that Robin did not, and he felt so saddened that Robin would end it all before he got that gift – the gift of being a grandfather. For the first time to me, he seemed truly and completely at peace.

Jim with his granddaughter Emma

Jim with his wife Betsy, daughter Jessica and granddaughter Emma

Made in the USA
San Bernardino, CA
09 January 2020

62893084R00292